Chemistry for You
BOOK ONE

Acknowledgements

Acknowledgements are due to the following for permission to reproduce photographs and diagrams: Australian News and Information Bureau p.46; BBC Hulton Picture Library p.60; Blackwood Hodge p.8; J. Bown p.60; British Airways p.111; British Ceramic Research Association Ltd. p.138; British Gas pp.8, 127; British Petroleum pp.26, 27, 97, 104; British Steel pp.54, 78; British Sugar pp. 8, 24; British Tourist Authority pp. 16, 79, 100; Copper Development Association pp.66, 67, 71; Daily Telegraph p.54; Brian Davis, Bath City Council p.138; De Beers pp.124, 125; Dunlop Ltd. p.130; European Ferries Ltd. p.6; Farmers Weekly p.46; Griffin and George Ltd. pp.13, 24, 34, 38; Hawker Siddeley p.71; Imperial Chemical Industries PLC pp.7, 13; Imperial War Museum p.19; Institute of Geological Sciences p.142; John Lewis Partnership p.72; Lead Development Association pp.71, 82; May and Baker Ltd. p.17; John Moss p.16; National Coal Board pp.8, 26, 126, 127; National Water Council p.102; Nuffield Foundation (from *Revised Chemistry Handbook for Pupils*, Longman 1978) pp.128, 132; Nu-Swift International Ltd. p.91; G.E.C. Overton pp.73, 83, 86, 116; Permutit Water Softeners pp.100, 101; Pilkington Brothers Ltd. p.87; Portsmouth and Sunderland Newspapers Ltd. pp.48, 60, 79, 122; Portsmouth Water Company p.102; R.H.M. Foods Ltd. p.104; Robson and Baxter Ltd. p.12; Schweppes Ltd. p.93; Science Museum pp.36, 112; Thames Water Authority pp.92, 103; The Times p.139; Unilever Research Laboratory p.96; West Air Photography p.7; C. B. Wilberforce p.60.

The author also wishes to thank M. J. Latchem for providing apparatus drawings for the experiments throughout this book.

Hutchinson & Co. (Publishers) Ltd
An imprint of the Hutchinson Publishing Group
17–21 Conway Street, London W1P 6JD

Hutchinson Group (Australia) Pty Ltd
30–32 Cremorne Street, Richmond South, Victoria 3121
PO Box 151, Broadway, New South Wales 2007

Hutchinson Group (NZ) Ltd
32–34 View Road, PO Box 40–086, Glenfield, Auckland 10

Hutchinson Group (SA) (Pty) Ltd
PO Box 337, Bergvlei 2012, South Africa

First published 1982
© W. E. Latchem 1982

Designed by The New Book Factory, London
Typeset by Parkway Illustrated Press, London and Abingdon
Printed in Great Britain by The Anchor Press Ltd
and bound by Wm Brendon & Son Ltd
both of Tiptree, Essex

British Library Cataloguing in Publication Data

Latchem, W.E.
  Chemistry for You 1.
  1. Chemistry
  I. Title
  540   QD33

ISBN 0-09-144501-9

Chemistry for You

BOOK ONE

W E Latchem

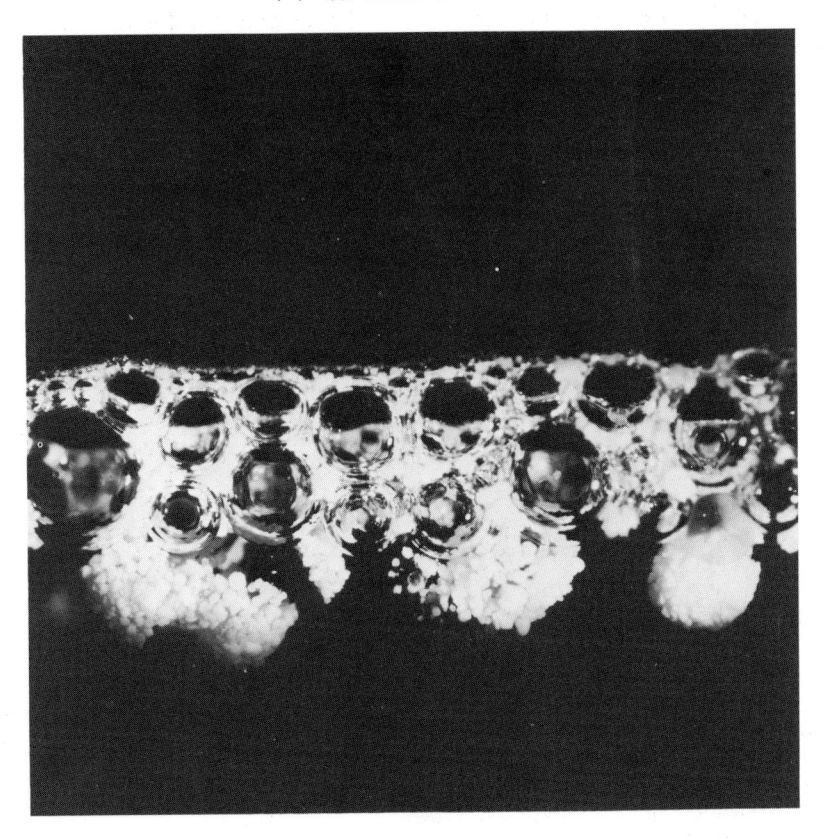

Hutchinson

London Melbourne Sydney Auckland Johannesburg

Chemistry for You Book Two

1. What is Chemistry? Tell me again!
2. Atoms and molecules
3. Modern Atomic Theory
   Radioactivity
4. Sulphur dioxide and sulphuric acid
   preparation, manufacture, properties, uses
5. Electrolysis: mechanism, products, uses
6. Inside the atom
   proton, electron, neutron
   atoms and ions
7. The halogens
   hydrogen chloride, hydrochloric acid, chlorides
   chlorine
   the halogens as a chemical family
   Chemistry and disease
8. Other chemical families
   the noble gases
9. Why and how elements combine
   ionic bonding
   covalent bonding
   The Periodic Table
10. Carbon chemistry
    hydrocarbons, alcohols and acids, esters
    polymers and man-made fibres
    carbohydrates such as starch and sugar
    The oil industry
    World food supplies
11. Nitrogen and its compounds
    nitrogen in foods, ammonia, ammonium salts
    nitric acid and nitrates
    nitrogen oxides
    Fertilizers
12. The rate of chemical reaction –
    how fast and how far
13. Energy in chemical changes
    Fuels and energy
14. The chemistry of metals
    sodium, iron, copper, aluminium:
    their properties and important compounds
    other metals in less detail
    Iron and steel
    Corrosion
    Cosmetics
    Careers

Contents

This book is made up of units, usually of two pages, which deal with one topic. Several related topics make up a section. Experiments are numbered with the section number.

**Important note
Experiments marked *
should only be
done by a teacher.**

Section	Topics	Pages
1	What is chemistry? Making substances pure, testing their properties, making new substances from them	6–31
2	Burning substances Air and oxygen: the products of combustion The manufacture and uses of oxygen	32–53 54–55
3	Water and hydrogen What you should know : a summary with questions	56–63 64–65
4	Metals and the activity series Making metals from ores; oxidation and reduction Chemistry and building	66–85 86–87
5	Carbon dioxide Our water supply	88–91 92–93
6	Natural water: the hardness of water Our water : out of the tap and down the drain	94–101 102–103
	Ideas in chemistry : a summary with questions	104–105
7	Atoms and molecules Relative atomic mass: the mole, equations	106–121
8	Non-metals: carbon The coal industry	122–125 126–127
9	Allotropy: sulphur Pollution	128–137 138–139
10	Acids and salts	140–149
	Questions	150–152
	List of elements	153
	Games and puzzles	154–156
	Periodic table	157
	Glossary	158–160

Chemistry? What's that?

Chemistry is part of Science. In Science we find out about ourselves and all the things around us.

To find out we must ask questions.

Look at the picture. Pick out ten things you can see in it. Write out a list of them on paper. Can you answer questions about them?

Try these questions:
    Is sea water really blue?
    How could I find out if the water is sea water?
    Where do clouds come from?
    Steel sinks in water. Why does a steel ship float?
    What moves the ship through the water?
    Where does its fuel come from?
    What are the cliffs made of?
    What is it that makes grass green?
    Why is sea water salty?
    Does anyone make salt from sea water?
    Why does the steel in the ship rust?

Science tries to answer these questions. It answers thousands of others too. In Science we find out about things as they are. We also find ways of changing them.

Human beings like asking questions. They began thousands of years ago. So today we know a great deal. We know about our world and ourselves. Science? There is 'a lot of it about'.

This is why Science is divided into parts.

About 4000 years ago people made metals. They built monuments like Stonehenge.

About 2500 years ago they made glass. They made cheap metals look like expensive ones. This made them think a metal like lead could be turned into gold. They tried to find something which would make it happen. This made them ask what the world is made of.

About 2300 years ago Democritus said it was made of atoms.

2000 years ago the Romans had invented central heating. They used coal as a fuel. They built straight roads. They used bronze and silver coins. They invented sewage systems.

1700 years ago the first jet engine was made!

The first Chemistry book in this country was written in 1144 AD. It was written in Latin.

In 1250 AD Roger Bacon may have discovered gunpowder. He was the first modern scientist.

Since then millions of people have worked in Science. They asked questions. They found answers. They made new materials. They invented new ways of treating disease. Men have walked on the moon. Space craft have reached the farthest planets. They have sent back photographs.

Photographs are only just over a hundred years old. People travelled by balloon before aircraft were thought of. Radio and television are not many years old. Plastics are recent, too.

Most of these inventions need 'stuff'. Silver, bronze, gunpowder, medicines, coal, plastic....

This is what we deal with in Chemistry.

Stonehenge is about 4000 years old.

Fox Talbot was an early photographer.

Chemistry and substances

The world is made of 'stuff'. It has soil, rock, sand, water, air.... The name given to all this 'stuff' is **matter**. Matter can be solid, liquid or gas. Sand is a solid, water is a liquid and air is a gas. Solid, liquid and gas are called the **states of matter**.

One particular kind of matter is called a substance. Iron is a substance. So is water. Salt is a substance, too. We have matter all around us. Most of it is a mixture of substances.

Where do substances come from?

They come from the earth.

Coal is mined. Oil is found underground. Each of them is a mixture of many substances. Metals are made from the rocks of the earth.

They come from the air and sea.

Air is a mixture of gases. They can be separated. The sea contains many substances.

They come from plants.

Plants give us food. They provide materials for our clothes. Rubber comes from a tree. Sugar comes from plants. Some plants give oils. They are used in making soap and cosmetics. Some of the first medicines and drugs came from plants.

A drilling platform. The burning gas is being tested.

An opencast coal site.

Harvesting sugar beet.

Harvesting sugar cane.

Lea Hall colliery and Rugeley power station.

In Chemistry we find out about substances. We do this by asking three kinds of question.

1 How can we get a substance on its own? This means taking others away from it. In Chemistry we first make substances pure.

2 How do we know, or recognize, a substance? I have a white substance. How do I know whether it is chalk, salt, sugar or ...?

3 How can we use substances to make new ones?

As an example, take the substance sugar. It is made from sugar beet or sugar cane.

Sugar beet is grown in cold climates. It is harvested. Soil is washed off. The beet is sliced and treated with hot water. The sugar passes out of the beet into the water.

The liquid is separated. Lime is added to it. This gets rid of some substances. They fall to the bottom of the liquid as sludge. The sludge is taken out by filtering.

The clear liquid is heated. It loses water. Sugar forms in it. It is removed by centrifuge. After washing it is dried ready for use.

A thick treacly liquid is left. It is called molasses. Treacle, rum and alcohol are made from it. With beet pulp it makes cattle food.

Sugar cane grows in hot climates. It is treated in the same way. The sugar formed is brown. Charcoal is used to turn it into white sugar.

So 1 We have made pure sugar.
    2 We can recognise it by its taste.
    3 We can use it to make other substances.

Using taste is dangerous. A white substance may be sugar. But it may be a poison. We need to find **other ways to recognize substances.**

Copy this into your book. Fill in the blanks.

In Science we _____ out. To do so we ask _____. Chemistry is a _____ of Science. In Chemistry we deal with _____. We ask three kinds of questions:

1 How can we make substances _____?
2 How can we _____ a particular substance?
3 How can we use substances to make _____ ones?

The world is made of 'stuff'. All this stuff is called _____. It can be solid, _____ or _____. These are the different _____ of matter.

We get substances from the _____. They also come from the _____, the _____ and the _____.

I am Willie, this is Grace.
We think experiments are ace.
We hope that you enjoy them too –
That's why it's Chemistry for You.

Experiments

In Chemistry we find out about substances. Sometimes we can do this just by looking. Using eyes (and ears) is called observation. It may be all we need to answer some questions. To answer others we need to do tests. A test in which we do something is an **experiment**.

In Chemistry we use observation and experiment.

An experiment must be planned with care. We first decide what we want to know. What question do we need to ask and answer?

Next we work out what we need to do. Then we plan exactly how we mean to do it. The plan must say what materials we need. Last of all, we make sure the method is safe.

During the experiment watch what happens. Make notes so that you do not forget anything.

Use the results to answer the question asked.

We often do this in everyday life. Look at the drawing on the right. It shows a problem which asks a question. This is how we might work out how to answer it.

I have to deliver a newspaper at this house. The notice shows that this could be tricky. Does the dog bite?

I must give the dog a chance to bite (but not me!). I could go in wearing cricket pads. Or I could wait and watch the postman go in.

The dog might bite me above the cricket pads. I shall wait for the postman. This is safer.

The postman went through the gate. The dog rushed at him. It licked his hand.

It seems that the dog does not bite.

> X. Perry, a chemist from Gwent
> Was trying to make a new scent.
> When he smelled the first pong
> He said, 'I've gone wrong!
> This isn't what X. Perry meant.'

Does the dog bite?

Try this!

One question on page 6 was: Is sea water really blue or is it colourless like tap water? Plan an experiment to find out.

These questions are to help you plan.
How will you get sea water?
What will you put the sea water in? A bottle? A plastic cup? A white plastic cup? A glass tumbler?
How will you take sand or seaweed from the water?

Safety

Chemistry is like the dog. There is a chance that it may be dangerous. Always follow the simple rules given below.

The drawings below are labels. They show dangerous substances. Look for them on containers, tankers and trucks.

| explosive | toxic (poisonous) | corrosive | oxidizing agent (oxidant) | flammable (will burn) | harmful or irritating |

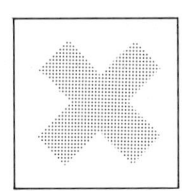

Safety rules

DO keep working areas clear (no satchels, cases etc.).
DO listen when you are told what to do.
DO work with care and watch results.
DO remember that clothes and hair will burn.
DO point test tubes in a safe direction. That is,
DO point them away from others as well as yourself.
DO wear eyeshields if there is any risk to eyes.
DO **report any accident at once.**

Some don'ts

DO NOT run, push or be silly in a laboratory.
DO NOT taste or smell anything unless your teacher says you may.
DO NOT try your own experiments without permission.

Summary

The world is made of stuff. This 'stuff' is called matter. Some matter is solid. Some is liquid and some is gas.

A substance is one particular kind of matter. Iron is a substance. So is water. Sugar is, too. Chemists make substances pure. Substances are made from the matter around us. They come from the earth, the air, the sea and from plants.

Chemists must know how to recognise a substance. They make new substances from those we already have.

Chemists find out by observation and experiment.

Things to do

Look at the labels on substances at home. Make a list of those with 'Pure' on the label. Look for the warning signs shown on this page.

Try this – how to find out

Sea water comes only from the sea. It can be carried best in a clean bottle. Strain it through cloth to remove seaweed or sand. A white cup makes it easy to see colour.

> Willie, for everyone's protection,
> Points test tubes in a safe direction.
> Grace, when stuff from test tube flies,
> Has eyeshields to protect her eyes.
> George treats the bunsen flame with care
> He wouldn't like to lose his hair.
> So be as safe as you can be.
> Don't use just one but use all three.

Making substances pure

We get substances from the air, the sea and plants. They also come from the earth. One of these substances is rock salt.

Drop a lump of rock salt on the bench. You can hear how it gets its name. Observation means using ears as well as eyes.

A machine cutting rock salt in a Cheshire mine.

Experiment 1.1 What does rock salt contain?

Put a small lump of rock salt in a mortar. Crush it to a powder with a pestle. Look at it through a magnifying glass. Try a microscope as well.

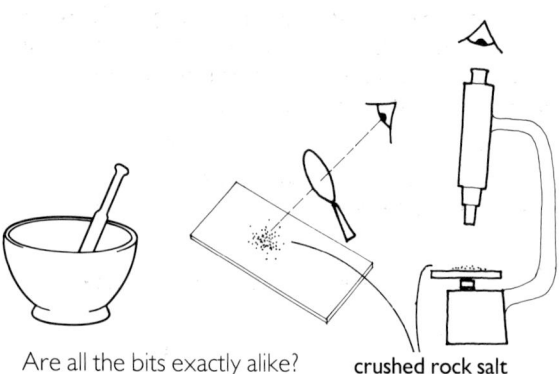

crushed rock salt

Are all the bits exactly alike?
Are they all the same colour?
Are they all the same shape?
Do any of the bits look like sand?

Observation shows that rock salt is a mixture. Most of it is salt. Some bits look like sand.

To get salt from rock salt we must take away the sand. How? Make use of some way in which they differ.

Two nuts fall off your bike. It happens on the beach. Get them back. How? Make use of some way in which nuts differ from sand.
Pick them out by hand? Nuts and sand look different.
Put the sand through a sieve? Nuts are bigger than sand grains.
Run a magnet over the sand? Steel moves towards a magnet.

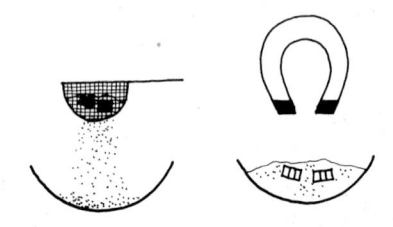

What difference is there between grains of sand and salt?
Can we pick sand grains out with tweezers?

Experiment 1.2 To separate the sand from the salt

Take a small beaker. Put in half a spoonful of crushed rock salt. Add water to a depth of 1 cm.

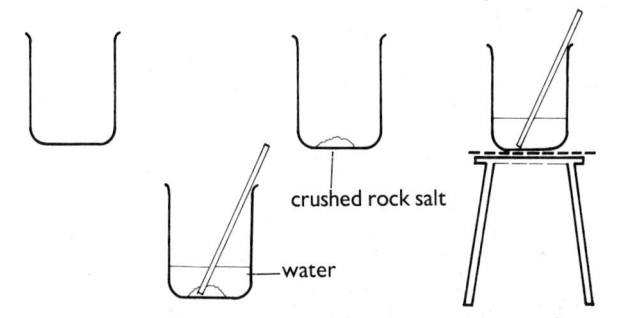

crushed rock salt
water

Heat the beaker on a wire gauze on a tripod. Stir the water with a glass rod. Stop heating when the salt has gone.

Fold a filter paper as shown. Put the cone into a funnel. Put an evaporating dish under it. Pour the liquid from the beaker into the cone.

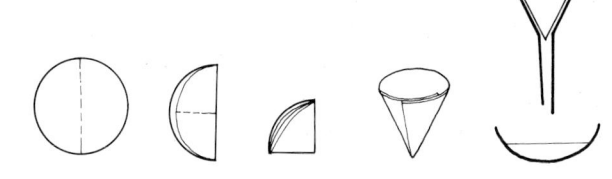

Where is the sand and where is the salt?

The paper cone **filters** the liquid. The liquid which runs through it is called the **filtrate**. The salt is in the filtrate. The salt **dissolved** in the water. A substance dissolved in a liquid is a **solution**. In the dish is a solution of salt in water. The sand is trapped in the filter paper cone. Pour a little water over it. This will wash any salty water out of it.

How can we get salt from this solution?
What will happen if we heat it in the dish?

Pure salt crystals.

Remember to wear eyeshields.

Experiment 1.3 To get salt from the solution

Put the dish on wire gauze. Heat it gently on a tripod. Stop when most of the water has gone.

Take up some of the hot liquid in a dropper. Put drops on a glass slide. White bits should form in the drops. If not, heat the dish again. Look at the bits with a microscope. Taste them. (It is safe!)

Do the white bits in the liquid taste of salt?
Is there any sand mixed with them?
Are they like those shown in the photograph?

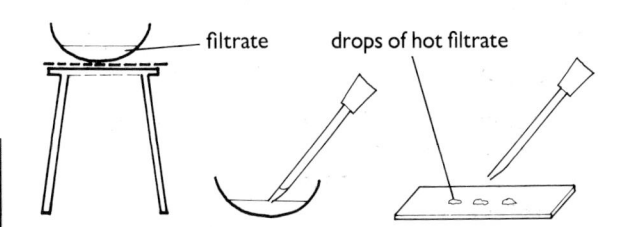

filtrate   drops of hot filtrate

Heating the solution makes it lose water. It comes out of the dish as steam, or water vapour. This is called **evaporation**. Some water is left. It may not be enough to dissolve all the salt. Some bits of salt come out of solution. They have a definite shape, like cubes. They are called cubic **crystals** of salt.

Solutions

Salt put into water disappears. It spreads through the water. Each drop of water has salt in it. Salt has dissolved in water.

Any substance dissolved in a liquid makes a solution. The liquid is called the **solvent**. The dissolved substance is the **solute**.

Experiment 1.4 To find out more about solutions

1. Half fill a test tube with distilled water. Put in a little salt. Stopper the tube. Shake the mixture for a minute or two.

Add more salt. Stopper the tube and shake it. When no more salt dissolves, add a little more. Heat the tube gently. Find out if more salt dissolves in the hot water.

Put drops of hot solution on a glass slide. Watch them through a microscope as they cool.

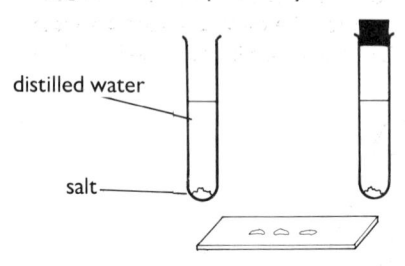

Now try copper sulphate instead of salt.

> Do both substances dissolve in water?
> Is there a limit to how much will dissolve?
> Why do crystals form when hot solutions cool?
> Salt and copper sulphate crystals differ. How?
> Does hot water dissolve more solute or less?

2. Put distilled water in a test tube. Add a little chalk. Heat the tube gently. Filter the mixture. Put drops of filtrate on a slide. Heat them as shown in the drawing.

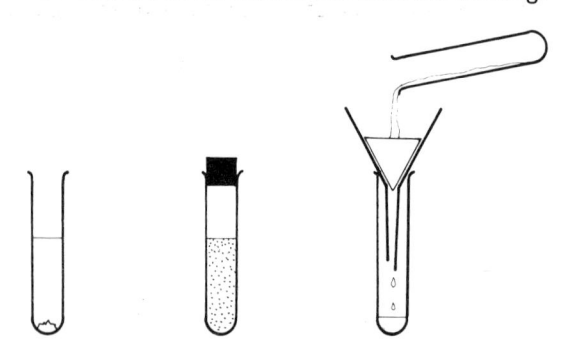

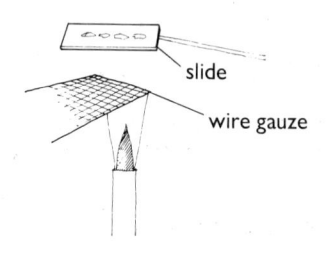

> Does chalk appear to dissolve in water?
> The filtrate runs through the paper. Is it clear?
> Is any solid left on the glass slide?
> Does chalk dissolve in distilled water?

1. If enough salt is added to water some will not dissolve. There is a limit to how much solute will dissolve. If no more solute will dissolve the solution is **saturated**. More solute dissolves in hot water than in cold. Cool a hot saturated solution. It will hold less solute. Some solute will be thrown out. It may appear as crystals.

2. Heating the filtrate leaves no solid. Chalk does not dissolve.

George dreamed of a job in the city.
He put rock salt on chips. What a pity!
He first should have planned
To take out the sand.
Then the chips taste just salty, not gritty.

Other solvents and solubility

Experiment 1.5 To try other liquids as solvents

Put out all bunsen burners. Put ethanol (meths) in three test tubes. In one put a small amount of salt. Stopper the tube and shake it. Warm the tube by standing it in hot water.

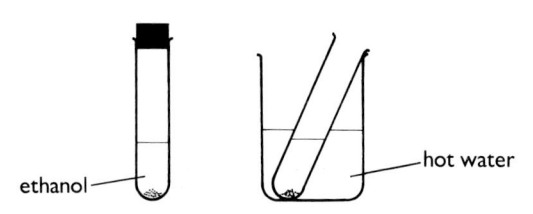

ethanol — hot water

Try copper sulphate in the second tube in the same way. To the third tube add a crystal of iodine. Add a second and third crystal.

Shake a crystal of iodine in water.

> Which of the three solids dissolves in ethanol?
> Does iodine dissolve better in ethanol or in water?

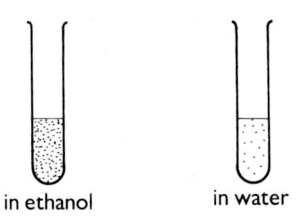

in ethanol   in water

Salt and copper sulphate dissolve in water. They do not dissolve in ethanol. Iodine dissolves in ethanol. The solution is red-brown in colour. It dissolves much less in water. Any liquid can be used as a solvent.

Substances which do not dissolve are **insoluble**. Chalk is insoluble in water. Salt is insoluble in ethanol. Salt is **soluble** in water. Iodine is soluble in ethanol.

Solids dissolve in liquids. Do liquids and gases dissolve?

Experiment 1.6 To find out if liquids and gases dissolve

1. Half fill a test tube with water. Add some oil. Stopper the tube. Shake it. Let it stand. Now use ethanol in water instead of oil.

*2. Take a round-bottomed flask. Fill it nearly full with water. Set it up as shown. Connect a filter pump to it. Draw air through the water for fifteen minutes. Some air may dissolve.

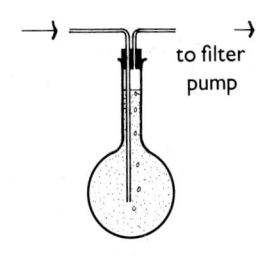

to filter pump

Fill the flask to the top. Fit it with a stopper and tube. Heat it. Let any air in the tube escape. Then fill a gas jar with water. Turn it upside down in the trough. Hold it over the tube.

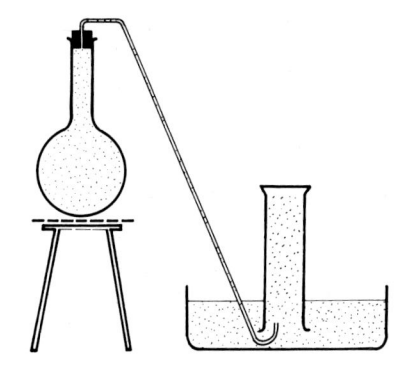

> Do oil or ethanol dissolve in water?
> Does any gas come out of the heated water?
> Solids dissolve in liquids. So do some liquids and gases.

Salt of the earth

When rain falls it runs through soil and rocks. Substances dissolve in the water. This water runs into streams and rivers. More substances dissolve. The rivers carry them to the sea.

This means that sea water has many substances dissolved in it. The main one is salt. An area of sea is sometimes cut off. It becomes an inland sea. One example today is the Dead Sea. Rivers flow in; nothing flows out. It evaporates like the salt solution in our dish.

Millions of years ago there were inland seas. One covered the middle of the British Isles. The climate was hot. The sea lost water. When all the water had gone, salt was left. It was not pure. It had dust and other substances in it.

The salt became covered with dust. Other changes turned the dust into rock. So the salt layers are now found underground. The photograph on page 12 shows rock salt being mined in Cheshire. Substances in the earth are called **minerals**.

Not much salt is mined. Most of it is brought to the surface in a different way. Water is pumped down to the salt layer. The salt dissolves. The solution, called brine, is pumped up. It is evaporated to give salt crystals.

Salt is also made from the sea. Sea water is run into shallow 'pans'. In hot climates it loses water quickly. Sea salt is formed. It contains other substances besides common salt.

About 80 million tonnes of salt is used each year. Animals cannot live without it. Human beings need it too. We use it to flavour food. Salt preserves food, too. Food treated with salt is 'cured'. Cured meat and fish keep longer.

Salt is used in making other substances such as soap, weed killers, household bleach and soda.

Chemists make salt and other substances pure. They find out about them and use them to make new substances.

Cheddar gorge.

A salt pan in Ethiopia.

Pure substances

A substance used in Chemistry should be pure. If not, we get wrong ideas about it. Suppose the only salt we knew was rock salt. We would think that salt is brown, salty and gritty.

Most substances used in Chemistry are kept in glass or plastic bottles. Each has a label. It gives the chemical name of the substance. The chemical name of common salt is sodium chloride.

This is the label of a salt bottle. It is much purer salt than we made. The label tells us how pure it is. 100 grams of this substance contain at least 99.5 grams of salt. It still has other substances in it. The label names them. The amounts of them are very small indeed.

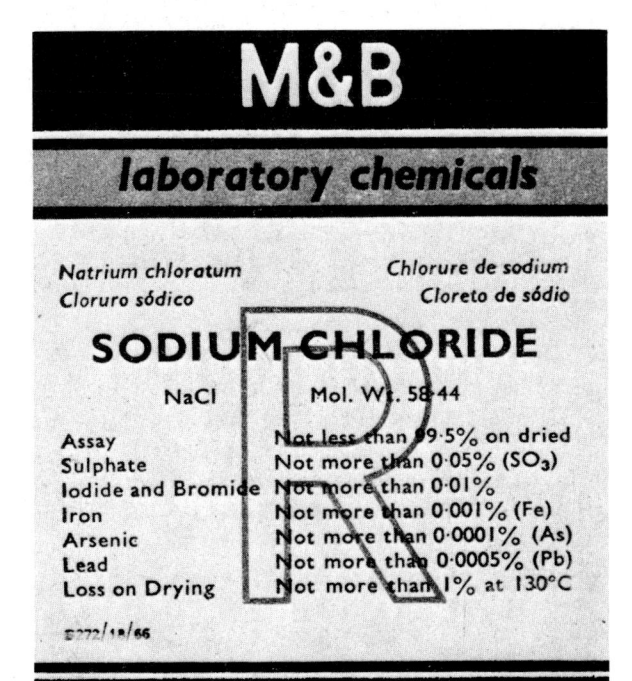

M&B

laboratory chemicals

Natrium chloratum   Chlorure de sodium
Cloruro sódico   Cloreto de sódio

SODIUM CHLORIDE

NaCl   Mol. Wt. 58·44

Assay   Not less than 99.5% on dried
Sulphate   Not more than 0·05% (SO$_3$)
Iodide and Bromide Not more than 0·01%
Iron   Not more than 0·001% (Fe)
Arsenic   Not more than 0·0001% (As)
Lead   Not more than 0·0005% (Pb)
Loss on Drying   Not more than 1% at 130°C

MAY & BAKER LTD DAGENHAM ENGLAND

The label from a bottle of the purest salt.

Summary

Substances found in the earth are called minerals. Rock salt is a mineral. It is a mixture. It has sand and salt in it. Salt dissolves in water. We say it is soluble. Sand is insoluble. It does not dissolve in water. We filter the solution to remove the sand.

Heating the salt solution makes it lose water. This is evaporation. The water gets less. In the end the solution is saturated. Some of the salt comes out on cooling. It forms cubic crystals. Other substances are left in the water.

All liquids are solvents. Solutes dissolve in them. A fixed amount of solvent can dissolve only so much solute. A saturated solution can dissolve no more solute. Most solids dissolve more in hot solvent than in cold. Gases and liquids dissolve in solvents. Gases escape on heating the solution.

Questions

1. In one sentence for each, explain the meaning of these words: solvent, solute, solution, soluble, saturated, crystals.
2. Work out a method of getting back
    a) iron nails lost in long grass,
    b) sugar which has fallen into chalk,
    c) iodine mixed with salt.
3. There is a muddy, weedy pond in your garden. How would you
    a) get clear water, free from mud and weed,
    b) find out if air is dissolved in the water,
    c) find out if any solid is dissolved in it?

Things to do

Make a list of foods which are cured with salt. Find out the crystal shape of salt in your salt cellar. Use a magnifying glass.

Find out if tap water is a solution. Leave some on a saucer on the radiator, or heat some on a glass slide.

Other substances but mainly water

Black ink is a common liquid. It may be a single black substance. It may be a solution of a black solid in a solvent. How can we find out?

Heat it. A black liquid evaporates. Nothing is left. A black solution evaporates, too. However, only the solvent boils away. The black solute will remain at the end.

Experiment 1.7 To find out about ink

Gently heat black ink in an evaporating dish.

The ink boils. It seems to give off steam. A black solid is left in the dish. Ink is a solution. It seems to be a black solid in water. How shall we know if the solvent is water?

What do we know about water? It has no colour or taste. When heated it turns into steam. When cooled it turns to ice.

Experiment 1.8 To find out more about water

Work in pairs. Fill a large test tube half full of ice. Hold it in a clamp and stand. Support a thermometer in the ice. Take its temperature.

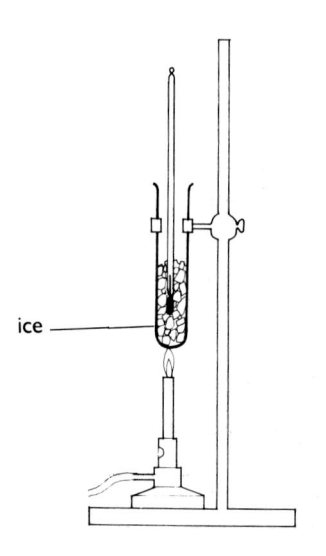

Gently heat the tube. Use a flame about 2 cm high. One partner looks at a watch. Every ten seconds he (or she) says 'Now'. The other calls out the temperature. The partner with the watch writes it down. Change over when the temperature is 50 °C.

Heat the water until it boils. Then take the temperature. Heat it more strongly. Find out if the temperature changes. Put in some salt. Take the boiling temperature again.
Add salt to fresh ice. Take the temperature.

Write down your results:
Melting ice was at _____ °C.
Ice and salt were at _____ °C.
Salt makes ice melt _____ quickly.
Boiling water was at _____ °C.
When strongly heated it boils at _____ °C.
Salt solution boils at _____ °C.

Ice is at 0 °C until most of it has melted. 0 °C is its melting point.
Ice and salt fall below 0°C. So the ice melts faster.
Water boils at 100 °C. 100 °C is its boiling point. Stronger heating does not alter it.
Adding salt makes the boiling point go up.

Properties

Is this man an aircraft pilot? He looks like one. But can he do what a pilot does? Can he fly a plane? Anyone can look like a pilot. All he needs is a uniform. The real test is to ask him to fly a plane.

We know people by what they look like: their appearance.
We also recognize them by what they do: their behaviour.
What they can do is the better test.
Behaviour is more important than **appearance**.

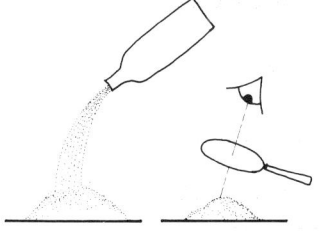

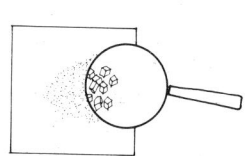

Is this substance salt? It is white. Its crystals are cubic. Its appearance is right.
What about its behaviour?
It tastes salty. However, tasting is dangerous. We need to know more properties of salt.

The properties of a substance are its appearance and behaviour.

There is a liquid in the beaker. Is it water?
What are the properties of water?
Pure water has no colour, no smell, no taste.
It melts at 0 °C. It boils at 100 °C.

Which are the best properties to use? The most useful properties are those which depend on what water can do. Of course, the water must be pure. Dissolved substances alter its boiling point. A change of pressure will alter it, too.

We have made pure salt from a salt solution. Can we get pure water from a salt solution?

When salt solution boils it turns into steam. The salt is left behind. How can we turn the steam back to water?
Three ways are shown in the drawings. Will any of them work? Which is the best method?

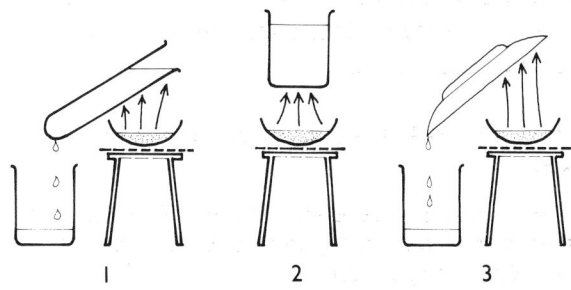

1   2   3

*Look at the picture. Tell me how
To prove this animal's a cow.
Its horns? Its udder? I would choose
To show that it gives milk and moos.*

*Try to tell me how I oughter
Find out if a liquid's water.
Its colour? Taste? No, let it freeze
And show it melts at 0°.*
        (Celsius, of course)

19

Pure water

To get water from a salt solution it must be boiled. The water turns into steam. Cooling the steam turns it into water again. On the last page were three methods of cooling. The best is method 3. It is the best way to collect the water.

However, the plate soon becomes hot. It no longer cools the steam. A German named Leibig found a better method. He passed the steam through a glass tube. This has a second tube round it. Cold water passes through this outside tube. It cools the steam all the time.

This is called Leibig's condenser.

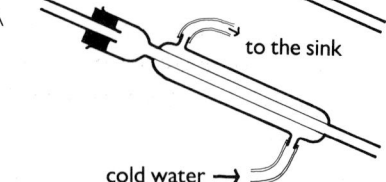

*Experiment 1.9 To make pure water

This is a distilling flask. Put salt solution into it.

Add a drop of ink. Put a thermometer into the flask.

Fit a condenser to the side neck of the flask.

Fit rubber tubing to top and bottom of the condenser. Connect the bottom to the tap. Turn on the tap.

Cold water fills the outside tube. It runs away to the sink.

Boil the solution in the flask.

Steam passes into the condenser. Cold water in the outside tube cools it. It turns back to water which is collected.

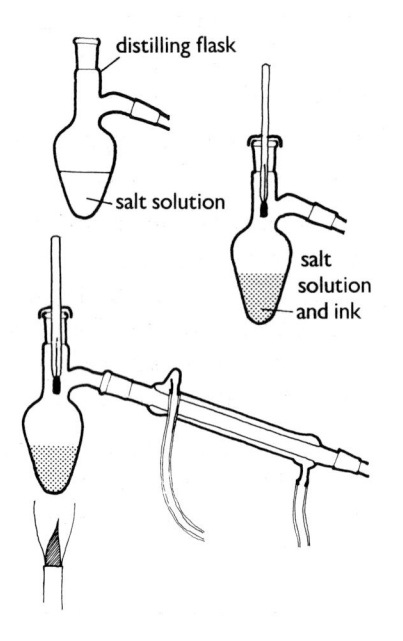

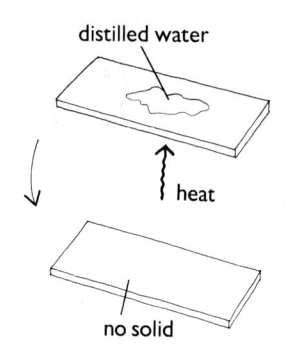

Is the water coloured?
Does it taste of salt?
What does the thermometer show?
This is the temperature of steam. Is the water pure?

This method is called distillation. The water formed is called distilled water. It boils at 100 °C and is pure. It has no colour. It does not taste of salt. The salt and the black dye are left behind in the distilling flask.

Note that it has no **solids** in it. If we heat it on a glass slide it will boil away. No solid will be left on the slide.

All liquids are solvents. They dissolve solids. They can also dissolve other liquids. Ethanol will dissolve in water, for example. Boiling a solution of liquid in liquid means both liquids turn into vapour. Some of each will be given off.

Copy this into your book. Fill in the blanks.

We know people by what they look like. This is called their _____. We also recognize them by what they can do. This is called their _____.

We recognize a substance in the same way. The appearance and behaviour of a substance are called its _____. Its _____ is a more useful property than its _____.

To show its true properties a substance must be _____. Water boils at _____ °C. Salt dissolved in it makes the boiling point _____. Ice melts at _____ °C. This temperature is its _____ point. Adding salt makes it _____.

Melting point and boiling point are useful _____. They are used to find out if a substance is _____.

When a liquid is heated it gives off _____. Cooling this turns it back into _____. When water boils it gives _____. The best cooling method is Leibig's _____. It has two tubes. Steam passes through the _____ one. Cold water runs through the _____ one. It is run into the condenser at the _____.

Heating a liquid and cooling the vapour is called _____. The condensed steam is called _____ water. It is _____. If pure water is boiled away, no _____ is left.

The engine roared. It wasn't nice!
The wheels kept slipping on the ice.
Willie knew what was at fault,
Under the wheels he scattered salt.
The car moved off! It didn't falter.
Salt had melted ice to water.

Questions

1. A wet road soon becomes dry. Does it dry more quickly in hot or cold weather? Where does the water go? What does it turn into? Water vapour rising into the air cools. What will it form? What are clouds made of? Where does rain come from?

2. Sea water evaporates. Will the vapour contain salt? Will rain drops contain dissolved salt? How pure is rain water? Can it be used instead of distilled water?

3. It is a cold night. The air temperature is −1 °C. There is ice on the road. Driving on ice is dangerous.

What is the melting point of ice?
Is the air hotter than this?
Will the ice melt in the air?
Where does the ice come from?

Salt is put on the ice.
What is the melting point of ice and salt?
Is the air hotter than this?
Will the ice melt now?

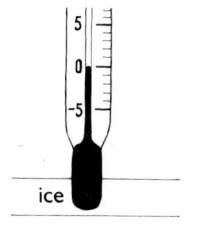

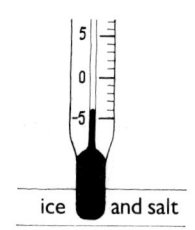

Separating other mixtures

Ink

Ink is a mixture. Black ink is a black solid in a solvent. Is the black solid a single substance? Or is it a mixture?

Experiment 1.10 To find out if the black solid is a mixture

Take a 10 cm square of white blotting paper. Stand it on a beaker or a petri dish. Put one drop of black ink in the middle of the paper.

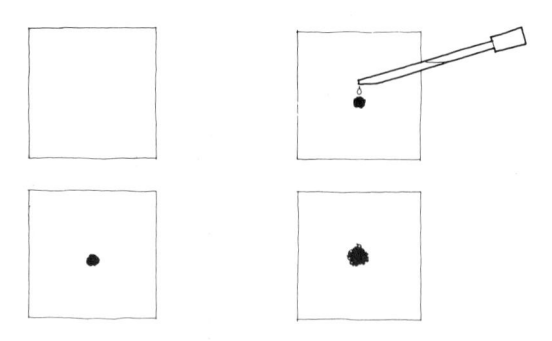

Fill a dropper with water. Put one drop of it on the ink blot. Let it soak in. Put a second drop in the middle of the blot. Let this soak in. Add drops until the colour gets to the edge of the paper.

> What happens?
> Is the result like the drawing?
> How many colours could you see?
> Is the black solid a mixture?

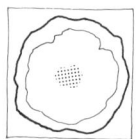

Try this method with inks of other colours.

The water soaks in. It spreads out through the paper. It takes the colour with it. Some coloured dyes are carried further than others. So each will end up as a ring of colour.

Black ink gives blue, orange and yellow. Did you see any other colours?

The method is called chromatography (crow-mat-og-raffy). The ring pattern is called a chromatogram (crow-mat-o-gram). It comes from Greek words meaning 'colour writing'.

The method was first used for coloured dyes. It can be used to separate substances with no colour. Can you see any problem with these?

Plants

Plants contain many coloured substances. Grass is green. Flowers and fruit are coloured. Green leaves go brown. How do we know that the coloured substances do not dissolve in water?

In wet weather grass is still green. The green dye does not dissolve in cold water. We need to find another solvent.

Experiment 1.11 To test the green substance in grass

Cut grass into short pieces. Put it in a mortar. Add some ethanol (meths). Grind the grass in it with a pestle. Pour the liquid into a small test tube. Let it stand or use a centrifuge.

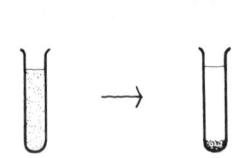

Collect the clear liquid in a dropper. Make two cuts in a filter paper as shown. Put one drop of the green solution in the middle of the paper. Let it dry. Add a second drop. Let this dry. Add a third drop on the same spot.

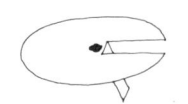

Put ethanol into a petri dish. Put the paper on the dish. Bend the paper tongue so that it dips into the ethanol. Leave it.

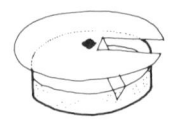

> How does the ethanol reach the green dye?
> Does this method work as well as using a dropper?
> How many coloured rings did you see?
> Is the green substance a mixture?

Ethanol dissolves the green substance in grass. The solution has bits of grass in it. These slowly settle to the bottom. We used three drops of solution. This gives more green substance than one drop. The colours are less faint.

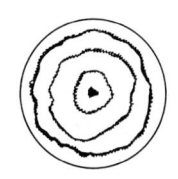

There are three rings of colour. The outer one is orange. This orange colour is xanthophyll. The middle ring is green chlorophyll. You may see a red inner ring of carotene.

Using chromatography

Chromatography separates coloured substances. It can be used to find out what a mixture contains. The drawings show a third way of making a chromatogram.

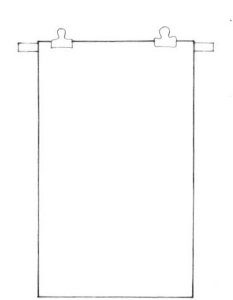

First get a piece of blotting paper (or filter paper) and hang it on a glass rod with two clips.

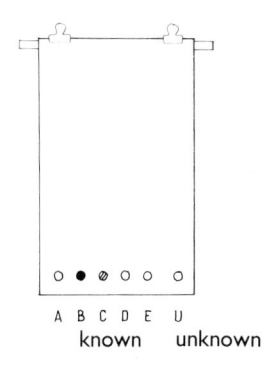

Now hang the paper in a container with some solvent at the bottom. The paper should dip into the solvent.

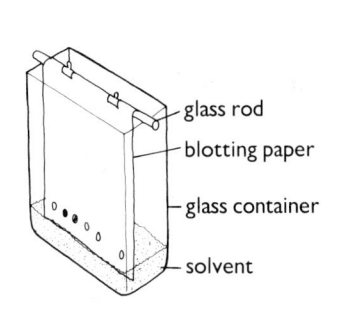

glass rod
blotting paper
glass container
solvent

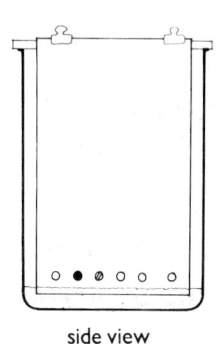

side view

The solvent rises up the paper. It carries the known dyes with it. The unknown is carried, too. Look at the results. The unknown gives two dyes. They look like B and C. They have been carried to the same height, too. Unknown dye = B + C.

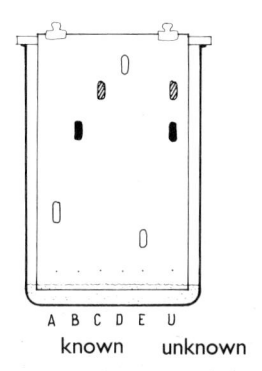

A B C D E   U
known   unknown

Put one drop of the unknown substance and drops of substances or dyes which you think might be in the mixture onto the bottom of the paper.

A B C D E   U
known   unknown

Substances with no colour behave in the same way. The problem is that we cannot see them. We can find where they are. We simply turn them into coloured substances. A liquid spray does this.

Powders may be used instead of paper. Chalk is an example. It is put into a long tube. The mixture is added at the top. Solvent is put in. It carries the dyes down the tube. The mixture is separated. We can find out what it contains.

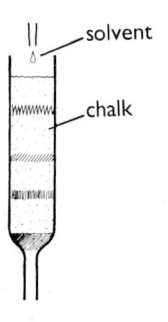

solvent
chalk

The centrifuge

This is a simple centrifuge. It is for use with test tubes. Notice the test tube holders.

The idea of a centrifuge is simple. Anything swung in a circle is thrown outwards. The same idea is used in a spin dryer. Wet clothes are put in a container with holes in it. It is rotated at high speed. Clothes and water are thrown outwards. The water goes through the holes. The clothes do not.

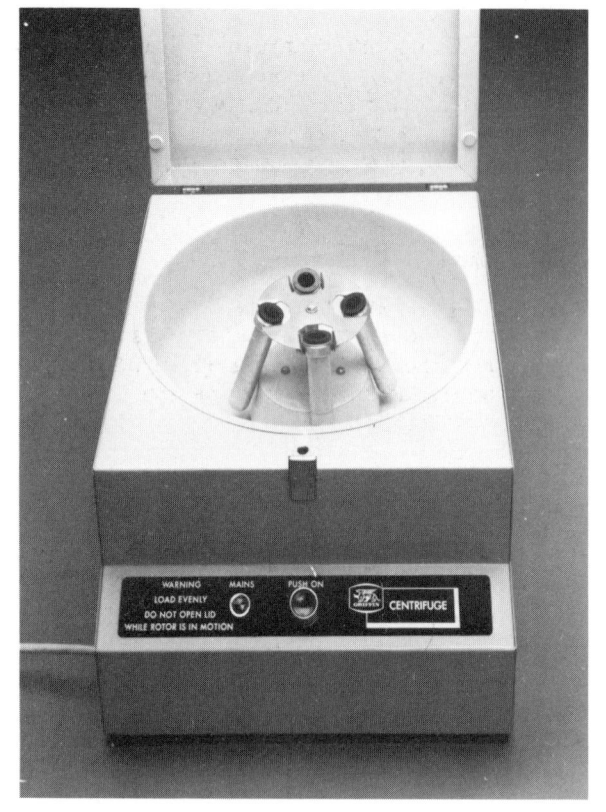

A centrifuge.

Centrifuges separating sugar crystals.

Centrifuges are used in industry. In design they are more like spin dryers. They can separate cream from milk. They separate salt crystals from a solution. They do what filtering does, but they do it much faster.

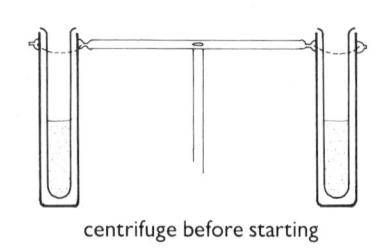

A centrifuge is used to separate solid from liquid. A laboratory one is shown in the photograph. On each arm it has test tube holders. They swing on pivots. The test tubes put into them contain the mixture.

The arms rotate at high speed. Holders and test tubes are thrown outwards. So is the solid. It ends up at the bottom of each tube.

centrifuge before starting

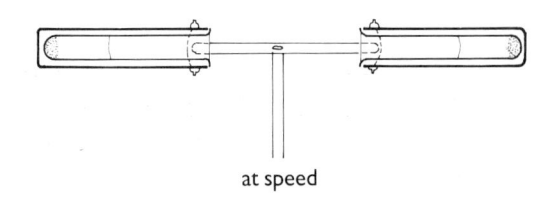

at speed

Things to do

1. Use ethanol to dissolve coloured substances out of flower petals. Find out if they are mixtures or single substances.

2. Test the dye in Smarties.
   Warm six of them in a little water. Pour off the coloured solution. Boil white wool in 1% ammonia solution. Wash it in water. Put a metre length in the coloured solution. Add a little ethanoic acid. The wool takes up the dye.

   Remove the wool. Put it into a little 1% ammonia solution. Let the dye come out. Boil the liquid away. Dissolve the solid in one drop of water. Use this in a chromatography experiment. The solvent is: 3 parts butan-1-ol, 1 part ethanol, 1 part of 1% ammonia solution.

Questions

1. Look at the drawing. The two tubes are full of powder. In one, a known mixture of substances has been used. They are A, B, C, D and E. An unknown substance was used in the other. The same solvent was used in each.

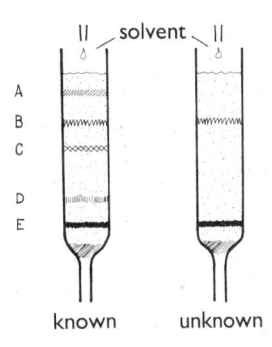

   a) Name one powder which could be used in the tubes.
   b) Which substance moved furthest through it?
   c) Which coloured band has moved least?
   d) How many bands are there in the second tube?
   e) Is the unknown substance a mixture?
   f) What does it contain?

2. Explain how you would separate these mixtures:
   a) mud and water,
   b) chalk and salt,
   c) tea leaves and tea,
   d) chalk and water,
   e) brass nails and iron nails.

Summary

The colour in ink is a dye. A drop of it is put on paper. A solvent is added. This washes the dye outwards. The paper holds some dyes more tightly than others. They will not travel so far. The method separates coloured dyes.

This method is called chromatography. The paper can be held upright as well as flat. Powders such as chalk can be used instead of paper. Other solvents are used as well as water. The result is called a chromatogram.

The method can be used for any substances. But colourless ones cannot be seen. Some way of finding out where they are is needed. They are turned into coloured ones.

A centrifuge takes solids out of liquids. The mixture is whirled round at high speed. The solid is thrown outwards. This takes it to the bottom of the liquid. The liquid is poured off. In other centrifuges liquid passes through the sides of the container. Solid is held inside.

Separating liquids

Crude oil

We get many substances from the earth. One of these is crude oil. It is also called petroleum.

Petroleum is found in some kinds of rock. The rock is porous. It holds the oil just as a sponge holds water. Above and below it are rocks which are not porous. Oil is found in rocks under the sea as well as under the land.

A hole is drilled down to the oil. Pipes are fed into the hole. Gas may exist above the oil. It may force the oil up pipes. In other wells the oil must be pumped up. It contains hundreds of substances. It is taken by pipeline and tanker to a refinery. Here it is distilled.

Experiment 1.12 To distil crude oil

Use a test tube with a side neck. Fill it to a depth of 2 cm with crude oil. Push rocksill into the oil. This soaks up the liquid.

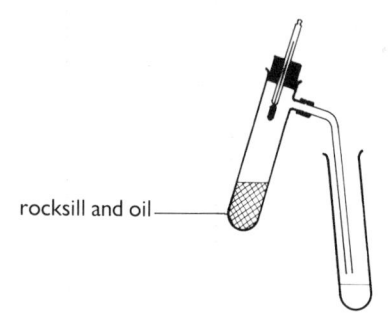

rocksill and oil

Drilling for oil.

Stopper the tube. Use a thermometer in the stopper. Heat the oil gently. Stop when the thermometer shows 70 °C. Stopper the collecting tube. Replace it with a second tube.

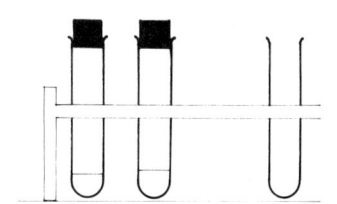

Test the liquid in each of the four tubes.
1. Tilt the tube. Find out how runny each liquid is.
2. Put a few drops on a watch glass. Leave it.
3. Put drops on a watch glass again. Try to light it.
If a liquid does not burn, put a cotton wool wick in it. Try to light the wick. Each liquid is called a 'fraction'.

Are the fractions coloured?
Which of them is the least runny?
Which fraction evaporates most quickly?
Which burns best and which is worst?

Heat the oil again. Collect liquid up to 120 °C. Change the collecting tube at 120 °C, 170 °C and 200 °C. Put a stopper in each tube.

There are many substances in crude oil. Some have low boiling points. They boil off first. They are the first fraction. Higher boiling point liquids come next.

Refining crude oil

A crude oil distillation unit.

The first fraction is runny. It evaporates fast. It burns well. It is not one substance but a mixture of many.

The second fraction is much the same. It evaporates less quickly. It burns just as well. It is a mixture.

The third and fourth are less runny. They evaporate slowly. The third burns with a smoky flame. The fourth needs a wick.

This is fractional distillation. A refinery deals with crude oil in the same way. But the method has to be continuous. Hot crude oil is passed into a tall tower. Superheated steam keeps it hot. Vapour rises and cools. Liquid falls.

The rising vapour passes through trays. These have bubble caps. They force the vapour to pass through liquid already formed.

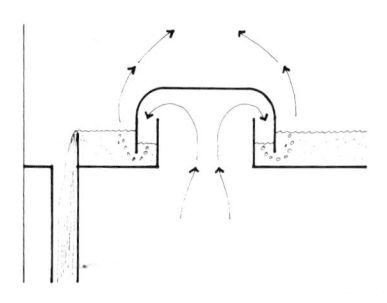

This cools the vapour. Some turns back to liquid. This liquid collects on the trays. It is run off.

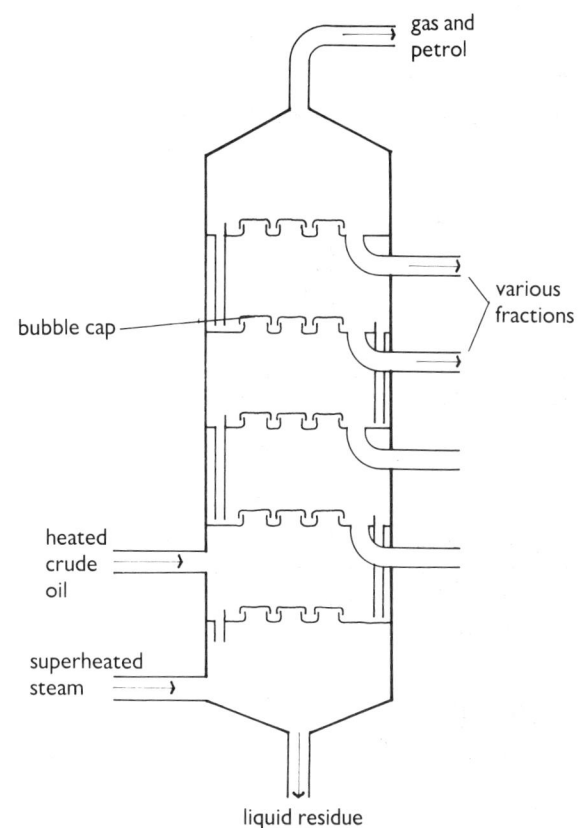

Vapour of liquids with low boiling points goes on. It turns back to liquid higher up the tower. This can also be run off. The crude oil is separated into fractions. The method goes on continuously.

We shall study this in more detail later in the course.

Making new substances

Chemists make pure substances. They find out what their properties are. They find ways of making new substances from them. One method of doing this is to heat substances we already have.

Experiment 1.14 The effect of heating wood

Use pieces of wood as long as a match but thicker. Hold one piece in tongs. Put it in the hot part of a bunsen flame. Take it out when it burns.

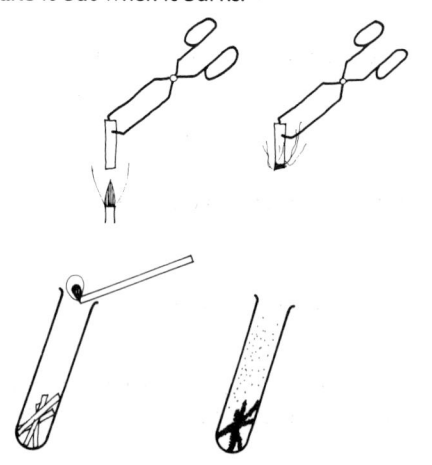

Put four pieces in a test tube. Hold it at the open end in a holder. Heat the wood. Put a lighted splint at the mouth of the tube. Stand the tube on a tile to cool. Take out the black pieces. Try to write with one. Put another in the bunsen flame.

> Does the wood burn with a flame in the air?
> Does it burn with a flame in the test tube?
> Have new substances been formed in the tube?
> Does the black solid write and burn?

Experiment 1.15 The effect of heat on other substances

  Coal
  Paraffin wax
  Chalk
  Salt
*Iodine
*Red lead
  Copper sulphate

Use a test tube for each. Look at each substance before heating. Look at what is left after heating. Describe any changes. Light a splint. Hold the flame at the mouth of each tube.

> Do any of the heated substances burn?
> Does anything come out of the tube?
> Which tubes have new substances in them?
> Which are the same after heating as before?
> What happens to the lighted splint?

Wood begins to burn in the flame. It burns with a flame when taken out. A small amount of grey ash is left.

In the test tube the wood does not burn. There is no flame in the tube. The wood turns into black sticks. They make a soft black mark on paper. They also burn.

A dark brown tar forms in the test tube. Something burns at the mouth of the tube. The splint sets it on fire. We can see nothing coming out. So it must be a gas.

wood heated → charcoal + wood tar + a gas which burns

Coal gives the same kind of result as wood. The black lumps left in the tube are coke.

coal heated → coke + coal tar + a gas which burns

Paraffin wax melts to a liquid. It turns back to wax on cooling. No new substance is formed.

Chalk and **salt** No change can be seen in either substance.

Iodine A black crystal of iodine turns into a violet substance. This is iodine vapour. No liquid is seen. As it goes up the tube the vapour cools. It turns back to shiny black crystals.

Red lead The red powder changes to a yellow one. The flame of the splint burns brighter. This means something is coming out of the tube. Nothing can be seen. It must be a gas.

red lead heated → a yellow substance + a gas

Copper sulphate crystals The blue crystals slowly turn white. Steam comes out of the tube. The splint goes out. Drops of liquid form in the tube.

copper sulphate crystals → a white powder + steam (?)

Heating does not change some substances. They just get hotter. Some, like wax, get hot enough to melt. Cooling reverses the change. The liquid turns back to solid.

Heating some substances forms new ones. Wood and coal break down into many new substances. The yellow solid from red lead may be a new substance. A change of colour does not always mean a new substance. A gas given off does. The white substance from copper sulphate may be a new one.

A change which gives new substances is a chemical change.
If no new substance is formed the change is a physical one.

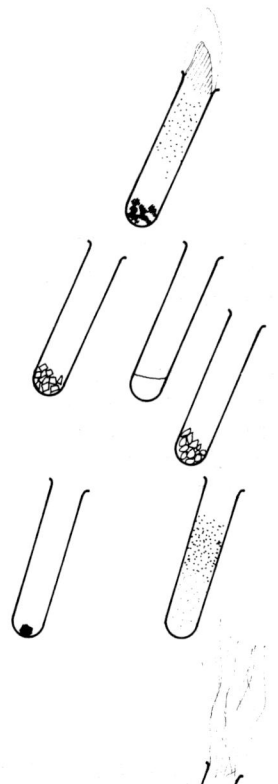

Heating metals

Write down the names of all the metals you know.

> How do you know that they are metals?
> What are the properties of metals?
> Do they all have a shiny surface?
> Do they float or sink in water?

Check your list with the one on the next page. Give yourself a mark for each metal in your list.

All metals have a shiny surface. If it is not shiny a metal can be polished. The shine is called **metallic lustre**. It is quite different from the shine on plastic or glass.

Metals can be recognized by appearance. But behaviour is more important. So we shall find out what metals can do.

Experiment 1.15 To heat metals (wear eyeshields)

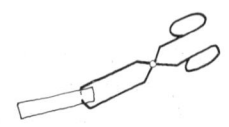

1. Clean a strip of copper with emery paper. Hold it in tongs. Heat it gently. Leave it on a tile to cool.

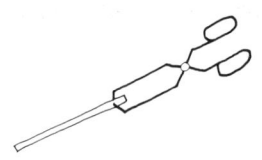

2. Do the same with a 1 cm strip of magnesium.

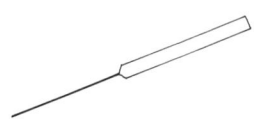

3. Take a platinum wire sealed into glass. Use the glass as a holder. Heat the wire strongly.

*4. Rub a small lump of lead with emery paper. Put it on a crucible lid. Put the lid on a pipe clay triangle, on a tripod. Heat it gently, then strongly.

5. Rub iron wire with emery paper. Hold it in tongs. Heat it.

> Which metal is exactly the same after heating?
> In what ways have the other metals changed?
> Which metal burns with a bright, white flame?

All the metals get hot. Platinum becomes white hot. It does not melt. When it cools it is the same as before.

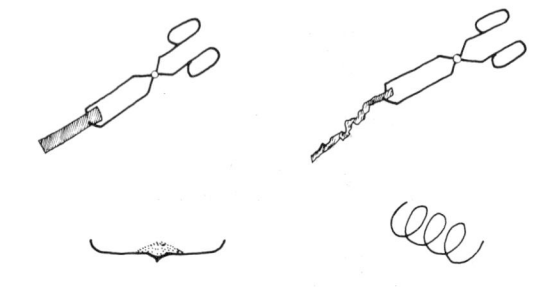

Magnesium burns with a bright, white flame. The result is a dull white powder. It is not a bit like magnesium. Copper becomes coated with a black powder. Lead melts. It slowly changes to a yellow powder. Iron is a grey metal. It forms a blue-black substance.

Summary

Heating makes substances get hotter. Some, like wax, become hot enough to melt. Cooling will reverse the change. No new substance is formed. This kind of change is called a **physical change**. Such changes are easy to reverse.

Heating melts ice to water. Cooling turns the water back to ice. No new substance is formed. Ice to water, water to ice are physical changes.

Heating changes some substances into new ones. Heating coal splits it up into new substances. Shiny magnesium metal burns. It leaves a white powder. This is very different from the metal. It seems likely to be a new substance.

This kind of change is called a **chemical change**. It is not easy to reverse. A chemical change forms at least one new substance.

Mad to light magnesium wire,
Willie sets the house on fire.
Willie's wallet, full of cash, is
Lost in the fire and burnt to ashes.
Though all his notes have gone, it's strange –
Willie has some chemical change.

Questions

1. Look at each common change listed below. Decide if a new substance is formed. Decide if the change is easy to reverse. Say whether the change is a chemical or a physical one.
   a) milk going sour,
   b) iron rusting,
   c) boiling water turning into steam,
   d) frost forming on a cold night,
   e) a wet road drying in the wind,
   f) a forest fire,
   g) salt dissolving in water,
   h) clouds forming in a clear sky,
   j) bread turning into burnt toast.

2. Copy this into your book. Choose the best answer from the ones in brackets. Put this answer in.

   New substances are formed by (physical/chemical/simple) changes. Heating wood in air makes it (hot/burn/boil). It turns into a (brown/grey/yellow) ash. This (is/is not) a new substance. The ash (can/cannot) be turned back into wood. Burning wood is a (physical/chemical) change.

   When lead is heated it (burns/melts). This is a (physical/chemical) change. More heating turns the lead into a (black/yellow/blue-black) powder or ash. This powder (is/is not) like lead. If it is a new substance the change is a (chemical/physical) change. We heated five metals. The one which burns with a bright white flame is (copper/lead/platinum/magnesium/iron).

List of metals
Aluminium
Barium
Calcium
Copper
Chromium
Gold
Iron
Lead
Magnesium
Mercury
Platinum
Silver
Tin
Zinc   and others

Burning

Heating substances can give new ones. When heated, some substances burn with a flame. Burning is a chemical change. It happens every day. We need to know more about it.

What do we know about it now?
Wood burns with a flame in air. So does magnesium. There is no flame when wood is heated in a test tube. Why is this?
Can anything burn inside a test tube? Try it and see!
A gas jar is easier to use than a test tube.

Experiment 2.1 To burn a candle inside a gas jar

Put a candle on a gas jar cover. Light it. Invert a gas jar over it. The jar is full of air.

> What happens to the candle flame?
> Can air get into or out of the jar?
> We know what happens to the candle. What happens to the air?

Experiment 2.2   To find out what happens to air during burning

Light a candle. Stand it on a big cork. Float it on water in a trough. Put a bell jar over it. Stopper the jar.

The flame goes out. Light a splint. Hold it near the stopper. Take the stopper out. Put the flame in the jar.

The jars in these two experiments are full of air. In both the flame goes out. No air can get in or out. Water rises into the bell jar. This means some air has gone. The air left in the jar puts out a flame. Air has two parts. One lets things burn. The other does not.

Why

In Science we try to explain why. The explanation is called a theory. It must explain all the facts. A fact is something we know to be true. We make theories all the time. Each theory uses the facts known at the time.

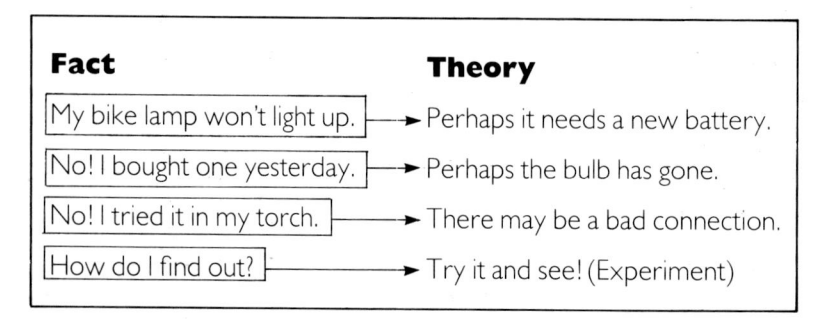

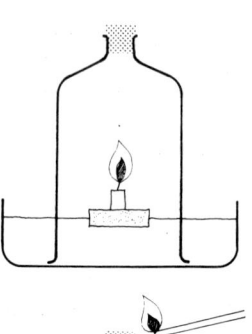

Fact	Theory
My bike lamp won't light up.	→ Perhaps it needs a new battery.
No! I bought one yesterday.	→ Perhaps the bulb has gone.
No! I tried it in my torch.	→ There may be a bad connection.
How do I find out?	→ Try it and see! (Experiment)

A theory of burning

A good theory explains all the facts we know. It can also show us how to find new ones. It suggests experiments to do.

The bell jar experiment gives us facts about burning. Do all burning substances give the same results?

Magnesium burns well. With care we can use it in a bell jar. Hook a spiral of it on a wire. Stick the wire into the stopper. Light the magnesium. Put it quickly into the bell jar. At the same time put in the stopper. The results are the same as before.

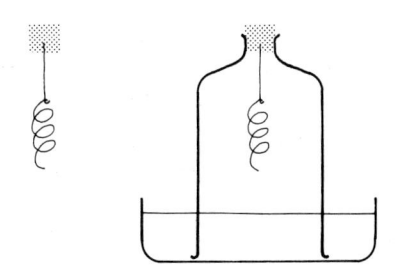

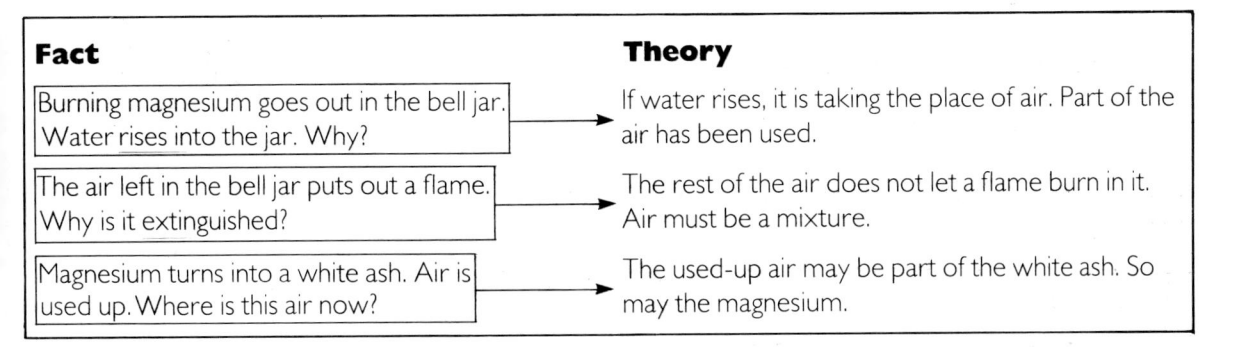

Fact	Theory
Burning magnesium goes out in the bell jar. Water rises into the jar. Why?	If water rises, it is taking the place of air. Part of the air has been used.
The air left in the bell jar puts out a flame. Why is it extinguished?	The rest of the air does not let a flame burn in it. Air must be a mixture.
Magnesium turns into a white ash. Air is used up. Where is this air now?	The used-up air may be part of the white ash. So may the magnesium.

Full theory

Burning substances use part of the air. The rest of the air will not let flames burn in it. Air is a mixture. The air used up may be part of the substance formed.

Burning magnesium gives a white ash. The theory says

   white ash = magnesium + used-up air

If so, the white ash has more matter in it than the magnesium. Finding out if this is so will test the theory.

Matter, mass and weight

The world is made of matter. The amount of matter in a substance is called its **mass**. Mass is measured in kilograms (kg). 1 kg = 1000 grams.

Hold 1 kg of iron. Let go of it. It falls towards the earth. The pull of the earth on it is its **weight**.

Put 1 kg on a spring balance. The pan goes down. Put 2 kg on the pan. It goes down twice as far. A balance can be used to measure mass or weight.

A top pan balance is best. It shows the mass on a moving scale.

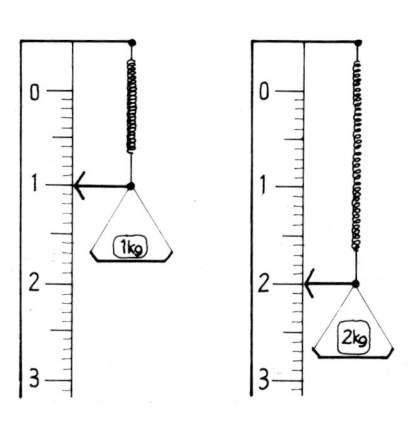

What happens to the air in burning

Experiment 2.3 To compare the mass of the white ash and the magnesium

Half fill a crucible with magnesium turnings. Put on its lid. Put it on a top pan balance. Read off its mass.

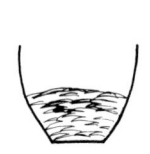

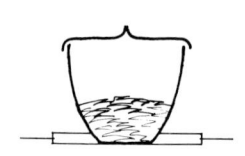

Put it on a pipe clay triangle, on a tripod. Heat it gently, then strongly. Lift the lid with tongs regularly. Try to prevent any smoke escaping. Let it cool. Put it back on the balance. Read off its mass.

   Is white ash formed in the crucible?
   Does the mass change?
   If so, is it smaller or larger?

The magnesium turns into white ash. The lid is lifted to let air in. It must be put back quickly. If not, some white ash escapes as smoke. The ash has a bigger mass than the magnesium. It seems that

   white ash = magnesium + used-up air

A top pan balance.

We have heated other metals. Some, like platinum, show no change. Copper, lead and others give coloured powders.

Experiment 2.4 To find out if other metals show a change in mass

Put a strip of copper foil on a balance. Read off its mass. Hold it in tongs. Heat it in the bunsen flame. Let it cool. Measure its mass.

   What happens to the copper?
   Is the mass the same, smaller or larger?
   Does heated copper use up part of the air?
   Is this air part of the black ash formed?

This experiment has a snag. Black ash forms on the copper. However, it easily flakes off. Losing it may make the mass seem less. Take the results of the whole class. Most of them will show an increase in mass. Heated copper uses air.

   But does air have a mass? It seems not to fall to the earth.
   How can we find out?
   We can compare an empty flask with a flask full of air.

Willie's brother licks his chops,
Eats and eats and rarely stops.
As he gobbles up more matter,
George, of course, becomes much
   fatter.
Because he eats so much, alas,
His weight gets bigger,
   and his mass.

34

Experiment 2.5 To find out if air has mass

Fit a round-bottomed flask with a stopper. The stopper carries a piece of glass tubing. On it there is a rubber tube and clip.

Connect the rubber tube to a pump. Pump out the air. Close the clip on the rubber tube. Put the flask on a balance. Read off its mass. Open the clip. Find out if the mass changes.

What do you observe when the clip is opened?
After opening, is the mass greater or smaller?
What is the mass of the air in the flask?

The pump takes air out of the flask. Opening the clip gives a rushing noise. This is air rushing back into the flask. As a result the mass becomes greater. The increase is the mass of the air. It is very small.

Summary

Burning uses up air. Only part of the air is used. The rest of the air will not allow burning. Air is a mixture of gases. One part lets things burn. One part does not.

Burning forms new substances. They have a larger mass than the substance burnt.
This is true of magnesium which burns with a flame. It is also true of copper which does not. The used-up air is part of the new substance.
   the black ash = copper + used-up air

The mass of a substance is the amount of matter in it. It is measured in grams (g) and kilograms (kg). Mass is measured on a balance.

Questions

1. I burn magnesium in a closed space. When it goes out I put in a lighted splint. Explain how this shows that air is a mixture of gases.

2. Metals heated in air often leave an ash. Is the mass of the ash greater than the mass of the metal? Describe how you would find out.

3. Charcoal glows red hot when heated in air. Almost nothing is left. Where is the new substance if no ash remains?

4. Air is pumped out of a flask. Its mass is found to be 150 grams. Air is let in. The mass is found to be 151.2 g. What is the mass of the air in the flask?

5. Fill in the blanks.
   A piece of lead is put on a balance. This measures its _____. The lead is heated for a long time. The ash formed is _____ in colour. Its mass is _____ than the mass of the lead. The lead has used up part of the _____. The yellow ash contains _____ and _____ air. It is a _____ substance. Heating gives a _____ change.

Oxygen and burning

Copper heated in air turns black. Our theory to explain this is:

    copper + used-up air → black powder

The metal mercury is a silvery liquid. If it is heated a red powder forms on it. This is a chemical change. It is very slow. It may take days of heating to complete it.

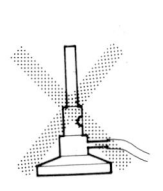

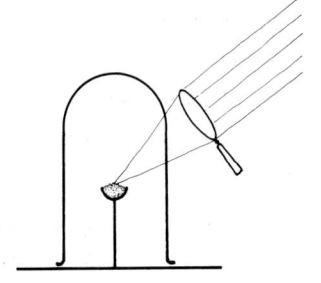

In 1774, John Dalton heated this red powder. He had no bunsen burner. It was not invented until 1855. He put the red powder in a glass vessel. He used a lens to focus the rays of the sun on the powder. We shall get the same result with a bunsen burner.

The apparatus which Lavoisier used.

*Experiment 2.6 To heat the red powder

Do the heating in a fume cupboard. Put the red powder in a test tube. Heat it gently. Light a splint. Hold the flame at the mouth of the tube. Blow out the flame. Put the glowing red end of the splint inside the test tube. Let the tube cool. Tap its contents into a dish.

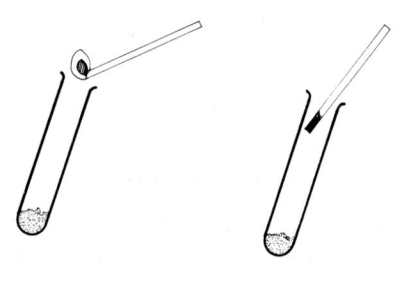

What happens to the flame of the splint?
What happens to the glowing splint?
Did you see anything coming out of the tube?
What is there in the test tube and dish?

A silvery metal forms. Drops of mercury fall into the dish. Mercury vapour is poisonous. This is why a fume cupboard is used.

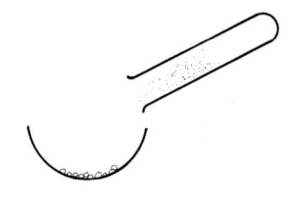

The lighted splint burns more brightly. The glowing splint bursts into flame. A substance coming out of the tube causes this. But we saw nothing. This substance must be a gas.

The red powder splits up into mercury and a gas. This gas makes flames burn brighter. **It relights a glowing splint.**

Dalton told a French scientist about the gas. His name was Lavoisier. He saw a way of testing our theory of burning.

He used the apparatus shown. The vessel with a curved neck is a retort. It had some mercury in it. Lavoisier heated it on a charcoal fire.

After some days a red powder formed in the retort. The liquid rose inside the bell jar.

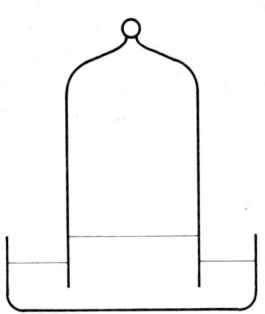

Some of the air had been used up by the mercury. Lavoisier took out the retort. He took every bit of red powder out of it. He heated the powder. It gave off a gas. All the gas was put back into the bell jar. The level of the liquid fell. It went back to the level at the start.

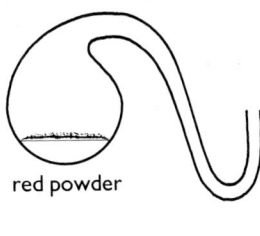

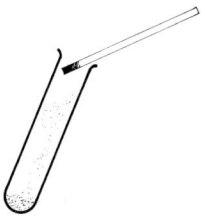

The gas put back was the used-up air. Lavoisier called it **oxygen**.

Now we know that:

Air is a mixture of gases. One gas allows substances to burn in it. This gas is oxygen.

The rest of the air is not oxygen. It does not let things burn in it. Most of it is a gas called nitrogen.

Burning substances use up oxygen. So do some heated metals. When all the oxygen has been used, burning stops.

metal + oxygen from air → a powder or ash

Elements and compounds

Heated mercury uses oxygen. It forms a red powder. In the red powder mercury and oxygen are joined together. We say that mercury **combines** with oxygen.

Heat splits the red powder up. Oxygen comes out of the tube. Mercury is left in it. The powder **decomposes**. This kind of chemical change is called **decomposition**.

Mercury cannot be split up. No one has been able to decompose it. Substances like this are called **elements**.

An element is a single substance. It cannot be split up into simpler substances.

Copper is an element. So is magnesium. Oxygen is an element too.

Elements combine. The result is called a **compound**. Magnesium combines with oxygen. The white powder formed is a compound. A compound contains two, or more, elements chemically combined.

The names of compounds

The name must say which elements it contains.
In the white powder are magnesium and oxygen.
Its name is **magnesium oxide**.
If it contains only two elements the name ends in -**ide**.
Why not call it oxygen magneside? Try saying it!

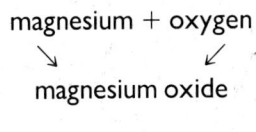

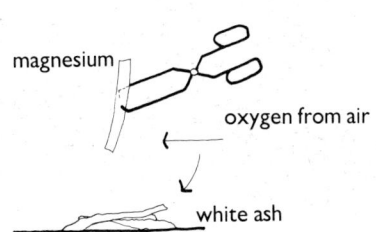

magnesium + oxygen
↘   ↙
magnesium oxide

How much of the air is oxygen?

To find the answer we must
- measure some air
- take away its oxygen
- find out how much air has gone.

Try to plan an experiment to do this. Call it 2.7.
How can we measure a gas?
The best way is to find its volume. We cannot see the air to measure it.
We can use a vessel with volume markings on it.

How do we take away oxygen? Heat a metal in the air.
As oxygen is used, more air will get in. Close the vessel!
Then how shall we heat the metal?
How can we measure how much air has gone?
A syringe solves all these problems.

This is a syringe. It has air in it. Markings on the side tell us how much.

This is a glass tube. It is full of tiny bits of copper. Their colour is salmon pink.

Join the syringe and tube with rubber tubing. Join an empty syringe at the other end. Small bits of glass rod hold the copper in place.

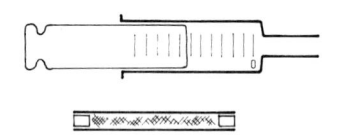

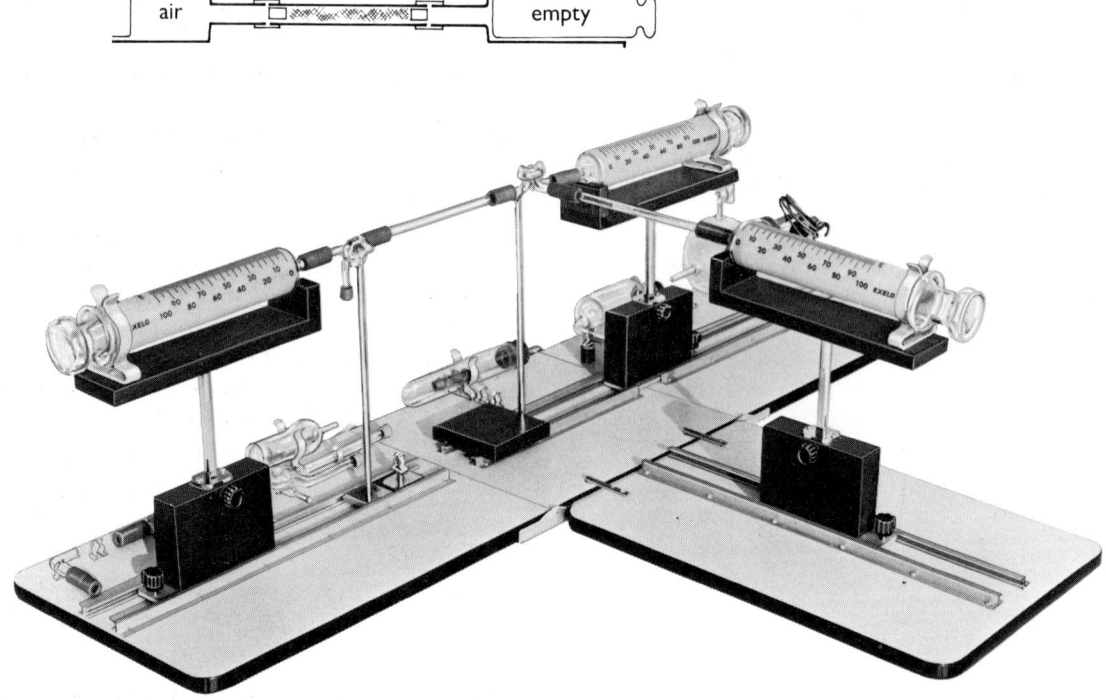

A gas syringe.

Experiment 2.7 How much of the air is oxygen?

1. Heat a small length of the copper. Push the air out of the syringe. It goes through the copper. It enters the empty syringe. Heat the next section of copper. Push the air back through it.

Repeat this. Stop when there is no change in the volume of air. Let the tube cool. Note the volume of air left in the syringe.

> What happens to the heated copper?
> Does the last section of heated copper change?
> What does this tell us about the air?

The copper turns black. It takes oxygen from the air. So the volume of air gets less. The last section of heated copper stays pink. There is no oxygen left in the syringe.

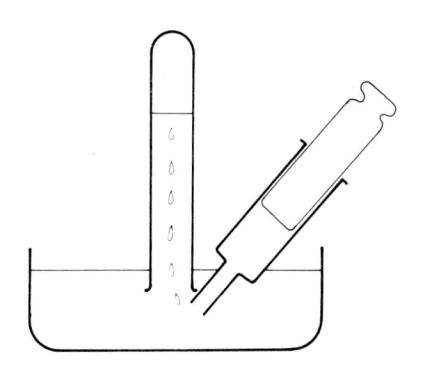

2. Push the gas out of the syringe. Collect it in a test tube. Test it with a lighted splint. Does the flame go out?

Here is a set of results: (the volumes are in cm^3)
Volume of air at the start = 41.5
Volume (cold) at the end = 33.0
Volume of oxygen used up = 8.5
41.5 cm^3 of air contain 8.5 cm^3 of oxygen.

The percentage of oxygen is $\frac{8.5 \times 100}{41.5} = 21\%$

Roughly $\frac{1}{5}$ of the air is oxygen. About $\frac{4}{5}$ is nitrogen.

Summary

When heated, mercury turns into a red ash. It combines with, and uses up, part of the air. Heating the red ash gives back a gas. Lavoisier proved that this gas is the used-up air. It is called oxygen. Substances burn more brightly in it than they burn in air. It makes a glowing splint burst into flame. Heated copper also takes oxygen out of air. We used this to show that 21% of air is oxygen. Air is roughly $\frac{1}{5}$ oxygen and $\frac{4}{5}$ nitrogen. Nitrogen puts out almost all burning substances.

Nitrogen, oxygen, copper, mercury are elements. They cannot be split up into other substances. Copper and oxygen combine. The black ash formed is not an element. It can be split up into copper and oxygen. It is a compound.

The compound is called copper oxide. The name ends in -ide. This shows that it contains only two elements. The name also shows which ones.

Questions

1. Copy this into your book. The brackets contain answers. Choose the *best* one. Write only this one into your book. Do not copy in the others.

    Magnesium is (an element/a compound/a mixture). It burns giving a (black/white/red) ash. It combines with (nitrogen/oxygen/gas) in the air. The ash is (an element/a compound/a mixture). It is called (oxygen magnide/magnesium oxide).

    Heated mercury gives a (black/red/white) ash. This is a (physical/chemical/colour) change. The change is (very fast/slow/very slow). The ash is called (mercury oxide/oxygen mercuride). When heated the red ash splits up. It gives a gas called (oxygen/nitrogen/mercury). The split-up is a (physical/chemical/colour) change. It is called (combination/decomposition).

    Air is a (compound/mixture) of several gases. Oxygen is about ($\frac{1}{5}$/$\frac{4}{5}$/ 79%) of the air. Substances burn in oxygen (feebly/very well). Oxygen (puts out/relights) a glowing splint.

2. Make a list of all the substances we burn. Do they use oxygen from the air? Why is the air never short of oxygen?

3. Burning substances need oxygen from the air. Explain how a fire blanket works.

Pure oxygen

Oxygen is made in two ways. It can come from oxides or from air.

Air is a mixture of gases. To get oxygen the other gases must be taken away. Oxygen is manufactured by this method.

Oxides are compounds. Heat decomposes some of them giving oxygen. Mercury oxide is one of these. But it is expensive. Hydrogen peroxide is cheap and easy to use.

*Experiment 2.8 To make and collect oxygen

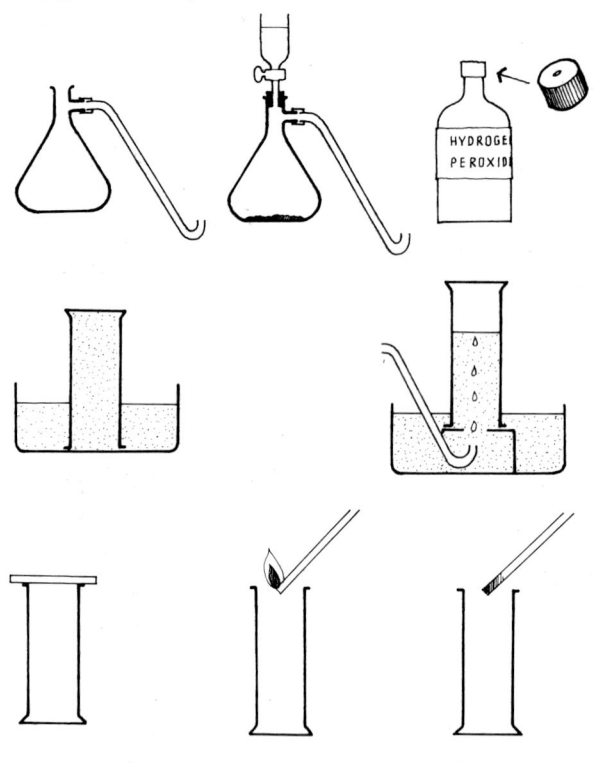

The drawing shows a conical flask (shaped like a cone). It has a side neck. Connect a glass tube to it. Put black manganese (IV) oxide into the flask. Fit a dropping funnel into the stopper. Fill this with hydrogen peroxide solution.

Fill a trough with water. Fill a gas jar with water. Turn it upside down in the trough.

Open the tap in the funnel. Let some hydrogen peroxide drop into the flask. Close the tap.

Gas comes out of the glass tube. Stand the gas jar on a shelf. Put the tube under it.

When the jar is full of gas, slide a cover over it. Take it out. Fill six more gas jars.

Use one jar to find out if the gas is oxygen. Put in a lighted splint. Blow the flame out. Put the glowing splint in the gas.

We shall burn elements in oxygen. Oxides will be formed. We shall try to dissolve each oxide in water. We shall test the water. The tests are litmus paper and Universal Indicator.

On page 22 we dissolved the green substance out of grass. Litmus is made in the same way. It is the dye in one kind of moss. The dye is mauve in colour (like pickling cabbage). Filter paper is soaked in the solution of it. Drying it gives litmus paper.

Universal Indicator is a solution. It contains coloured dyes.

They are both called **indicators**. They indicate, or show, what a liquid contains.

Burning in pure oxygen

Hydrogen peroxide splits up on its own. It gives oxygen very slowly. This oxygen gets out through a hole in the bottle cap.

Manganese (IV) oxide speeds up the change. It is still there at the end. Substances which do this are called **catalysts**. The oxygen comes from the hydrogen peroxide.

A glowing splint bursts into flame. The gas is oxygen.

*Magnesium   Hold a strip of magnesium in tongs. Light it at the bunsen. Hold it in a gas jar of oxygen. *Do not look at it.* Watch it only through blue glass.

In each test: Look at the results in the gas jar. Add water. Put a cover on the jar. Shake it. Put in a litmus paper. Add drops of Universal Indicator.

*Calcium   Hold a piece of calcium in tongs. Burn it in the same way. *Do not look at the flame.*

*Iron   Put a bunsen flame near the top of a gas jar. Hold a tuft of iron wool in tongs. Touch the flame with it. Put it quickly into the oxygen.

*Carbon   One form of carbon is charcoal. Hold a stick of it in the flame. Put the red-hot end into oxygen.

*Sulphur   Put sulphur in a combustion spoon. Hold it in the bunsen flame. When it burns, hold it in oxygen.

*Phosphorus   Put red phosphorus in another spoon. Get it burning gently. Put the spoon into a gas jar of oxygen.

Have this table ready to put in the results.

element	metal or non-metal	colour of flame	oxide is	dissolves in water	litmus colour	Univ. Ind. colour
calcium	metal	brick red	solid	perhaps	blue	violet
carbon	non-metal	white	gas	perhaps	mauve	yellow

All these elements burn brilliantly in oxygen. Some of the oxides are solid. Others cannot be seen. They are likely to be gases. In water litmus is mauve; Universal Indicator is green. Water is added to each gas jar. It may change the indicator colour. If it does, the oxide has dissolved in the water.

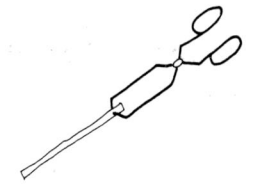

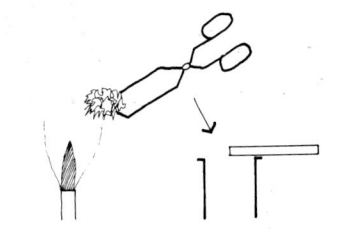

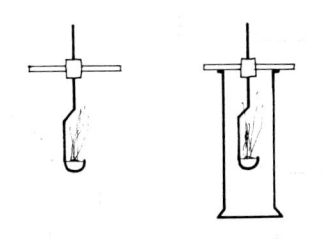

Acid and alkali

The burning elements form oxides. Some of these dissolve in water. The oxide in water gives a solution. Most solutions make litmus red or blue. They also change the colour of Universal Indicator.

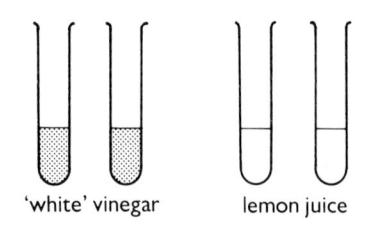

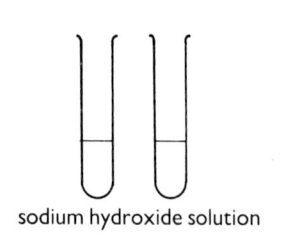

'white' vinegar

lemon juice

sodium hydroxide solution

Experiment 2.9 To find out what substances affect indicators

Put vinegar in two test tubes. Put lemon juice in two others. Add drops of litmus to one of each. Add drops of Universal Indicator to the other two.

Try the taste of vinegar and lemon juice. (Yes, it is safe.) What effect do they have on the indicators?

Vinegar and lemon juice taste sour, sharp or acid. They are acidic solutions. Each contains a substance called an acid.

Put sodium hydroxide solution in two test tubes. Test each of them with one of the indicators.

Sodium hydroxide solution is alkaline. It contains a substance called an **alkali**. The family name of alkalis is **hydroxide**.

Indicators

Acid turns litmus red. Alkalis turn litmus blue. Many dyes change colour in this way. They are called indicators. They indicate, or show, that acids or alkalis are present.

Universal Indicator is a mixture of dyes. It shows many colours. There are usually seven. They are the colours of the rainbow.

| Red | Orange | Yellow | Green | Blue | Dark Blue | Violet |

acid colours

stronger   weaker

alkali colours

weaker   stronger

Red shows a stronger acid than orange or yellow. Violet shows a stronger alkali than blue or dark blue.

Alkalis

In Experiment 2.8 we burnt elements in oxygen. Check the metals in the table of results. They were magnesium, calcium and iron.

All three gave oxides. Two of the oxides dissolve in water.

> *Calcium burns in a blinding flash*
> *And changes to a dull white ash.*
> *In the dull white ash I find*
> *Metal and oxygen combined.*
> *So, bless my cotton socks, I'd*
> *Better call it calcium oxide.*

What indicator colours did the solutions give?
Are they acid or alkaline solutions?

Take calcium, for example. Its oxide dissolves in water. The solution turns litmus blue. It has an alkali in it. The name given to an alkali is hydroxide. This one is calcium hydroxide.

Check the Universal Indicator colour it gives. Is the alkali strong or weak?

We can write in short:

calcium + oxygen → calcium oxide
calcium oxide + water → calcium hydroxide

Now check the results for a non-metal. Try carbon.

Carbon burns with a white flame. We cannot see the oxide. It must be a gas. It is called carbon dioxide.

Carbon dioxide dissolves in water. We know this because the water in the gas jar turns Universal Indicator yellow. This shows it is a weak acid. It is called **carbonic** acid. The name shows which element it came from.

We can write in short

carbon + oxygen → carbon dioxide
carbon dioxide + water → carbonic acid

Half-way or neutral

The half-way colour for litmus is mauve. It will be mauve if there is no acid or alkali. The liquid is **neutral**.

What will happen if we mix acid and alkali?

Experiment 2.10 To mix an acid and alkali

Burn a stick of charcoal in oxygen. Shake the oxide with water.

Burn calcium in air or in oxygen. Shake the oxide with water. Filter the mixture. Add litmus paper to the clear solution. Pour it into the carbon dioxide gas jar. Put black paper behind the jar. What do you see? What happens to the litmus?

The clear liquid becomes 'milky'. The clear liquid is calcium hydroxide solution. Carbon dioxide makes it milky.

> *Carbon in oxygen burns white hot.*
> *What kind of oxide have we got?*
> *Nobody saw one in my class.*
> *Carbon dioxide must be a gas.*
> *It can't be seen but it's there all right.*
> *It turns lime water from clear to white.*

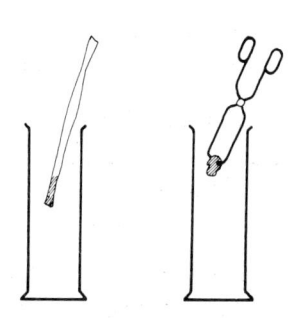

Mixing acid and alkali

Pure water has no acid in it. It is not acidic. It has no alkali in it. It is not alkaline. In pure water litmus is mauve. This colour is half-way between red and blue. Litmus shows that water is **neutral**. The half-way colour of Universal Indicator is green. Green shows neutral.

Carbon dioxide in water forms an acid. Calcium oxide in water forms an alkali. Mixing the two gives a white substance.

Calcium hydroxide solution is 'lime water'. Carbon dioxide makes it 'milky'. Only carbon dioxide can do this. We cannot see carbon dioxide. We can recognise it because

Carbon dioxide makes lime water milky.

Experiment 2.11 To mix another acid and alkali

Use acid and alkali from the bench bottles. One-third fill a test tube with sodium hydroxide solution. Add drops of Universal Indicator.

Fill a dropper with dilute hydrochloric acid. Add drops of it to the alkali. Shake the test tube. Add more acid. Stop adding it when the indicator changes colour.

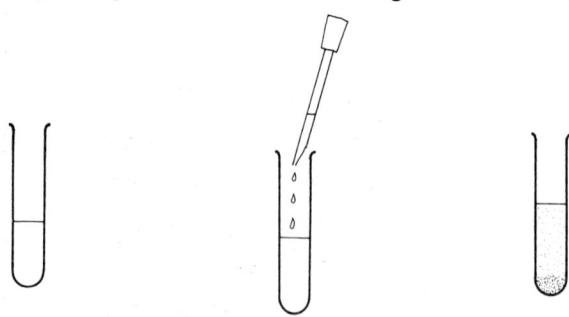

Add a pinch of charcoal to the test tube. Heat it. Filter the liquid into a dish. Heat the dish. Stop when most of the water has gone. Put some of the liquid on a glass slide. Look at it through a microscope.

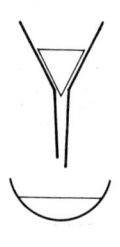

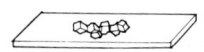

Pure salt crystals.

What colour is the indicator in alkali?
How many indicator colours did you see?
Was the final colour green?
What does charcoal do to the solution?
Are crystals formed on the glass slide?
Do their shapes show what the solid may be?

You may have got all the colours from red to violet. It is difficult to get a neutral solution. We shall try again later with another method.

Charcoal takes out the colour. Heating the solution gives a white solid. It may appear as crystals. Are they like those in the photograph?

acid + alkali → a new substance (salt?)

Calcium + oxygen → calcium oxide is a summary. It means 'Calcium combines with oxygen. Calcium oxide is formed.' We can write these **word equations** for any reaction.

Iron + oxygen → magnetic iron oxide
This oxide does not react with water.

Sulphur + oxygen → sulphur dioxide
Sulphur dioxide + water → sulphurous acid

Some metals have more than one oxide. Copper has two. Their names must show which one we mean. We have used **black** copper oxide. There is a better naming method. We shall learn it later. It uses Roman numbers; I, II, III, IV and so on.

Summary

Oxygen is made from air or from oxides. The best oxide for lab use is hydrogen peroxide. Manganese(IV) oxide is a catalyst. It makes hydrogen peroxide decompose quickly. The oxygen is collected 'over water'. The gas is oxygen because it relights a glowing splint.

Elements burn more brightly in oxygen than in air. Oxides are formed. Some metal oxides dissolve in water. Each solution turns litmus blue. It is alkaline. It contains an alkali.

Non-metal oxides may dissolve in water. These solutions are acidic. Each contains an acid. Acids turn litmus red. Universal Indicator is a mixture of dyes. It shows the colours of the rainbow. They run from red to violet. Red shows acid, violet is alkaline, green shows neutral.

A word equation sums up a chemical change.
phosphorus + oxygen → phosphoric oxide
Acid plus alkali can give a neutral solution. A new substance is formed. In this way, carbon dioxide makes lime water 'milky', or cloudy.

Questions

1. Sodium is a metal. It burns well in air. Choose the best answer in each statement below.

   a) In oxygen sodium burns (brilliantly/well/fairly well/feebly/not at all).
   b) Sodium oxide dissolves in water. The solution turns litmus (red/mauve/blue/violet).
   c) This solution is (acidic/alkaline/neutral).
   d) In this solution, Universal Indicator becomes (red/orange/yellow/green/violet).

2. Explain why any substance burns more brightly in oxygen than in air.

3. You are given an element. How would you find out if it is a metal or a non-metal?

Things to do

Use vinegar as an acid. Use washing soda as an alkali. Find out if any of these are indicators: beetroot juice, blackcurrant juice, elderberry juice. Use one of them to test Milk of Magnesia, tap water, Alka-seltzer.

Hydrogen peroxide gives oxygen. Manganese(IV) oxide speeds up the change. Find out if the change is speeded up by (a) black copper oxide, (b) magnetic iron oxide, (c) blood.

*Acid gives red,
Alkali blue
If you use litmus
This rhyme is true.*

Other burning substances

Burning is very common in everyday life.

We burn things by accident. Houses, forests, oil tankers and clothing are all set on fire by chance.

We burn some substances to keep ourselves warm. Coal, coke, gas, wood and oil are used in this way. They are called fuels. They give heat energy. This keeps houses and other buildings warm.

We need transport. Cars, buses, lorries, ships and trains all burn fuel.

We burn fuel to cook food. We may use electricity for cooking and transport. However, fuels are used in power stations to make electricity.

When fuels burn they form oxides. These oxides are called the 'products of combustion'. When magnesium burns we can see the oxide. It is a white powder. When fuels burn we do not often see the oxides. This means that they are gases or vapours.

Smoke comes from not burning a fuel completely. It wastes fuel and pollutes the air.

A candle burns in air. What is 'candle oxide'?
Petrol burns. What is 'petrol oxide'?

Burning stubble in a wheatfield.

Coal arriving at a power station.

A bush fire in Australia.

The products of combustion

Experiment 2.12 To find out what these products are

Stand a candle on a tile. Hold a funnel over it. Connect the funnel to the test tubes. Connect a filter pump to the other end of the apparatus.

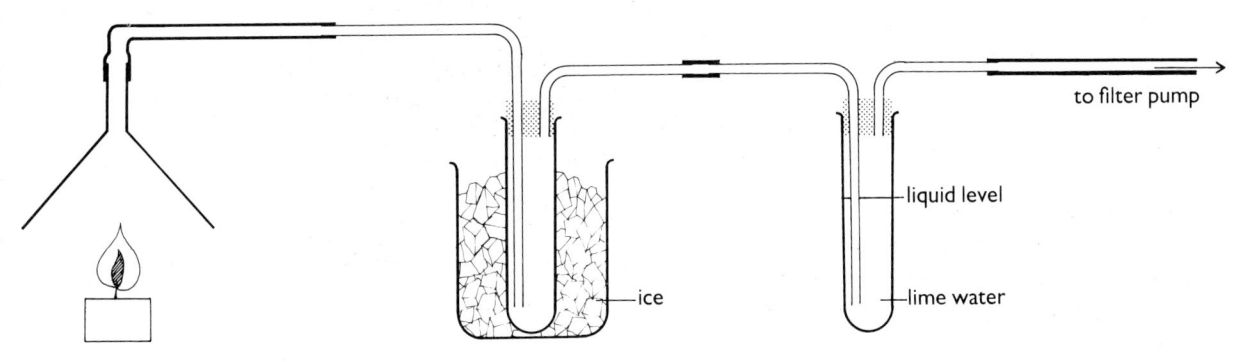

The first test tube is empty. It has ice round it.
The second test tube is half filled with lime water.
Light the candle. Turn on the filter pump.
Use other fuels instead of a candle.

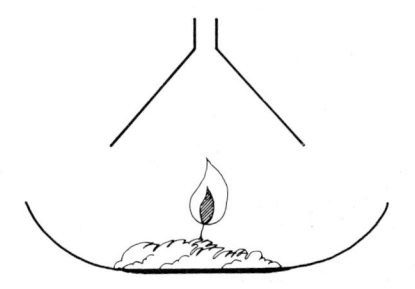

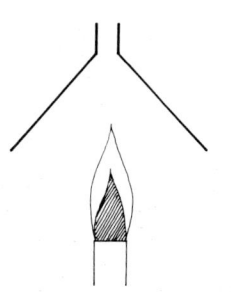

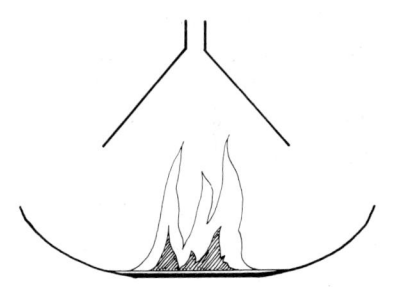

The pump draws air through the apparatus. The air takes the products of combustion with it. They pass through the tubes.

>What do you see in the first test tube?
>Can you guess what this substance might be?
>What happens to the lime water?

Remember that most products of combustion are gases or vapours. The lime water 'turns milky'. This happens with all the fuels we burn. One of the products of combustion is carbon dioxide.

a fuel burning — takes oxygen out of the air
             — puts carbon dioxide into the air

The first test tube is cold. It will cool any vapours. It may turn some of them back into liquids. The liquid which collects in this tube is colourless. It looks like water.

Is water formed when fuels burn?

All burning fuels give carbon dioxide. Many also give a liquid. This has no smell or colour. It looks like water.

> How can we find out if it is water?
> What properties of water do we know?
> What is its boiling point?

Experiment 2.13 To heat copper sulphate crystals

Put the blue crystals into a test tube. Fill it to a depth of 1 cm. Heat it gently. Collect any liquid in a cooled, dry test tube. Boil this liquid. Record its boiling point.

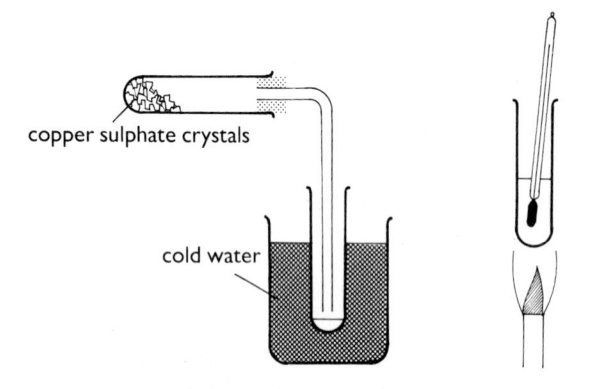

Let the solid get quite cold. Then add water.

> What happens to the heated blue crystals?
> Does boiling point show the liquid is water?
> What does water do to the white substance?
> Do the water and solid become hot?

Experiment 2.14 To heat cobalt chloride crystals

Heat cobalt chloride crystals as in Experiment 2.13.

The results show one difference. What is it?

Heating both substances gives a liquid. Its boiling point is 100 °C. This shows that it is pure water.
The blue crystals lose water. They turn into a white solid. Only water can turn this back to blue. It becomes hot.
Cobalt chloride crystals lose water. A blue solid forms. Only water can turn it pink again. Any water will do.

Water turns white **anhydrous** copper sulphate blue. Anhydrous means 'without water'. Cobalt chloride paper is useful. Both are used as a test for water. The colour change is given by the liquid from burning fuel. That liquid is water.

Soak filter paper in pink cobalt chloride solution. Dry it. Hold it high above a bunsen flame. It loses water. The paper turns blue. It proves that water is present by turning pink.

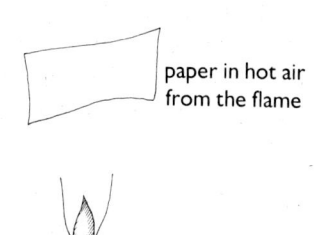

Traffic burns fuel.

Fuels and the air

When they burn, all fuels use oxygen from the air. The products of combustion are mainly carbon dioxide and water. If not enough air is present smoke may form. Poisonous carbon monoxide may be produced. The result is air pollution.

Everyone burns fuels. It happens all over the world. It happens all the time. In Britain alone there are over 17 million cars and lorries. They burn petrol and diesel oil. Trains and tractors use diesel oil too. Jet aircraft and paraffin heaters use kerosene. Ships and central heating use heavier oils. About 2 million tonnes of coal are burnt every year. They give us coke, gas and electricity. There are many gas fuels. Natural gas and calor gas are used for cooking and heating.

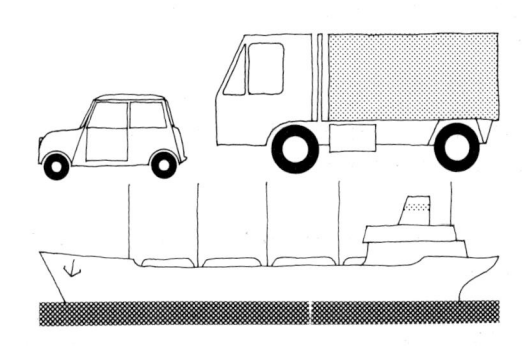

Burning fuel takes out oxygen
↑
the air
↑
Burning fuel puts in carbon dioxide and water

This raises three questions:
Why has all the oxygen in air not been used up?
Why is the air not full of carbon dioxide?
Is there any carbon dioxide in the air at all?

Summary

Human beings find it useful to burn fuels.
They keep us warm. They allow us to cook food.
They provide energy to run our transport.
They burn in power stations making electricity.
They put carbon dioxide and water into the air.

Water can be recognised by its boiling point. Other tests are with white anhydrous copper sulphate and blue anhydrous cobalt chloride. They prove that water is present. They do not prove that it is pure. Boiling point does that.

Burning fuels can pollute the air. Without enough oxygen they form smoke and carbon monoxide. They use up the oxygen of the air. They put into air carbon dioxide and water vapour.

Questions

1. Give three reasons why we burn fuels.
2. Burning fuels affect the air around us. What changes do they cause? How do they cause these changes to happen?
3. A candle burns in air. Draw the apparatus used to collect the products of combustion. Label the drawing.
4. I have a colourless liquid. How would you prove that it contains water? What test will show that it is pure water?
5. What do we mean by air pollution?

Carbon dioxide and the air

***Experiment 2.15 To find out if air contains carbon dioxide**

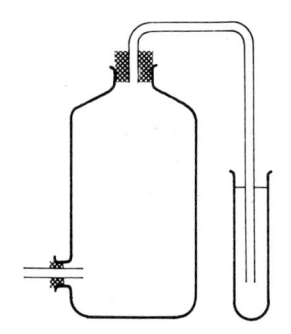

This is a large jar full of air. Connect it to the water tap.

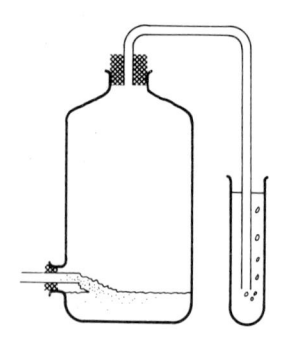

Run water into the jar. This will push air out at the top.

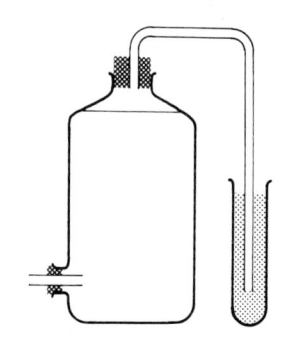

Let this air slowly bubble through lime water.

We are using the kind of air we breathe in.

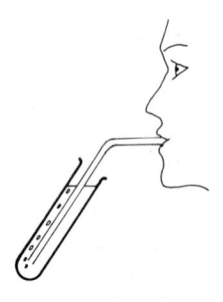

Use the same amount of lime water again. Take a deep breath. Blow gently into the lime water.

We are using the kind of air we breathe out.

> What happens to the lime water?
> In which test tube was it more milky?
> Which air has more carbon dioxide?

A whole jar of air made the lime water just cloudy. The amount of carbon dioxide in it must be small. Very little breathed-out air was needed. The lime water was very milky. This air has far more carbon dioxide.

There are about 2500 million people on earth. Nobody knows how many animals there are. They all breathe in air. This air has little carbon dioxide in it.

They breathe out. This air contains much more carbon dioxide. We all put carbon dioxide into the air.

What about a bite to eat?

What is your temperature?
Are you hotter than the air around you?
Does your body lose heat to the air?

37.3 °C   20 °C or less

Do you run? Do you ride a bike? Do you play games? Do you stand still? To do all these needs energy. Where does it come from?

*Experiment 2.16 To burn a cornflake

Hold a large cornflake in tongs. Light it at the bunsen flame. Hold it in a gas jar of oxygen. Let it burn. Shake lime water in the jar.

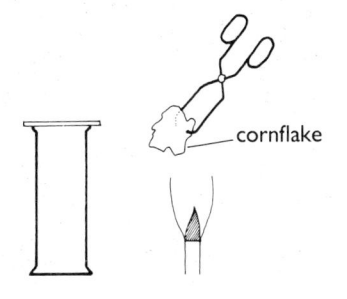

cornflake

What does the lime water prove?

Most foods behave like the cornflake. They burn. This means that they give heat. They also give carbon dioxide.

Food is digested inside us. Chemical changes turn it into substances we can use. These are carried by the bloodstream.

We breathe air into our lungs. Oxygen from it passes into the blood. It is carried round the body. Food and oxygen meet in muscle tissue. The food 'burns', or **oxidizes**. It uses oxygen.

We use food as a fuel. Oxidizing it gives heat. This heat keeps us warm. It provides energy for movement. But burning, or **oxidation**, also forms carbon dioxide. This passes into the blood. It is carried back to the lungs. We breathe it out.

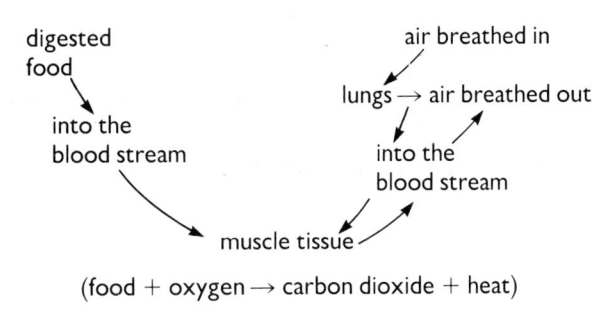

digested food → into the blood stream → muscle tissue ← into the blood stream ← lungs → air breathed out
air breathed in → lungs

(food + oxygen → carbon dioxide + heat)

*Running is one of Willie's crazes.
It makes him get as hot as blazes.
What gives the heat when Willie hustles?
Food oxidizing in his muscles!*

Summary

There is little carbon dioxide in the air. The air we breathe out contains much more. Food burns or oxidizes inside us. It uses oxygen from the air we breathe in. This produces carbon dioxide and heat. The heat keeps us warm. It provides energy for movement. The carbon dioxide passes into the blood stream. It is breathed out by the lungs.

We use oxygen from the air

The air round the earth is called the atmosphere. It is a mixture of several gases.

I have just breathed in. My lungs now contain 1000 cm^3 of this air. The table shows the main gases in it. It shows their volumes, too.

My blood takes oxygen from this air. It puts carbon dioxide into my lungs instead. I breathe out. The table shows the gases in this air, too.

Thousands of millions of animals live on Earth. They include us. We all breathe. We cannot live without oxygen. Look at the change we make in the atmosphere.

Name of gas	The air I breathe in	The air I breathe out
oxygen	208	170
nitrogen	780	780
carbon dioxide	0.3	40
others	19	19

We burn fuels. Burning also takes oxygen out of the air. Burning, like breathing, puts carbon dioxide into the air. Yet their proportions stay the same. The atmosphere shows little change. So some other change must happen as well.

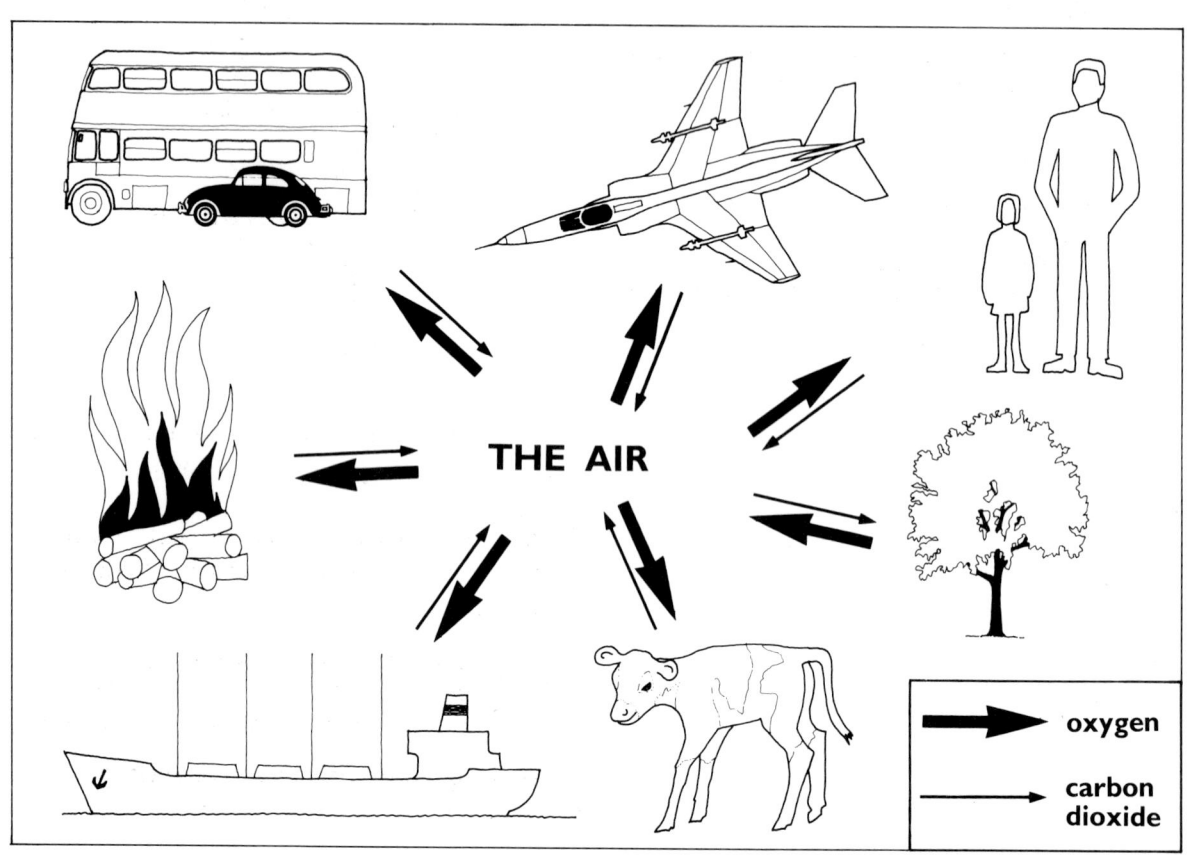

The carbon cycle. Man, animals and machines all take oxygen out of the air. Only green plants put it back in.

Green plants put back oxygen

***Experiment 2.17 Plants and the atmosphere**

1. Put water weed under the funnel. Stand the trough in sunlight or daylight. Collect gas in the test tube. Test it with a lighted splint. Then test it with a glowing splint.

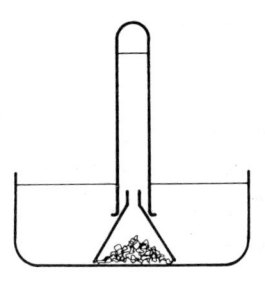

What gas does water weed produce?

2. Put the plant on a stand. Light the candle. Stand the bell jar over both. Stopper the jar. Leave the apparatus in the window in light.

Set up the apparatus a second time. Put it in a cupboard. Leave both for three days. Test the air in each with a lighted splint.

What do the lighted splints show?

The water weed gives oxygen. It does this best in sunlight. The candles go out. They have used up all the oxygen. The plants live in this air. The one in daylight gives oxygen. The splint stays alight in this jar. In the other it goes out.

Green plants
- take carbon dioxide from the air
- take in water through their roots
- use these substances to make starch or sugar.

This chemical change happens in the leaves. Green chlorophyll speeds it up. The energy needed comes from sunlight.

The change is called **photosynthesis**. It means the building up of carbon compounds using light. *Photo* means light and *synthesis* means build.
As well as starch, oxygen is formed. It passes into the air.

carbon dioxide + water + energy → starch + oxygen

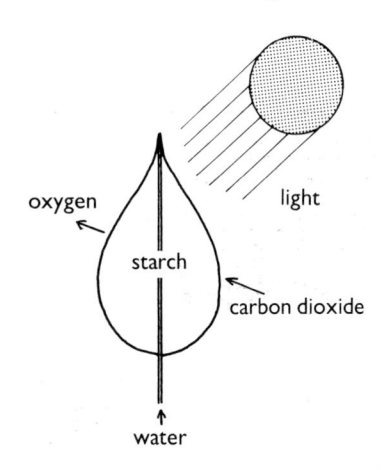

Animals oxidize their food. Fuels burn. Both changes use up oxygen and give carbon dioxide and energy.
Photosynthesis does the opposite. It just balances breathing and burning. This means the atmosphere is not changed.

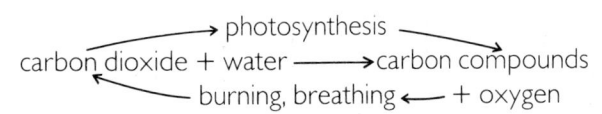

$$\text{carbon dioxide + water} \underset{\text{burning, breathing}}{\overset{\text{photosynthesis}}{\rightleftarrows}} \text{carbon compounds + oxygen}$$

These changes are called the **carbon cycle**, or **energy cycle**.

The manufacture and uses of oxygen

Substances burn more brightly in oxygen than in air. We need oxygen to live. These two facts explain its uses.

A fuel gas, such as acetylene, burns in air. In oxygen its flame reaches 3000 °C. This melts metals. Melting a metal is one way to cut it. Liquid metal is used to join metals by welding.

Space rockets burn fuel. Tonnes of it burn each second. This needs huge amounts of oxygen. It is carried in the rocket as liquid. The gases formed drive the rocket upwards.

Iron is made in a blast furnace. Oxygen and air are blown in. White-hot liquid iron comes out. It is not pure. Oxygen is blown into it. Elements such as carbon and phosphorus burn away. The iron is pure. It can be made into steel.

Joining metals by welding.

Tapping a blast furnace.

Putting hot iron into a vessel so that oxygen can be blown through it.

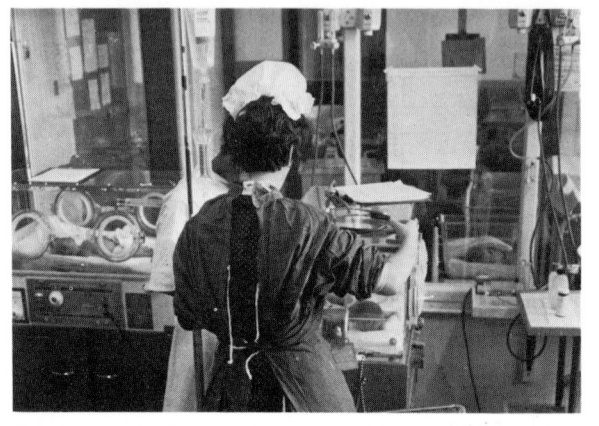

Breathing normal air gives us enough oxygen. Higher up the air gets thinner. It does not give enough oxygen. Mountain climbers and fliers take it with them, stored in cylinders.

People who are ill may be very weak. Breathing may tire them. They may have lung diseases. They may be under anaesthetic. Oxygen is fed into the masks through which they breathe.

Divers use compressed air to give oxygen. Its nitrogen dissolves in the blood. It comes out only slowly. It can give the diver 'the bends'. A mixture of oxygen and helium avoids this. It is used by climbers as well as divers.

A baby in an incubator with an extra oxygen supply.

The manufacture of oxygen

Manufacture means making large amounts. Oxygen is made from air. Water and carbon dioxide are taken out first. They are frozen to solids.

You have used a bicycle pump. Air compressed by the pump gets hot. Letting this air escape will cool it. A pump is used in making oxygen.

The pump gives hot compressed air. This passes into water-cooled pipes. It is now cold compressed air. It escapes through a valve. This cools it still more. It is used to cool the air coming down to the valve. This comes out even colder.

At last the air is cold enough to turn to liquid. This is liquid air. It is at about −200 °C. It is a mixture of liquid oxygen and nitrogen.

As it warms, nitrogen boils off. It boils at −196 °C. Liquid oxygen remains. Its boiling point is higher. It is −183 °C. (Higher ?) Oxygen is stored as a liquid. For most uses it is sold in steel cylinders, under pressure.

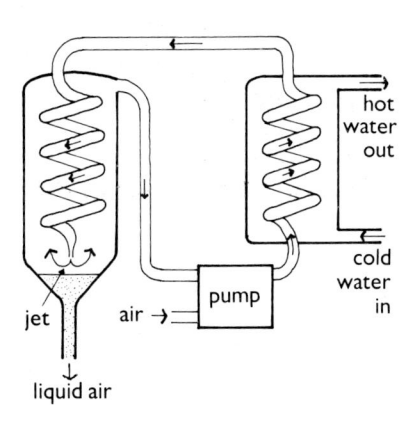

Copy this out. Fill in the blank spaces.

The air round the Earth is called its _____. It contains two main gases, _____ and _____. 78% of air is _____. 21% is _____. 0.03% of the atmosphere is _____ _____.

Oxygen is taken out of air in two main ways. It is used by animals _____. It is also used by fuels _____. Both changes also put the gas _____ _____ into the atmosphere.

Green plants take _____ _____ out of the air. Their roots take in _____. They use these two substances to make _____ or _____. This change also gives the gas _____. It happens in the _____ of the plant. This puts _____ into the air. The change is called p_o_o_y_t_e_i_. It means building up in _____.

Photosynthesis balances _____ and breathing. The gas proportions in air remain _____.

Oxygen has many uses. Gas fuels burn more _____ in it than in air. The flame is very _____. It can melt _____. It is used in cutting and _____ metals. Oxygen is used in space _____. It is carried as a _____. It makes fuel burn very _____. The gases formed _____ the rocket.

Questions

1. Give three reasons for using oxygen masks.
2. What is oxygen used for in making iron and steel?
3. Substances A, B, C, D and E are heated in oxygen.
   A burns to a white powder. This dissolves in water. The solution turns litmus blue.
   B burns giving carbon dioxide and water.
   C burns giving an oxide. This oxide is a gas. It dissolves in water. It turns litmus red.
   D shows no sign of change.
   E does not burn. A black ash forms on it.

   Which substance, A, B, C, D or E, is a metal? Which substance, A, B, C, D or E, is most like (a) copper, (b) salt, (c) platinum, (d) a candle, (e) a cornflake, (f) magnesium, (g) wood, (h) sulphur, (j) calcium, (k) charcoal, (m) petrol?

Water – is it an oxide?

Read these sentences. Write down the missing words.

A substance which burns uses _____ from the air. The new substance formed is called an _____. It is made up of the burning substance + _____. Most burning fuels give carbon _____ and _____. Water is formed by burning. So it may be an _____.

Check your answers with those at the bottom of the page.

Magnesium is an element. It combines with oxygen when it burns. The white ash is magnesium oxide. In it two elements are combined. Any oxide contains oxygen and some other element.

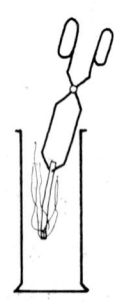

If water is an oxide it contains oxygen. This is combined with some other element. Which one? Take oxygen away from water. This will leave the other element. What substances take away oxygen? Those which burn well. Magnesium burns brilliantly.

water = X oxide
water − oxygen → X

Experiment 3.1 To try to get an element from water

Clean magnesium ribbon with fine sandpaper. Cut off a 3 cm length. Fold it loosely in three. Drop it into water in a test tube. Watch what happens. Now warm the test tube. If the metal moves, tap the tube gently.

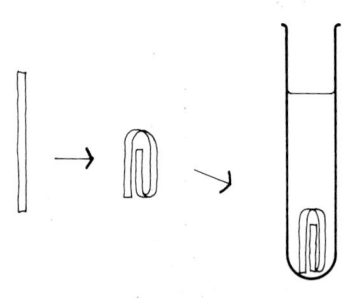

What do you see happen in the test tube?
Can you see any signs of a gas forming?
Does the magnesium move in the water? Why?
Does the magnesium change in any way?

Magnesium is a good taker of oxygen. It has a shiny surface. It sinks in water. Tiny bubbles form on its surface. They act like balloons. They carry the magnesium upwards. Tapping the tube shakes the bubbles off. The metal sinks.

Invent a way of collecting the bubbles of gas.

Look carefully at the magnesium. It has lost its metallic lustre. Tarnish has formed on the surface. This could be magnesium oxide.

Answers
oxygen
oxide
oxygen
dioxide
water
oxide

Collecting the bubbles

The bubbles are a gas. They are very small. They are given off slowly. How can we get more gas more quickly?

Experiment 3.2 To collect the gas

Take all the bits of magnesium used by the class. Clean them with sandpaper. Put them in a trough. Put a funnel over them as shown.

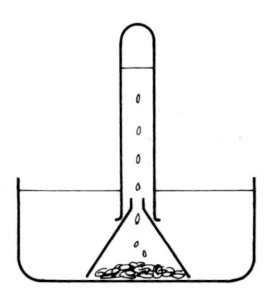

Fill a test tube with water. Invert it in the trough. Put it over the funnel. Let enough gas collect. Test it with a lighted splint.

> Do you see any new results?
> What happens to the lighted splint?

The gas still comes off at a slow rate. It takes some time to collect enough. The splint goes out. There is a small explosion. This is often called a 'squeaky pop'.

Experiment 3.3 To try to get the gas more quickly

What other metal burns brilliantly? What is it which
'... burns with a blinding flash
And changes into a dull white ash'?

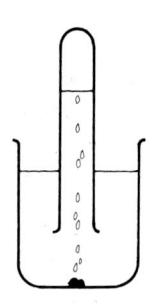

Two-thirds fill a small beaker with water. Invert a test tube full of water in it. Drop in a tiny piece of calcium. Hold the test tube over it. Collect the gas. Test it with a lighted splint. Put a litmus paper in the water.

> Does calcium react faster than magnesium?
> Does it give the same gas as magnesium?
> Litmus turns blue. What kind of substance is there in the water? What is its name?

Both metals take oxygen from water. Shiny magnesium becomes dull. We say it 'tarnishes'. The tarnish may be the oxide. The calcium reacts faster. The test tube soon fills with gas.

The water contains an alkali. The family name of alkalis is 'hydroxide'. The water is a solution of calcium hydroxide.

The gas is **hydrogen**. A lighted splint gives a small explosion. Hydrogen is an element. Water is hydrogen oxide.

Hydrogen

Calcium + water →
calcium hydroxide + hydrogen

Water is hydrogen oxide. Hydrogen means 'water producer'!

From the last experiment we know some properties of hydrogen. It is a gas. It has no colour or smell. Bubbles of it rise through water. So it does not dissolve much in water. To discover other properties we need larger amounts. It is best made using metals and acids.

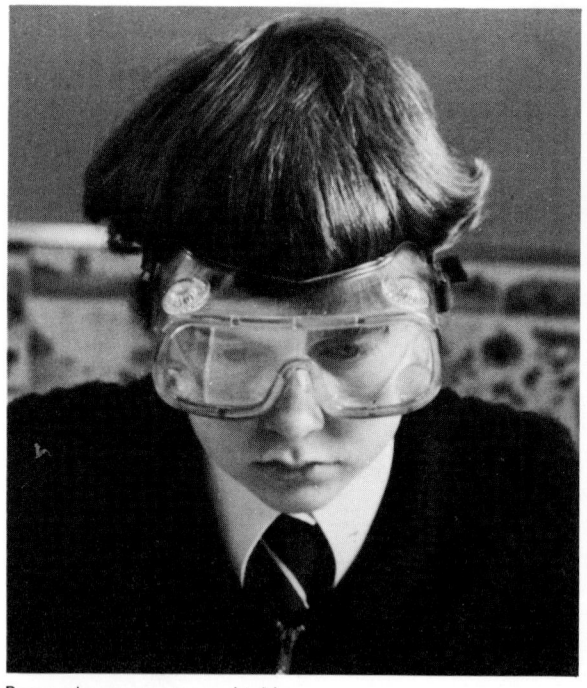

Experiment 3.4 The action of acids on metals

Put a strip of metal in a test tube. Add dilute hydrochloric acid. If bubbles appear, test them. Put a lighted splint at the mouth of the tube. Wear eye shields. Use a test tube holder.

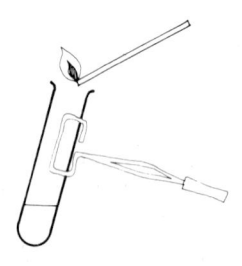

Remember to wear eyeshields.

We need to collect hydrogen in gas jars. So we choose a metal which gives hydrogen fairly quickly.

*Experiment 3.5 Other properties of hydrogen

Put lumps of zinc in the flask. Add a few drops of copper sulphate solution. Pour dilute hydrochloric acid down the thistle funnel. Add enough to cover the bottom of the funnel.

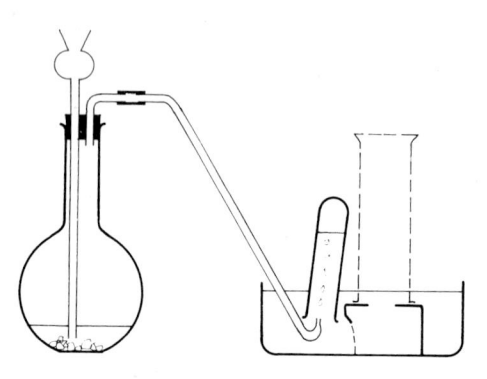

Try this with copper, zinc, aluminium, lead, tin, iron and magnesium. There may be no reaction. If so, heat the tube gently. Do not let the liquid boil.

Write your results in the form of a table. Make a list of the metals. Put at the top the one which reacts best. Put the others in order of how quickly they give hydrogen.

Metal used	Is heat needed to get gas?	Is hydrogen formed?	How quickly is it formed?

First collect the gas in test tubes. Test each tube with a lighted splint. Wait until the gas gives no 'squeaky pop'. Then collect it in gas jars over water. Why do we test it in this way?

*The properties of hydrogen

Put safety screens round the gas jars in tests 1 and 2.

1. Take a gas jar of hydrogen. Hold a lighted splint near the top. Quickly take off the lid.

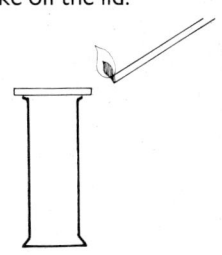

2. Take the lid off a gas jar of hydrogen. Count ten. Put in a lighted splint.

3. Take a test tube half full of water. Collect hydrogen in it. Test it with a lighted splint.

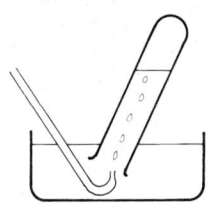

4. Add detergent to water. Put in a little glycerol. Stir it. Dip the hydrogen delivery tube into it. Blow bubbles. Shake them off the tube. Chase them with a lighted splint.

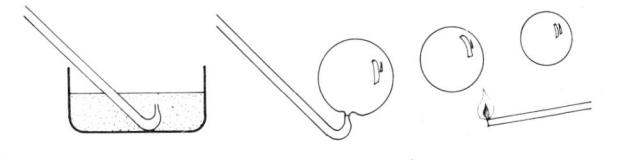

5. Fill a balloon with hydrogen. Use a cylinder of gas. Tie the balloon with string at the neck. Let the balloon go.

What do the tests tell us about hydrogen?

In 1. pure hydrogen burns quietly. In 3. it is mixed with air. The splint makes it explode. In 2. the splint burns quietly. Counting ten gives time for the hydrogen to escape.

The bubbles and the balloon are full of hydrogen. They rise into the air. Hydrogen is less dense than air. This is why it escapes from the open jar. Air takes its place.

An air–hydrogen mixture explodes. This is why we first collect it in test tubes. A gas jar of the mixture would be dangerous in test 1. Burning or exploding it forms an oxide.

*Experiment 3.6 To show that hydrogen oxide is water

Use the apparatus shown. Put safety screens round it. Use hydrogen from a cylinder. Put a delivery tube at A. Collect the gas in test tubes. Test it until there is no explosion.

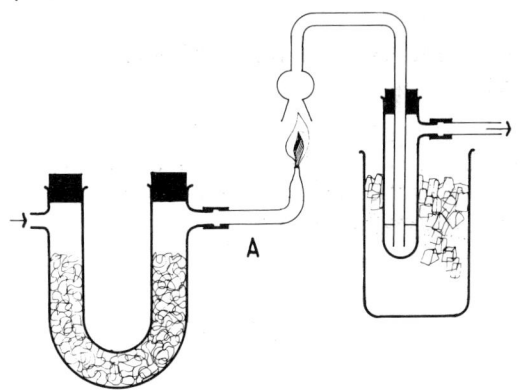

Now put a jet at A. Light the hydrogen. Gently turn on the pump. Collect liquid in the tube cooled by ice. Test to see if it is water.

1. Add the liquid to white copper sulphate.
2. If there is enough, find its boiling point.

The U-tube holds anhydrous calcium chloride. It dries the hydrogen. Why is drying needed?

> Grace got so excited when
> The balloon was filled with hydrogen,
> She didn't let go of the string.
> Grace and balloon were on the wing
> So fast that no one could have stopped her.
> They brought her down by helicopter.

The uses of hydrogen

The uses of any substance depend on its properties. Hydrogen is lighter (or less dense) than air.

Balloons filled with hydrogen will rise through the air. Weather balloons can do this. They have been used to carry instruments into the air. They measure factors such as wind speed and air pressure. These affect weather.

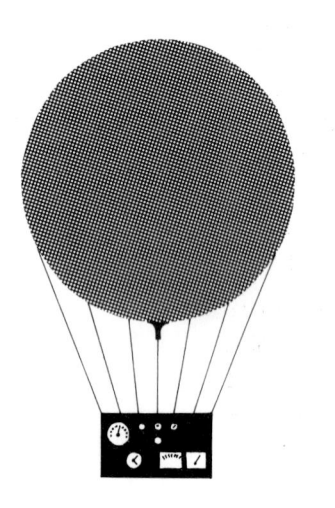

Airships are balloons fitted with engines and steering. They were first used early in this century. The later ones were rigid. That is, they had a metal frame covered with material. They were moved by propellors and driven by diesel engines.

These airships carried people and goods. The Germans called them Zeppelins. They used them in the first World War.

Britain and America also built airships. The British R34 crossed the Atlantic in 1919. It was the first to cross from Britain to USA.

A hydrogen balloon.

The burnt out remains of the R101.

A weather balloon being launched.

A barrage balloon.

In time bigger and better airships were built. Two famous British ones were the R100 and R101. The Germans built a very large one in 1936. They called it the Hindenburg.

All airships and balloons have one fault. The hydrogen which lifts them burns. If air mixes with hydrogen a light will explode it. Accidents to airships could be disastrous.

The R101 made its maiden voyage in 1930. It set out for India. It hit a hillside in France. An explosion and fire followed. The airship burnt out. Forty-eight people died.

The Hindenburg burnt out, too. It was destroyed by an explosion in 1937. It was caused by a bomb. Many lives were lost as a result. Aircraft became bigger and faster. They could carry more fuel. So they could travel farther without stopping. Airships became less useful. They now use helium. This is a light gas, too, but it does not burn.

Barrage balloons were used in the last war. They were to protect places from air attack. The attacks were made by low-flying aircraft. They used bombs and machine guns.

The balloons were filled with hydrogen. This took them into the air. They were moored by steel cables. These made air attacks difficult. However, hydrogen burns. Many balloons were shot down in flames.

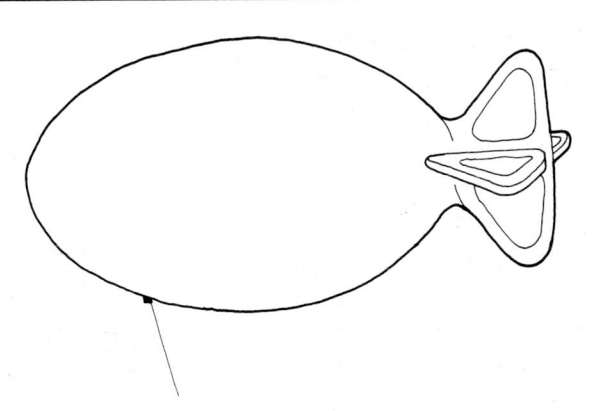

Hydrogen has other uses. Vegetable oils are easy to obtain. They come from soya beans, coconuts and ground nuts. The oils are not suitable as food. Hydrogen can convert oils to solid fats. Fats mixed with other food stuffs make margarine.

Ammonia is a very important substance. It is used in making fertilizers, explosives and nitric acid. Huge amounts of it are made from hydrogen and nitrogen.

hydrogen + nitrogen → ammonia → fertilizers / nitric acid / explosives

Hydrogen is also used in the manufacture of methanol. This is one of the fuels used in rockets.

The first US space shuttle took off in April 1981. It had a crew of two and carried liquid hydrogen and oxygen. At take-off the hydrogen was burnt in the oxygen. In $8\frac{1}{2}$ minutes, 1500 tonnes of hydrogen was used up, or about 3 tonnes per second. It produced heat and steam. The huge thrust from these launched the shuttle.

One more property of hydrogen

Calcium burns brilliantly in air. This means it must be very good at taking oxygen from the air. It can even take oxygen from water. This was how we discovered hydrogen.

Calcium + hydrogen oxide → calcium hydroxide + hydrogen

This is a chemical change. It is also a battle for oxygen. In water, hydrogen is joined to oxygen. Calcium takes away the oxygen. Calcium wins. It is more active than hydrogen.

Some games are like this. Football is a battle for the ball. George has the ball. Willie takes it away from him. Willie wins the ball. He is more active than George.

But hydrogen burns in air. It must be quite good at taking oxygen. Can it win oxygen from other metals?

*Experiment 3.7 To test how active hydrogen is

Use a test tube with a hole at the closed end. Put a layer of black copper oxide in it. Keep it away from the stopper. Hold the tube in a clamp. Pass hydrogen through it for some time.

Light the hydrogen at the hole. Gently heat the copper oxide. Start heating at the stopper end.

> Is there any change in the black oxide?
> Is any other substance formed in the tube?
> What is left in the test tube?
> Why is the hydrogen not lit at the start?

Copper oxide is copper combined with oxygen. It turns into an orange-pink substance. This might be copper. If it is, hydrogen has taken oxygen from the copper.

A mistiness appears in the tube. This could be water. If it is,
copper oxide + hydrogen → water + copper

Hydrogen has won. It has robbed copper of its oxygen. Hydrogen is more active than copper. It takes oxygen from it. Calcium is more active than hydrogen. It takes oxygen from it.

Perhaps we can work out a league table. The most active element would be at the top. The others would be placed in order of activity. Can you put calcium, copper and hydrogen in order? We can add others to the list. Where will magnesium be?

We can play a match between magnesium and hydrogen. This time give the ball (sorry, the oxygen) to magnesium. Find out if hydrogen can take this oxygen away.

Plan the experiment: What two substances must we start with?
Where shall we play the match?
Can you guess the result?

*Experiment 3.8 To find which is more active, magnesium or hydrogen

Repeat Experiment 3.7. Put magnesium oxide in the tube. Pass hydrogen through. First heat gently, then strongly.

Is there any sign of change in the tube?

No water forms in the tube. The white oxide shows no change.
No new substance is formed. No chemical change takes place.
Hydrogen does not rob magnesium of oxygen. Magnesium wins.
Where will magnesium be in the activity list?

Summary

When fuels burn, water is formed. So water may be an oxide. Some metals burn well in oxygen. They may be able to take oxygen from water. Calcium and magnesium can. Calcium reacts faster. A gas is formed. It is called hydrogen.

calcium + water → calcium hydroxide + hydrogen

Pure hydrogen burns quietly. Water forms. Both changes show that water is hydrogen oxide. Hydrogen mixed with air can explode. This is why a lighted splint gives a 'squeaky pop'.

Calcium and magnesium are more active than hydrogen. They take oxygen from it. But hydrogen reacts with hot copper oxide. It takes oxygen from it. Hydrogen is more active than copper.

copper oxide + hydrogen → copper + water

Taking oxygen from a substance is **reduction**. Hydrogen can **reduce** copper oxide to copper.

Zinc and dilute hydrochloric acid give hydrogen. It is collected over water. Balloons filled with hydrogen rise. It is less dense than air. Hydrogen is used to make other substances.

Copy this out. Fill in the blanks.

Water is hydrogen _____. Calcium will _____ with water. The final solution turns litmus _____. It contains an _____. The word equation is
    calcium + water → calcium _____ + _____

Hydrogen can be made from an acid and a _____. Dilute _____ and _____ can be used. The gas is collected in gas jars 'over _____'. It is tested with a _____ splint. It gives a small _____ or _____ pop, if mixed with _____. If it is _____ hydrogen burns quietly.

Hydrogen is _____ _____ than air. Balloons filled with it _____. Hydrogen takes _____ from hot copper oxide. The oxide is _____ to copper.

    copper oxide + _____ → copper + _____

Elements can be put in order of how _____ they are. The most _____ metal comes at the _____.

Magnesium is below calcium but above hydrogen.

63

This is what you ought to know

In this book we have begun to study Chemistry. We have learnt the answers to many questions.

1. *What is chemistry?*
Chemistry is part of Science. In Science we find out. To find out we ask questions. We answer them by observation and experiment.

2. *What is the world made of?*
The stuff of which the world is made is called **matter**. One particular kind of matter is called a **substance**. We recognize a substance by (a) what it looks like, (b) what it can do. These are its **properties**.

3. *When does a substance show its properties?*
To show its true properties a substance must be **pure**. This means taking away other substances from it. There are many ways of doing this.

4. *How do you make a substance pure?*
A substance may dissolve in a liquid. If it does, it is **soluble**.
The result is called a **solution**. The liquid is called a **solvent**.
The dissolved substance is called a **solute**.
To get back the solvent, **distil** the solution.
To get back the solute, **evaporate** the solution.
The solute may come out of the liquid as **crystals**.
To take out an **insoluble** substance, filter the liquid.
Chromatography separates substances of the same kind.

5. *How do you test for a pure substance?*
To find out if a substance is pure, measure its **boiling point**. Its **melting point** can be used too. An impurity will raise the boiling point. It will lower the melting point.

6. *What is a chemical change?*
A substance can be used to make new ones.
A change in which a new substance is formed is a **chemical change**.
If no new substance is formed the change is a **physical one**.
Chemical change is also called **chemical reaction**.

7. *What is burning?*
Heating can cause chemical or physical change. Heated in air some substances burn with a flame. **Burning** is a chemical reaction. **It uses up part of the air**.
This part of the air is **oxygen**. The rest is mainly **nitrogen**.

8. *What are the properties of oxygen?*
Pure oxygen can be made by heating some oxides. The oxide splits up or **decomposes**. Oxygen and the element remain.
Magnesium burns to a white ash. This contains magnesium and oxygen.
The white ash is called **magnesium oxide**.

Substances which burn in air burn more brightly in oxygen. **This is why oxygen relights a glowing splint**.

9. *What are the properties of oxides?*
A **metal oxide** may dissolve **in water**. If it does, the solution turns **litmus blue**. It contains an **alkali**. The name given to these alkalis is **hydroxide**.

Non-metals give **oxides**. They may dissolve **in water**. If they do, the solution turns **litmus red**. It contains an **acid**. Acids react with alkalis. They may give a **neutral** solution. It contains new substances. In it **litmus** will be **mauve** in colour. Universal indicator has a range of colours. Its neutral colour is green.

10. *What are the properties of hydrogen?*
Burning fuels give **carbon dioxide** and **water**. Calcium takes oxygen from water. **Hydrogen** is formed. **Water is hydrogen oxide**. Hydrogen is less dense than air. It rises through the air. **Pure hydrogen** burns quietly. **Mixed with air it explodes**. Hydrogen can take oxygen from some **metal oxides**. This leaves the metal.

11. *How can we write down a chemical reaction?*
A chemical reaction can be summed up by a word equation:
    calcium oxide + water → calcium hydroxide

Questions

1. Read each sentence. Choose the *best* answer from **A, B, C, D** or **E**.

    Salt dissolves in water. We say it is:
    A insoluble; **B** soluble; **C** solution; **D** solvent; **E** dissolvable

    Water boils at: **A** 0°C; **B** 100°C; **C** 212°C; **D** 105°C; **E** 32°C

    Substances dissolved in water make its boiling point, compared to normal:
    A higher; **B** the same; **C** lower

    A metal burns in air. In oxygen it would burn
    A more brightly; **B** less brightly; **C** not at all; **D** feebly; **E** slowly

2. Fill in the blank spaces.
    magnesium + oxygen → _____ _____
    calcium + water → calcium _____ + _____
    This last solution turns litmus _____. It is an _____.
    carbon + oxygen → _____ _____
    Sulphur dioxide in water turns litmus _____. The solution contains an _____. Fuels use _____ from the air. They form _____ _____ and _____.
    Animals breathing use _____ from air. They put into the air _____ _____. Plants take _____ _____ from air and put back _____.

3. Three jars contain different gases. Each is tested with a lighted splint.
    In A the splint burns brighter. The gas is _____.
    In B there is a squeaky pop. B is _____.
    In C the splint goes out. C is _____ or _____ _____.

    Which gas, A, B or C, will you test with lime water?
    Which will you test with a glowing splint?

Metals

Hydrogen reacts with heated copper oxide. A liquid forms in the test tube. It makes white copper sulphate blue. It boils at 100 °C. These tests show that it is water.

An orange pink powder is left in the tube. It looks like copper. It has the colour of a new penny.

copper oxide + hydrogen → (copper?) + water

How can we find out if the powder is copper? What are the properties of metals?

Metals are shiny. The shine is called metallic lustre. Is the powder shiny? No, but it may be tarnished. Polish it! Have you ever tried polishing a powder? We need to know some other properties of metals.

What others do you remember? The uses of a substance depend on its properties. Make a list of the uses of copper from the pictures.

Copper is used in making coins. Observation shows that they sink in water. They are 'heavy'.

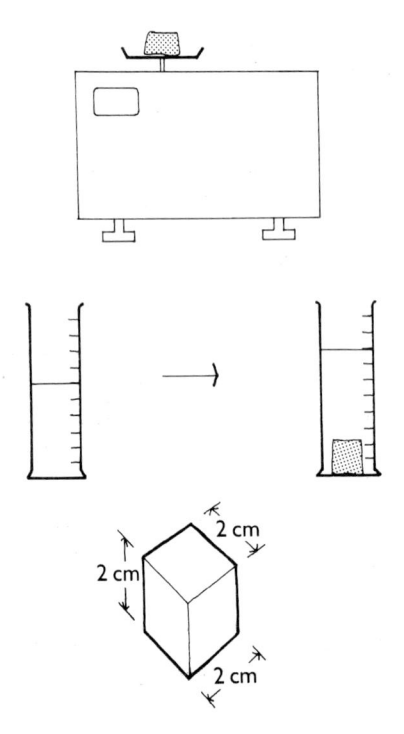

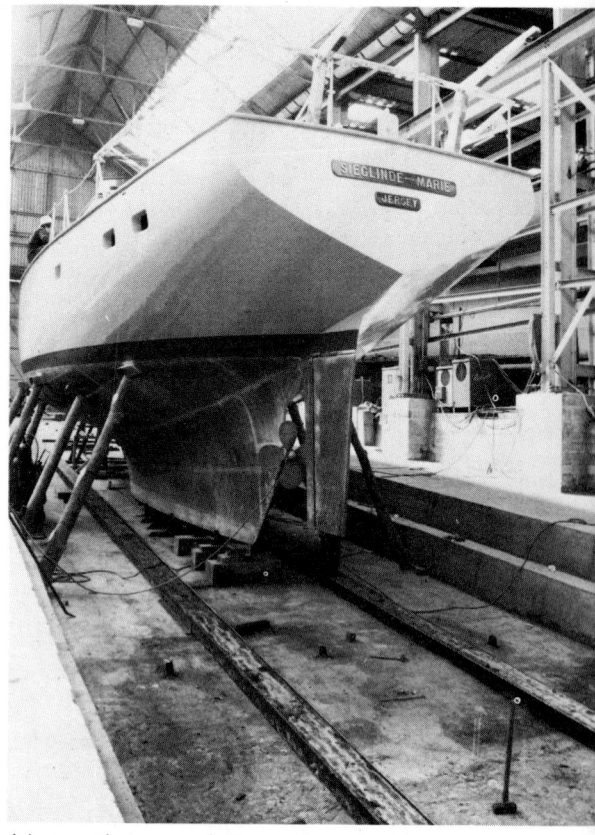

A boat with a copper hull.

Experiment 4.1 To find out about the heaviness of substances

Take cubes or lumps of substances. Use as many metals and non-metals as you can. Put each one on a balance. Read off its mass.

Measure the side of each cube in centimetres. Another way is to take a measuring cylinder. Half fill it with water. Read the level of the water. Put in the lump. Read the water level again.

The balance gives the mass of the lump. This is the amount of matter in it. It is in grams (g), or kilograms (kg).

The amount of space a lump takes up is its volume. This is measured in cubic metres (m^3) or cubic centimetres (cm^3).

Work out the mass of 1 cm^3 of each substance, for example: the volume of the cube shown is 8 cm^3. Its mass is 80 g. If 8 cm^3 has mass 80 g then 1 cm^3 has mass 10 g. The mass of 1 cm^3 is called the density.

Check your list of uses of copper.

Copper is used in roofing. It is a covering for the hulls of boats. It is used in 'silver' and 'copper' coins. This is because it is not an active metal. Air and water have little effect on it.

Copper is used in wires and cables. It acts as a lightning conductor. All these carry electric current. Substances which do this are called conductors. Those which do not are insulators.

Experiment 4.2 To test electrical properties of substances

Connect the apparatus as shown. Touch the bare wires A and B together.

Take dry lumps or cubes. Use the same ones as in the last experiment. Touch one side of the lump with A. Touch the other side with B. Press the bare wires against the lump.

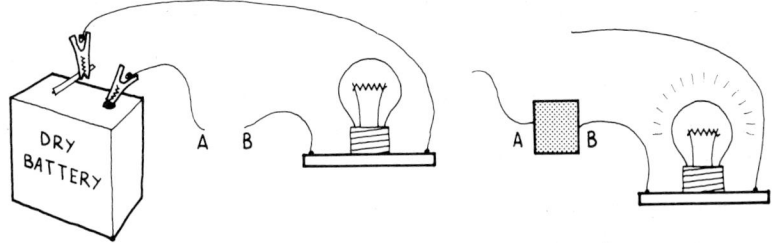

A copper roof and lightning conductor.

Why does the bulb light up when A and B touch?
What happens when a metal is between A and B?
Do all metals give the same result?
What happens when non-metals are used?
Do any non-metals give a different result?

When the bare wires touch, an electric current flows. It passes through the bulb. The bulb lights up.
Then a lump separated the bare ends of wire. If the bulb lights, that shows a current is passing through it. The current must be passing through the lump. The lump is a conductor. Current cannot pass through insulators. If the lump is an insulator, no current passes through the bulb. It does not light up.

Note down your results in a table:

Name of substance	metal or non-metal	element or not	mass of 1 cm^3 in g	conductor or not
copper	metal	element	8.9 g	conductor

Copper is an element. It cannot be split up into other substances. Brass is a metal. However, it is a mixture. We can split it up into copper and zinc.

Metals are **conductors**. Nearly all non-metals are **insulators**. The density of a metal is usually high. Non-metals have lower densities than metals.

A telephone cable containing many copper wires.

The activity series

You know some of the properties of metals now. Check what you know. Copy this out. Fill in the blank spaces.

Metals can _____ an electric current. They are _____. Density is the mass of _____. Most metals have _____ densities. They also have high _____ points. They have metallic _____.

Metals combine with oxygen to form _____. Some metals burn in air. One of them is _____. Metals which burn in air are very _____. Some cannot burn in air but can burn in _____. One is _____. It is _____ active than those which burn in air. Some metals take _____ from water. One is _____. It is very _____.

Some metals do not react with air, oxygen or water. One is _____. These metals are not _____.

All metals have similar properties. They differ in how active they are. We can put them in order of activity. The list is called the Activity Series. The most active metal is at the top.

So far we have these facts:

1. Metals heated in air (Expt 1.15) — Magnesium burns brightly. Copper turns black. Lead changes slowly to oxide. So does mercury. Platinum does not change.

2. Metals in oxygen (Expt 2.8) — Calcium burns with a blinding red flash. Magnesium burns brilliantly. Neither should be watched. Iron glows white hot.

3. Metals with water (Expt 3.3) — Calcium reacts rapidly. Magnesium reacts slowly. Look at the pictures. Do any of these metals react with hot water?

Take group 1. Put the five metals in order. Then do 2 and 3.

In each group the top metal is easy to place. In group 1 magnesium is most active. In groups 2 and 3 calcium is first. But in these groups magnesium is second. So the list begins:

calcium
magnesium
?
?
platinum

The least active metal is platinum. It takes bottom place.

All the other metals react in some way. It is not easy to put them in order. We need a way of comparing these middle metals.

The middle metals

To compare metals we must test them all in the same way. We match them all against the same element. The best one to use is hydrogen.

We can compare football teams in this way. We check the results of matches against the same team. The crazy teams all played Hydrogen Athletic. Look at the results. From them put the teams in order of how good (active) they are.

Lead United 1   Hydrogen Athletic 0
Magnesium United 9   Hydrogen Athletic 0
Iron County 2   Hydrogen Athletic 0
Copper City 0   Hydrogen Athletic 1
Zinc Rovers 4   Hydrogen Athletic 1
Aluminium Town 4   Hydrogen Athletic 0
Platinum Orient 0   Hydrogen Athletic 5

Comparing metals with hydrogen

Water is hydrogen oxide. Heat turns it into steam. This is a physical change. So steam is hydrogen oxide, too.

Test each metal with steam. Some may be able to take oxygen from steam. We can compare how well they do this.

Experiment 4.3 To compare metals using steam

Put water into a test tube to a depth of 2 cm. Push enough rocksill in to soak up the water.

Hold the tube in a clamp. Put in a small pile of metal powder. Put it half-way between rocksill and stopper. Set up the apparatus. Collect any gas in test tubes full of water.

Heat the metal gently. If nothing happens, heat it more strongly. Test the gas for hydrogen. Examine the pile after heating. Take out the stopper as soon as you stop heating.

Your teacher may test magnesium. This helps to place others.

    Which metals react with steam?
    Are any more active than magnesium?

Compare the metals in two ways:
1 How fast is hydrogen formed?
2 How hot does the metal become? Does it glow or burn?
What substance is left in the tube at the end?

The bunsen flame heats the metal. It also heats the water. The water turns to steam. This passes over the heated metal. If they react, hydrogen is formed. The metal oxide is left.

League table
Magnesium United
Aluminium Town
Zinc Rovers
Iron County
Lead United
Hydrogen Athletic
Copper City
Platinum Orient

Putting the metals in order

Did you get the football list right? The results give the order.

Matches between metals and hydrogen give results too.
Aluminium glows brightly in steam. It takes oxygen from it. Hydrogen forms rapidly. Aluminium oxide is left in the tube.
Zinc glows red hot. Hydrogen comes off quite rapidly. Zinc oxide remains. It is yellow when hot and white when cold.
Iron glows dull red. Its oxide is blue-black. It gives a steady flow of hydrogen.
Lead has little action on steam.

These metals are more active than hydrogen. They are put above it in the list. Magnesium reacts better than any of them. They all are below magnesium in the list.

Look at *Experiment 3.7. It shows hydrogen reducing copper oxide. Copper is less active than hydrogen. Its position is . . . ?

Did you notice how fair we were? We treated all the metals alike. Each was in powder form. Each one was heated gently then strongly. So each had the same chance to win oxygen. Pass steam over zinc again. This time use *lumps* of zinc.

The list
Calcium
Magnesium
Aluminium
Zinc
Iron
Lead
Hydrogen
Copper
Platinum

Some less common metals
We shall use lithium and sodium. They are very reactive. They must not be touched. Use tongs to pick them up.

*Experiment 4.4 The action of sodium on water

Take sodium from the bottle with tongs. Blot it with filter paper. Cut off a thin slice with a knife. Drop it into water in a glass trough. Cover the trough with a safety screen.

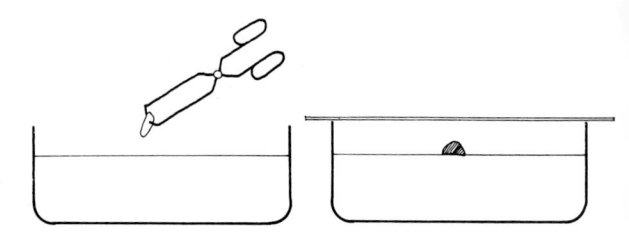

Cut a piece the size of a rice grain. All its sides must be freshly cut. Wrap it in fine wire gauze. Fill a test tube with water. Invert it in the trough. Drop the gauze into the water. Hold the test tube over it. Tap the gauze with the tube. Test the gas with a lighted splint.

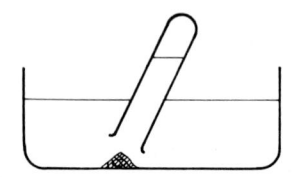

Float a filter paper on the water. Drop a piece of sodium on it. Cover the trough with a screen. Remove the screen at the end. Hold a bunsen flame in the smoke in the trough. Put a litmus paper and Universal Indicator in the water.

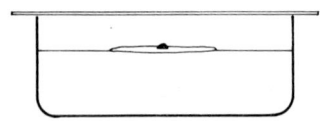

Do the same tests with the metal lithium

> Sodium has some metal properties. Which ones?
> In what ways is it not like other metals?
> Write a word equation for the reaction.
> What colour is the bunsen flame in the smoke?
> How does lithium compare with sodium?

Freshly cut sodium has metallic lustre. It tarnishes very quickly. This explains why it is kept under oil.
In water it melts to a silvery ball. It floats. It moves across the water. The wire gauze is used to sink it. The gas is hydrogen. The water contains an alkali, sodium hydroxide.

On filter paper the sodium cannot move. It cannot lose heat. It bursts into flame. It may even explode. The reaction gives heat. Lithium is like sodium. However, it does not get hot enough to melt.

We cut sodium with a knife. It floats on water. It melts. It is soft. Its density is low. So is its melting point. Not many metals are like this.

Sodium compounds colour the flame orange-yellow. Lithium compounds colour it scarlet. Potassium compounds give a lilac flame.

Summary

All metals have similar properties. However, some are more active, or reactive, than others.

Most metals combine with oxygen. Some burn in air. Some burn only in oxygen. Some react only slowly with air. Some do not react at all.

Some metals can react with water. They take oxygen from it. Hydrogen is set free. An alkali, or hydroxide, is formed in the solution. These are very active metals such as calcium. Sodium, lithium and potassium are very active. They tarnish rapidly in air. So they are kept under oil. All these reactions produce heat.

metal + water → alkali + hydrogen + heat

Other metals react if they are heated in steam.

metal + steam → metal oxide + hydrogen + heat

The heat makes the metal burn or glow. How active they are is shown by: (a) how brightly they glow, (b) how rapidly they give hydrogen.

Finding out

1. These photographs show different metals in use. What metals are being used? What properties make these metals suitable for these uses?
2. Make a list of all the metals you can find at home. How are they protected from tarnish?
3. Find out which metals are mentioned in the Bible. What metals did the Roman Britons use? Are all these metals high or low in the Series? Find out which metals occur 'native'.

A lead roof.

A Trident aircraft made from aluminium.

The Planetarium in London has a copper roof.

Metal versus metal

In Chemistry we make substances pure. Then we find out what their properties are. By making them react we are able to make new substances.

In doing this you have learnt about many substances. You have seen many chemical changes. How can you sort it all out and remember it?

A supermarket sells thousands of things. Suppose they were dumped on the shelves anyhow. It would be hard to find a Mars bar or meat. Shopping would take hours.

Similar things are put into groups. Mars bars are with all the other sweets. Meat is with meat, not mixed with toothpaste. It is easy to find quickly the things we need.

In the same way we group substances. We divide them into classes. On page 37 we used two. A pure substance is either an element or a compound. Tin is an element, tin oxide a compound.

On page 67 we put elements into two classes. They are either metals or non-metals. We know one from the other. They have different properties.

element or compound

metal or non-metal

Putting things in different classes is called **classification.**

Metals have similar properties. However, some are more active than others. We have put them in order of how active they are. This is classification, too. We can use it to predict results. People who do football pools predict. Before the game they say what the result will be. They use the League tables.

Can aluminium take oxygen from iron? Predict! Use the Activity Series to say what may happen.

*Experiment 4.5 The action of aluminium on iron oxide.

Dry iron (III) oxide in an oven. Dry aluminium powder too. Mix equal parts of each in a crucible. Stand it on a

A supermarket.

sand tray on heat-resisting mats. Use safety screens around it.

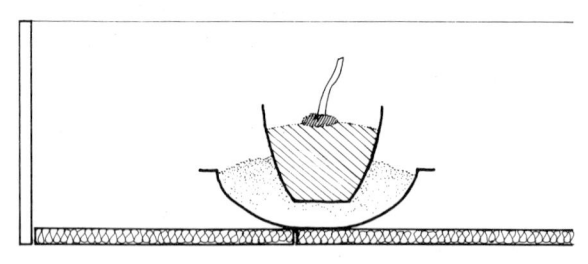

Put a small pile of sulphur on the mixture. Push a strip of magnesium ribbon into it. Light the ribbon from outside the screens.

Let the crucible cool. Scrape out its contents. Grind them to powder. Wrap a magnet in paper. Run it over the powder.

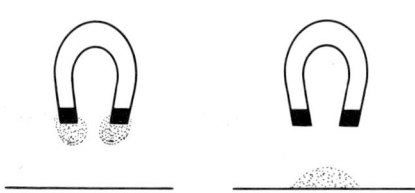

Magnesium and sulphur react. The heat this gives starts the reaction. Is it vigorous? Does it produce a large amount of heat?

Aluminium is higher in the Series than iron. Did you expect it to take oxygen from iron? That is, did you predict the result?

Taking oxygen away is called **reduction**. The magnet shows that iron is formed. We say that aluminium reduced iron oxide to iron. The reaction produces a great deal of heat. The iron formed is a white-hot liquid.

aluminium + iron(III) oxide → aluminium oxide + iron

(III) stands for three. The name is iron three oxide.

The reaction is called the Thermit reaction. It has been used in fire bombs. It can be used to weld pieces of iron. The space is filled with the mixture. Reaction is started. Molten iron is formed. This fills the gap with iron.

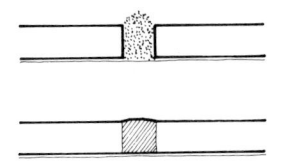

In the battle for oxygen, aluminium wins. It beats iron. Can magnesium reduce black copper oxide to copper? Predict!

The Thermit reaction.

Look at the Activity Series. Is magnesium higher than copper? Will reaction take place?

magnesium + copper oxide → magnesium oxide + copper ? ? ?

Is magnesium very much higher than copper in the Series? Will reaction be feeble, vigorous or very vigorous? Predict!

Now can you see how classification helps? Metals have the same kind of properties. They look alike. Their reactions are alike. This makes learning easier.

However, metals are not all equally active. Learn the Activity Series. It tells us how they differ. From it we can predict.

More reductions

Experiment 4.6 Can magnesium reduce copper oxide?

Dry some black copper oxide in an oven. Also dry magnesium powder. Mix small amounts of the two. Put the mixture in a crucible. Stand it on a pipeclay triangle. Put this on a tripod.

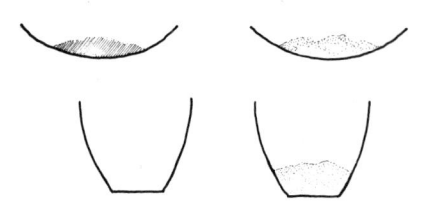

Stand the tripod on heat-resisting mats. Use safety screens. Light a bunsen burner under the crucible.

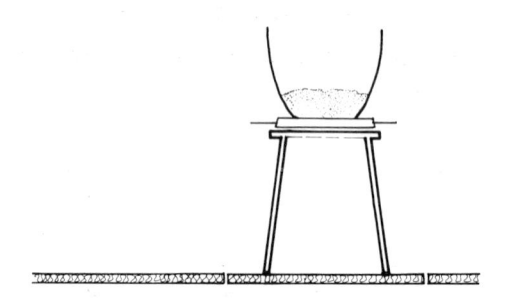

Did you predict the correct results?

Put some more mixture in a crucible. Add some magnesium oxide. Mix it in. Heat the crucible as before. Let it cool. Scrape out the contents.

Put them in a beaker. Add dilute acid. Warm the beaker. Filter the mixture when the magnesium oxide has dissolved.

The first reaction is almost explosive. Nothing is left in the crucible. We can only guess what is formed. Magnesium oxide added makes the reaction less vigorous. The acid dissolves it. There is a substance in the filter paper. It looks like copper.

We could predict this result. Magnesium is much higher than copper in the Series. It is much more active. It will take oxygen from copper oxide. It will do this very vigorously.

magnesium + copper oxide → magnesium oxide + copper

Experiment 4.7 Can iron reduce metal oxides?

Use black copper oxide, yellow lead oxide and zinc oxide. Mix each with iron powder. Fine iron filings can be used instead. Try to predict each result first. Do the lead oxide test in a fume cupboard.

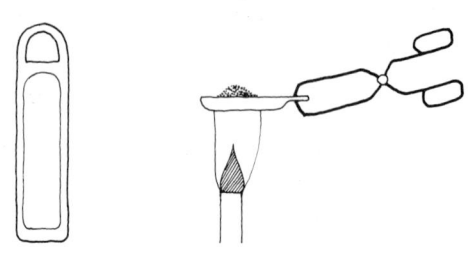

Put each mixture in a porcelain boat. Hold it in tongs. Heat it gently. If nothing happens, heat more strongly. Ceramic paper can be used instead of a boat. Wear eye shields.

Watch each mixture carefully.

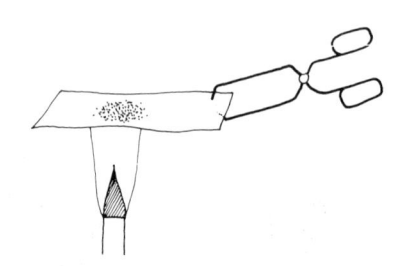

Replacement

Which mixture glows when it is heated?
Which mixture shows no change?
Did you predict all three results?

Iron is higher in the Series than copper. It will reduce copper oxide. Iron will reduce lead oxide too. But iron is lower in the Series than zinc. It does not reduce zinc oxide.

iron + copper oxide → iron oxide + copper

Iron has taken the place of copper. Can it do this with other copper compounds? What other copper compound do you know?

Experiment 4.8 Replacement reactions

1. Take iron wire or a pen knife. Rub it with emery paper. Put copper sulphate solution in a beaker. Hold the clean iron in it. Leave it for a minute or two. Take it out. Look at it.

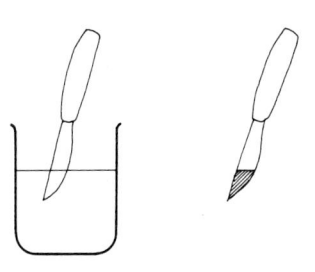

What do you see on the iron?
What substance has formed on its surface?
Has the iron taken the place of the copper?

2. Clean a piece of copper foil. Dip it into silver nitrate solution. Leave it for a while.

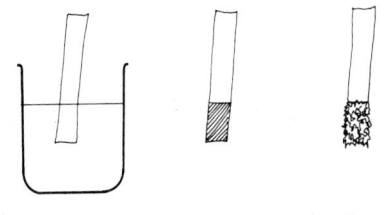

Dip clean zinc foil into lead nitrate solution. Rub lead foil with emery paper. Dip it into copper sulphate solution.

Metal forms on the copper. Is it silver?
Which is the more active metal, copper or silver?
Where should silver be placed in the Activity Series?
Does anything form on the surface of the zinc?
Which is higher in the Activity Series, lead or zinc?
Is there any sign of copper on the lead foil?

Each metal becomes coated. Copper appears on the pen knife. Iron is the more active metal. It takes the place of copper.

iron + copper sulphate → iron sulphate + copper

A white metal forms on the copper foil. It must be silver. Copper displaces silver. It is more active. Copper should be placed above silver in the Series. Lead crystals form on zinc. The surface of lead becomes copper-coloured.

Brother George and sister Grace
Were last in a three-legged race.
Active Willie, running ace,
Pushed George out and took his place.
The chief result of this displacement
Was the startling speed at which poor Grace went.

Making metals

Compounds of metals are found in the earth. They are called ores. Many ores are oxides. Those of iron and tin are.

A metal oxide can be reduced. Oxygen can be taken from it. This is an easy way to make a metal. It has one snag.

Take the Thermit reaction. Aluminium is more active than iron. It will reduce iron(III) oxide. But this leaves a mixture. The iron is mixed with aluminium oxide. To get iron, the oxide must be removed. This is not easy to do.

If only aluminium oxide were a gas! It would escape during the reaction. It would pass into the air. Iron would be left on its own.

Charcoal is a form of carbon. It burns well. This means that it takes oxygen well. It must be able to reduce. It may be able to reduce a metal oxide. Carbon dioxide is a gas!

Experiment 4.9   Reduction with charcoal

1. Mix powdered charcoal and black copper oxide. Use one part of charcoal to two of oxide. Heat the mixture in a test tube. Light a splint. Put the flame at the mouth of the tube.

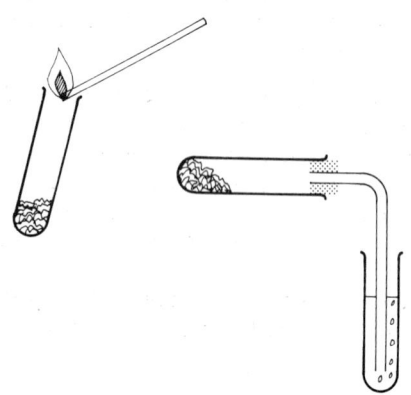

Heat the mixture again. Pass any gas into lime water. Let the tube cool. Scrape out the solid.

> The splint goes out. So a gas is given off.
> What gases put out a lighted splint?
> What does the lime water show?
> The solid left in the tube is brown in colour.
> Can it be copper? Write a word equation.

*2. Make a hole in a charcoal block. Put yellow lead oxide into it. Mix a little charcoal with it. Close the hole at the bottom of the bunsen.

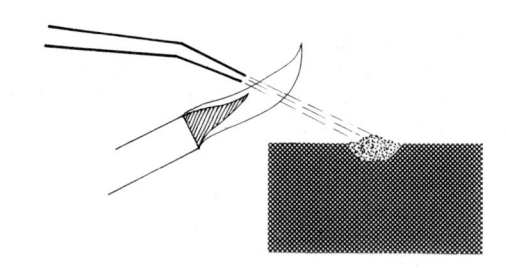

Use a mouth blow pipe. Put the jet at the back of the yellow flame. Blow the flame gently into the hole. Do this heating in a fume cupboard.

In 1, carbon dioxide is formed. It escapes into the air. The brown substance is copper. Carbon can reduce copper oxide.
In 2, a silvery metal forms. During heating it is a liquid. On cooling it becomes a solid. It writes on paper. It is lead.

3. Try to reduce other oxides with carbon.
Use the charcoal block method. Find out if a metal is formed.
Use the test tube method. Test for carbon dioxide.

> Which metal oxides are reduced?
> Are the metals high or low in the Activity Series?
> Did any substances on the block colour the flame?

Compounds of some metals colour the flame. We saw this in Experiment 4.4. Sodium compounds colour it orange-yellow.

Experiment 4.10 Flame colours

Put each substance in the edge of the flame.
Either: 1. Take a splint. Soak one end in dilute hydrochloric acid. On the wet end pick up a few crystals. Hold them in the flame.

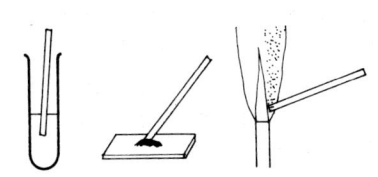

Or: 2. Take a flame test wire. This is platinum or nichrome sealed into glass. Dip it into the acid. Hold it in the flame. A clean wire will not colour the flame. Dip it in acid again. Use it to pick up some substance.

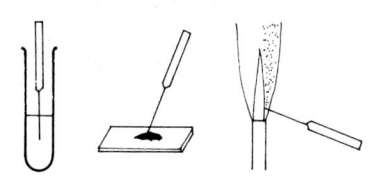

Use the substances shown in the table.

Substance	Colour of flame
sodium chloride	orange-yellow
potassium chloride	lilac
lithium chloride	scarlet
barium chloride	pale green
calcium chloride	brick red
strontium chloride	red
copper sulphate	green-blue

Summary

Metals can be placed in an Activity Series. Metals good at taking oxygen come at the top. They can take oxygen from metals lower down. Taking oxygen from a substance is reduction.

iron + copper oxide → iron oxide + copper

Iron reduces copper oxide to the metal copper. The mixtures become hot. Most chemical reactions give heat. Some become white hot.

Carbon is a good reducing agent. It turns into carbon dioxide. This escapes into the air.

tin oxide + carbon → carbon dioxide + tin

Metal compounds are found in the earth. They are called ores. Many ores are metal oxides. They can be reduced to the metal by carbon.

Metals can displace those below them in the Series. This can happen in solutions of compounds.

zinc + silver nitrate → zinc nitrate + silver

Many metal compounds give colours to a flame.

The Activity Series can be used to predict. We can say beforehand if a reaction will happen.

Questions

1. An oxide is heated on a charcoal block. A silvery metal is formed. What is this chemical change called? What metal could it be? How could you test it? Write a word equation.
2. Some possible changes are listed below. Use the Activity Series to say which would happen.
   a) Copper + zinc oxide → copper oxide + zinc
   b) Lead oxide + iron → iron oxide + lead
   c) Sodium chloride + tin → tin chloride + sodium
   d) Zinc in silver nitrate solution becomes coated in crystals of silver.
   e) Aluminium reacts with copper oxide to form copper. The reaction produces a lot of heat.

To rust or not to rust?

Most metals tarnish in air. They lose metallic lustre. The tarnish can be rubbed off. Then the shiny metal shows again.

Some metals tarnish quickly. They may need to be kept under oil. These metals are high in the Activity Series.

Some tarnish slowly or not at all. A new penny loses its shine very slowly. Gold keeps its lustre all the time.

Iron shows its tarnish most. The tarnish is red-brown in colour. This makes it easy to see on grey iron. It is called by the special name of rust.

The layer of rust easily flakes off. This exposes the iron underneath. This rusts too. In time the iron turns into a heap of rust. This is a chemical change. What makes it happen?

From everyday life we know that rusting needs water. What other substances does it use?

Derelict ships rusting.

Experiment 4.10 To find out if rusting uses air

Wet the inside of a test tube. Sprinkle iron filings inside it. Turn it upside down in water. Measure the height of air in the tube.

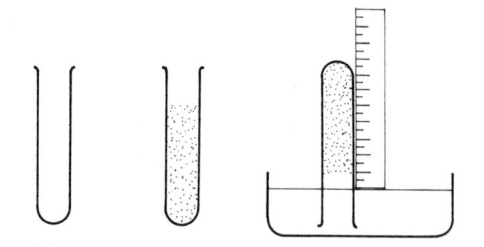

Leave it for a few days. Measure the height of air again. Test the air with a lighted splint.

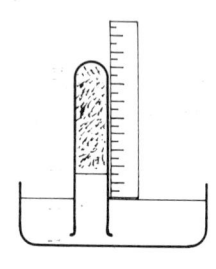

Unloading iron ore.

Iron rusts. Is air used by the change?
What happens to the lighted splint?
What percentage of air has gone?
What gas makes up this percentage of air?

These are some results:
First height of air = 14 cm
Height after rusting = 11 cm
Height of air used = 3 cm
Volume of air is roughly proportional to height.

The lighted splint goes out. About 21% of air is used. Both results show that rusting uses oxygen. Can you guess what substance rust is?

Tarnishing uses air. In it, most metals turn into their oxides. This is called **corrosion**. We say the metals **corrode** in air.

The manufacture of metals

On page 71 you were asked to make two lists. One was a list of metals found at home. The second was of those used in early times. The Bible shows which ones were used over 2000 years ago.

Both lists show how important metals are. Think of a home with no metals. No knives, forks or spoons! No cooker! No heating or lighting except by burning wood. What else would you miss?

Making metals is a huge industry. They are made from ores. An ore is a metal compound found in the earth. Getting a metal from its ore is called extraction. The properties of the metal decide which method to use.

Iron ore is mainly iron oxide. Millions of tonnes of iron are made from it every year in Britain. Coke is used to reduce the oxide. The iron is then turned into steel. Coke is carbon.

A bronze cannon which has been in the sea for nearly 500 years.

Gold and silver are at the bottom of the Series. They are very inactive. The actual metals are found in the earth. This explains why they were among the earliest metals to be used. Man did not need to find out how to extract them.

Copper and tin are low in the Series. Their ores are easy to reduce. So they were discovered early in history. Brass was used early. It looks like an element. It is a mixture of copper and zinc. Such mixtures are called alloys. Bronze is an alloy of copper and tin.

As we go up the Series the metals are more active. This makes them harder to extract. Sodium was first made in 1807. Aluminium was a rare metal until 1886. These top metals cannot easily be made by chemical changes. Most of them are made by electrical methods.

Properties of a metal decide its method of extraction. They also decide its position in the Series. This position tells us what kind of method might be used to extract the metal.

The Activity Series helps us to remember and to predict.

These coins were made 2000 years ago.

Breaking down other ores

Magnesium burns in oxygen. The two elements join together. They form magnesium oxide. The flame is white hot. In joining they produce a large amount of heat (and light).

magnesium + oxygen → magnesium oxide + heat

This reaction is called **combination**. The elements **combine**.

Suppose we want magnesium and oxygen back again. We try to split the oxide up. To do this we put back heat. They gave heat when they joined. We put it back to separate them. This kind of change is called **decomposition**.

We heat magnesium oxide very strongly. This has no effect. At 2500 °C it does not decompose. It does not even melt.

magnesium oxide + heat → no change

Lavoisier heated mercury in air. He heated it for days. The mercury and oxygen combine very slowly. They form red mercury oxide. No heat is given out.

We want mercury and oxygen back again. Heat the red oxide. Page 36 shows what happens. It splits up with ease. Only gentle heat is needed to decompose it.

It seems that:

Some elements combine vigorously. The reaction gives heat.
Then the compound formed is hard to split up.

It is hard to make some elements combine.
Then the compound they form is easy to decompose.

Compounds of metals high in the Series are hard to split up. Compounds of metals low in the Series are easy to decompose.

We shall try to decompose, or break down, some ores.

Willie really loves the sea,
He leaps into the waves with glee
And when the time for swimming's past
It's Willie who is dragged out last.
George is the other way about,
He's last one in and first one out.
He isn't active from the start,
But Willie and sea are hard to part.

Experiment 4.11 To heat the green ore called malachite

Take a small, clean, dry test tube. Fill it one third full of powdered ore. Heat it gently. If nothing happens, heat it more strongly.

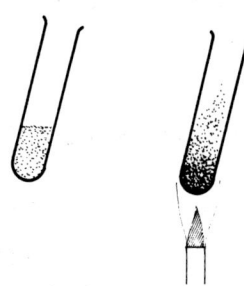

Does the powder need strong or gently heating?
What colour is the substance left in the tube?
The powder seems to 'boil'. Can you explain this?

The powder 'boils'. It is blown about in the tube. This shows that a gas is being formed. Some steam may appear. Only gentle heat is needed. Malachite may be the ore of a metal *low* in the Activity Series.

A black powder is left in the tube. The black powders we know are charcoal, manganese(IV) oxide and black copper oxide.
Charcoal takes litmus out of a solution (page 44).
Manganese(IV) oxide is used to make oxygen (page 40).
Hydrogen reduces heated copper oxide to copper (page 62).

Try one of these on the black powder from malachite. Which of the three tests would you try first?

Experiment 4.12 To find out if a gas is given off from malachite

How can we find out if a gas is formed from the green ore? Invent a method of doing this. Use it to collect the gas. How shall we know what gas it is?

Put malachite in a test tube. Fit it with a stopper. Put a delivery tube into the stopper. Collect the gas in test tubes.

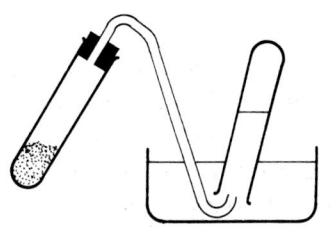

A lighted splint in different gases	In oxygen the splint burns more brightly. Oxygen relights a glowing splint.
	In hydrogen the splint goes out with a squeaky pop.
	In carbon dioxide or nitrogen the splint goes out. But carbon dioxide turns lime water milky.

Test the gas with a lighted splint. If it puts out a lighted splint, test it with lime water.

If hydrogen is passed over the black powder it becomes orange-pink. Water forms as well. The orange-pink powder is a conductor. It is copper. The black powder must be copper oxide.

copper oxide + hydrogen → copper + water

The gas puts out the splint. It also turns lime water milky. It is carbon dioxide. The black powder is copper oxide.

malachite heated →
black copper oxide + carbon dioxide

Malachite is copper ore. It is copper carbonate. Heating it gives copper oxide. This can be reduced to the metal copper.

Two other ores

Cerrusite

*Experiment 4.13 To heat cerrusite

Heat a little powdered ore in a test tube gently. If nothing happens heat more strongly. Put a lighted splint at the mouth of the test tube. Squeeze the teat of a dropper. Put the other end in the tube. Stop squeezing. The dropper takes up gas. Bubble the gas through lime water.

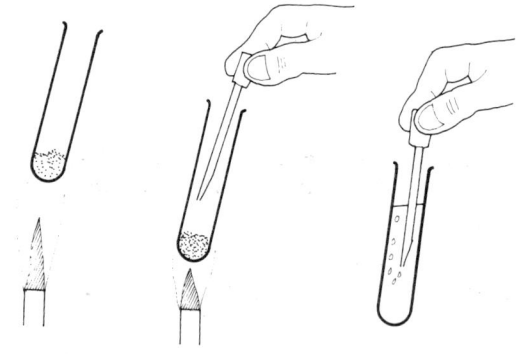

The white ore decomposes. What gas is formed?
A yellow substance forms. What might it be?
Did the ore need gentle or strong heating?

The ore needs stronger heating than malachite does. It splits up into carbon dioxide and a yellow substance. This looks like lead oxide. It could be. Lead oxide is yellow. Lead is higher than copper in the Series. Decomposing its compounds *would* need stronger heating.

*Experiment 4.14 To test the yellow substance

Heat a little of it with powdered charcoal in a crucible in a fume cupboard. Let it cool. Take any metal out of what remains.

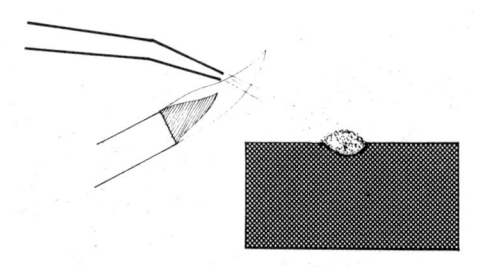

A silvery, liquid metal is formed. On cooling it turns to solid. It writes, so it must be lead. So cerrusite is lead carbonate.

lead carbonate → lead oxide + carbon dioxide

Lead is a soft, dense metal. It is not reactive and corrodes only very slowly. It has a low melting point. Which property explains the use of lead shown in the photograph below?

Lead and its compounds are poisonous. Our bodies absorb them but cannot get rid of them. Petrol contains a lead compound to cut down 'engine knocking'. So car exhausts cause lead pollution. We take it in as we breathe. The plants we eat contain lead compounds. Government reports say there is little to worry about. However, recent tests show that lead causes brain damage. Children are affected most. Lead-free petrol is used in the USA and other countries.

Lead is often used for roofing.

Chalk

Chalk is a common natural rock. It is fairly soft. Millions of years ago tiny creatures lived in the sea. Their skeletons fell to the sea bed. Pressure slowly turned them into rock. Smaller pressure made chalk. Bigger pressure gave limestone. Heat and pressure gave marble.

Experiment 4.14 The effect of heat on chalk

Put powdered chalk into a test tube. Heat it very strongly. Collect and test any gas.

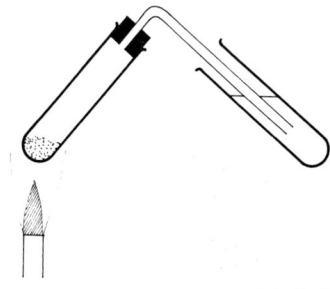

Can you see any change in the heated chalk?
How strongly must it be heated to give gas?
Can we heat it more strongly in the flame?

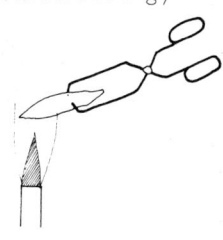

Hold a chip of chalk in tongs. Hold it in the hottest bunsen flame. Keep heating for ten minutes. Put it down on wire gauze to cool. Make sure that it is quite cold.

Does it appear to change in any way?
Does the flame alter during the heating?

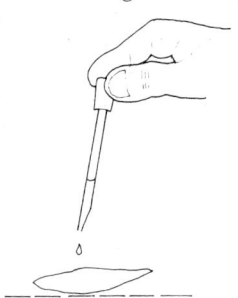

Add drops of cold water to the cold lump. Add water to a lump of chalk. Press a litmus paper on both after adding water.

Does water react with chalk?
Does it react with the lump left after heating?
What does the litmus paper show?

Very strong heating is needed to change chalk. A few bubbles of gas may be formed. It is carbon dioxide. The test tube may melt first! Chalk is more strongly heated in the flame. The lump glows white hot. The flame may be coloured during heating.

Water dropped on chalk soaks in. Nothing else happens. Water put on the cold lump turns to steam. Heat is needed to turn water to steam. This heat cannot come from the lump or the water. It must come from a chemical change.

The lump crumbles up into a powder. The powder turns litmus blue. It is an alkali.

A chalk cliff.

The limes

Limestone and marble

Experiment 4.15 To find out about limestone and marble

Repeat the tests of Experiment 4.14. Crush some marble and limestone. Heat each powder in a test tube. Pass any gas into lime water.

Hold a lump of each in the bunsen flame. Heat strongly for ten minutes. Let the lump get quite cold. Put it in a test tube. Add drops of cold water. Almost fill the test tube with water. Stopper the tube and shake it. Filter.

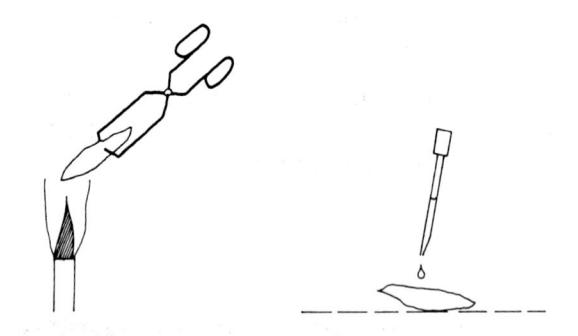

Test some filtrate with Universal Indicator. Breathe into the rest through a glass tube.

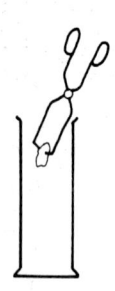

Do marble and limestone behave like chalk?
Can they be the same chemical compound?

Look again at page 41. We burnt calcium in oxygen. Calcium oxide was formed. It reacts with water. The substance formed is an alkali.

calcium oxide + water → calcium hydroxide

Calcium compounds colour the flame brick red.

Experiment 4.16 A flame colour from chalk

Hold a small lump of chalk in tongs. Put it close to a bunsen flame. Add a drop of dilute hydrochloric acid. Drop it on the chalk on the flame side. Do this with limestone and marble.

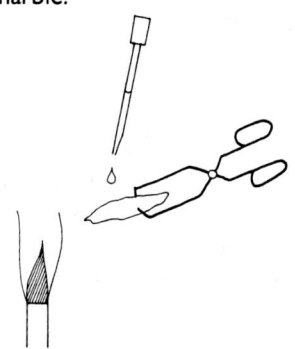

Do the acid and chalk react?
What changes are there in the bunsen flame?

Chalk, marble and limestone behave in the same way. Heat decomposes them. Carbon dioxide is formed. They are forms of the same compound. The compound is a carbonate, like malachite.

This carbonate is not easy to decompose. It effervesces with acid. It gives flashes of brick red colour to the flame. It is calcium carbonate. Calcium is high in the Activity Series. Its compounds are difficult to decompose.

calcium carbonate →
calcium oxide + carbon dioxide

Calcium oxide is called **quick**lime. It reacts vigorously with water. Heat is produced. Some of the water turns into steam. The calcium oxide crumbles to powder. This is an alkali.

calcium oxide + water → calcium hydroxide

Calcium hydroxide is called **slaked** lime. It dissolves slightly in water. Calcium hydroxide solution is lime water.

Limestone is an important mineral. In Britain about 50 million tonnes are used every year. About one fifth of this is used to make quicklime and slaked lime. This is done in lime kilns. All three are used in building (page 86).

Limestone is used in making iron and steel. Iron ore is mixed with limestone and coke. The mixture is fed into a blast furnace.

Quicklime is used in farming. The soil may be too acid. Quicklime neutralizes it.

Summary

Some metal ores are carbonates. On heating they decompose. Carbon dioxide is given off. The metal oxide remains. Copper is not very reactive. Its carbonate ore is malachite. It is easy to decompose. Black copper oxide is formed. It can be reduced to copper.

Chalk, marble and limestone are calcium carbonate. It is not easy to decompose. The oxide is quicklime. It reacts with water. Calcium hydroxide is formed. It is called slaked lime. Limestone, quicklime and slaked lime are important. They have many uses in building and industry.

Questions

1. I have a piece of white rock. I heat it very strongly. It gives carbon dioxide. A white lump remains. It reacts with water. The substance formed turns litmus blue. The rock is used for a flame test. The flame is coloured pale green. What is the rock? Explain all the changes.

2. Write down answers to fill the blank spaces. Chalk is calcium _____. It must be heated _____ to decompose it. Calcium oxide and _____ are formed. Calcium oxide is called _____ lime.

   calcium oxide + water → calcium _____

   The new substance turns litmus _____. It is an _____. It is also called _____ lime.

Heated quicklime glows. It gives white light. This was once used for spotlights. Important people on the stage were 'in the limelight'.

Chemistry and building

Have you ever seen a house being built? First of all the shape of the house is marked out on the ground. Then trenches are dug. This gives a base for every wall.
Each trench is filled with concrete. These are the foundations. On them the walls are built.

The walls may be of local stone. Bricks, breeze blocks and concrete blocks are more common. Each block is bonded to the ones round it. Thin layers of mortar are used to do this.

On top of the walls a wooden frame is put. Tiles or slates are put on it to form the roof.

Spaces are left in the walls. These are for doors or windows. Glass is used in window spaces. The walls are rough on the inside. They are covered with a smooth layer of plaster.

Clay, limestone and sand are used in building. Limestone is, like chalk, calcium carbonate. Sand is silicon dioxide. It belongs to the same family as carbon dioxide. Carbon dioxide gives carbonates. Sand forms silicates.

Clay is a mixture of aluminium silicate and sand. Mixed with water, it gives a paste like mud. Bricks and tiles are shaped from this. They are then baked in an oven called a kiln.

Cement is made from finely powdered limestone and clay. This mixture is heated in a rotating furnace at about 600 °C. It is cooled. It is ground to a fine grey powder. This is cement.

Cement is mixed to a paste with water. It is moulded into shape. Concrete is made of cement, small stones and sand. It is mixed with water and shaped like cement. Concrete and cement both dry out. They set to a hard mass like rock.
Reinforced concrete is set round a steel frame. This makes it much stronger.

Mortar is a mixture. It has six parts sand, one part slaked lime and one part cement. It gives a paste with water. This sets hard like cement. It is much cheaper. Slaked lime is an alkali. It combines with

Foundations and the start of walls.

These buildings in Stamford are made of local stone.

Buildings can be made in many different styles.

Glass is made in huge flat sheets.

carbon dioxide from air. This slowly forms limestone, making the mortar stronger.

Glass is a mixture. It is made from sand, soda and limestone. These are measured out and mixed. The mixture is heated in a furnace to about 1500 °C. It melts. The liquid is glass. It is as runny as treacle. Lumps of it, called gobs, are shaped in moulds. Air blows the glass into shape.

Flat glass is made by two methods. Liquid glass flows over rollers. These are cooled by water. Molten glass is also floated on liquid tin. This gives it a very smooth surface. Other substances are put in glass mixtures. They alter its properties to match the uses.

The mineral gypsum is calcium sulphate. It loses water when heated, like copper sulphate. The substance formed is Plaster of Paris. It is made into a smooth paste with water. It is spread on walls and ceilings. It slowly dries. It combines with the water. This gives gypsum.

Putty is used to fit glass into wooden frames. It is chalk mixed with linseed oil. The linseed oil reacts with air. It hardens out.

Carbon dioxide

In the last experiments we heated three carbonate ores. We shall now find the effect of adding acids to them.

Experiment 5.1 The reaction of acid with carbonate

Malachite is copper carbonate.
1. Put a small amount of it in each of three test tubes. Add dilute hydrochloric acid to one. Add dilute nitric acid to the next. Put dilute sulphuric acid in the third. Find out what gas is formed.

The drawings show ways of passing the gas into lime water.

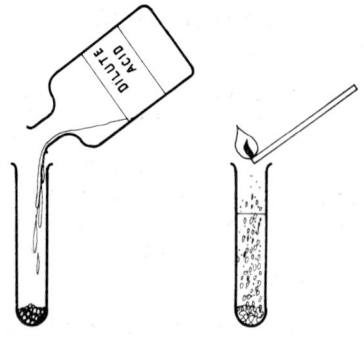

What tells you that a gas is formed?
Did you test it with a lighted splint?
Did you pass the gas through lime water?
What colour is the solution in each case?

2. Add the same dilute acids to (a) cerrusite, (b) chalk, (c) marble. Test the gas.

Do they all produce carbon dioxide?
Which of the carbonates give gas rapidly?
Which carbonate and acid give a steady stream?

The mixtures froth and bubble. This effect is called **effervescence**. It shows that a gas is being formed. We used the usual tests on it.

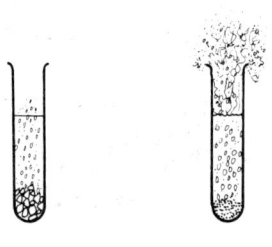

A lighted splint in different gases	In oxygen the splint burns more brightly. Oxygen relights a glowing splint.
	In hydrogen the splint goes out with a squeaky pop.
	In carbon dioxide or nitrogen the splint goes out. But carbon dioxide makes lime water milky.

All carbonates react with acid to give carbon dioxide. Some reactions soon stop. The powders give gas at a very rapid rate. They may foam out of the test tube. Lumps such as marble give gas more slowly.

We shall find out more about carbon dioxide. To do this we need gas jars full of it. For this we need a steady stream of the gas. Lumps of marble provide a steady flow.

Marble and sulphuric acid soon stop reacting. We shall use dilute hydrochloric acid.

The properties of carbon dioxide

Experiment 5.2 To make and test carbon dioxide

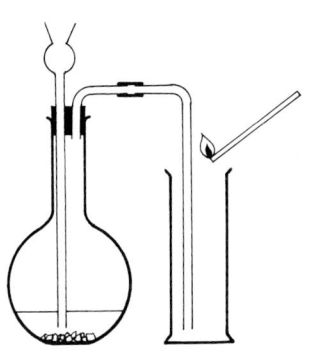

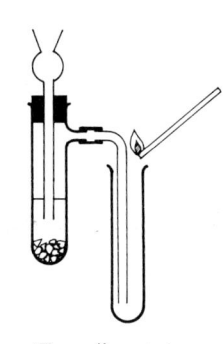

To collect the gas in gas jars

To collect it in test tubes

Hold a lighted splint at the top of the gas jar. When the jar is full of gas the flame goes out.

1. Shake carbon dioxide with water. Add a litmus paper. Put in some Universal Indicator.

   What do the indicators prove?

2. Invert a test tube of the gas in (a) water, (b) dilute alkali solution.

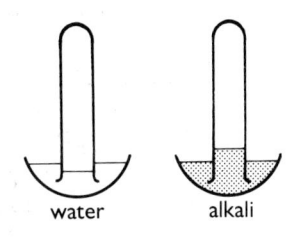

   water   alkali

   In which does the gas dissolve more?

3. Light a candle. Hold a gas jar of carbon dioxide over it. Take the cover off the jar.

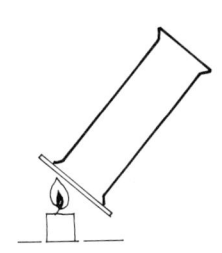

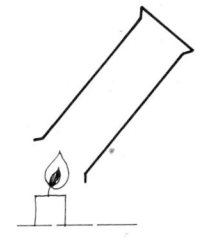

   What does this test tell us about the gas?

4. Light a piece of magnesium ribbon. Hold it well down in a gas jar of carbon dioxide.

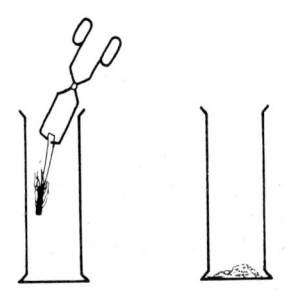

   Does magnesium go on burning?
   Is the powder left in the jar one substance?
   What could this substance be?

5. Bubble carbon dioxide through lime water (calcium hydroxide solution) for some time.

Carbon dioxide is more dense than air. It falls into the gas jar. It also falls over the candle. It puts the candle flame out. Magnesium burns in carbon dioxide. A white powder is left. It has specks of black in it. It may be magnesium oxide + carbon.

In water carbon dioxide forms a weak acid. It is carbonic acid. This is why it dissolves well in alkalis. It reacts with them.

The lime water test

Were you surprised when the lime water 'turned milky'? Surely not! We have used this test many times.

Carbon dioxide in lime water forms white chalk. The chalk floats in water. It makes it 'milky'.

calcium hydroxide solution + carbon dioxide → chalk + water

Did you expect it to become clear again? Putting in more carbon dioxide made it clear. If it is clear, the chalk has gone. But chalk does not dissolve in water. It must have formed a new substance.

chalk + water + more carbon dioxide → new substance

The new substance must be soluble in water.

Experiment 5.3 To heat the clear solution

Half fill a small beaker with lime water. Bubble carbon dioxide through it. Stop when the liquid becomes 'milky'.

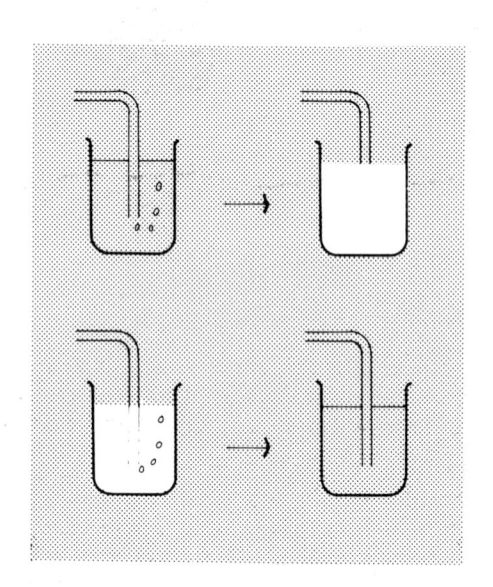

Bubble more carbon dioxide through it. Wait until it becomes clear. Gently heat this until the water boils. Watch what happens.

Boil it for four or five minutes. Let it cool. Pour away the water. Leave the solid in the beaker. Add dilute acid to it.

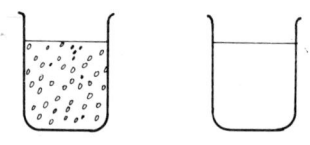

Do you live in a chalk or limestone area? If so, boil half a beaker full of tap water.

> What happens to the clear solution on boiling?
> Did you see bubbles of gas form in it?
> Does the white solid react with the acid?
> Does tap water behave in the same way?

When the clear solution is heated, bubbles form in it. This gas must be carbon dioxide. A white solid forms. This dissolves in acid. It also gives gas. It must be chalk.

Tap water from a limestone area gives the same results.

The clear solution contains a new substance. It is called calcium hydrogencarbonate. The equation is:

chalk + water + carbon dioxide → calcium hydrogencarbonate

The uses of carbon dioxide

In water carbon dioxide forms a weak acid.

About 1 cm³ of gas dissolves in 1 cm³ of water. Much more gas will dissolve under pressure. The solution is pleasant to the taste. Fizzy drinks contain carbon dioxide under pressure. The gas escapes when the bottle is opened.

Carbon dioxide is also the gas in wines like champagne. It is formed when wines and beer are made. Some of it remains in the liquid.

Carbon dioxide puts out burning substances.

Two effects put out a fire. One is cooling it. The other is keeping air from it. Water does both. However, it leaves an awful mess at the end.

A liquid carbon dioxide cylinder does both. It gives cold gas. This cools the fire and keeps out air. It leaves no mess. However, it is a gas. This means it does not stay over the fire. It is most useful for small fires. It is a non-conductor. It can be used safely on electrical fires. Mixed with foam it blankets the fire better. Powder extinguishers contain sodium hydrogencarbonate. Fire makes this give carbon dioxide.

Solid carbon dioxide is very cold. It turns to gas at −78 °C. It is used in refrigeration. It is colder than ice. It leaves nothing behind after use. This is important in food transport. It is used when low temperatures are needed.

Fizzy drinks contain carbon dioxide.

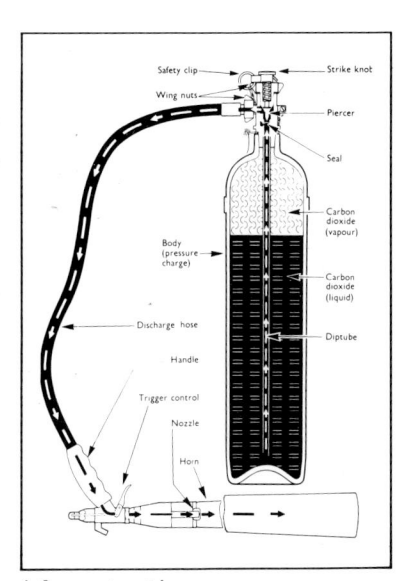

A fire extinguisher.

Questions

1. Fill in the blanks.

   Carbon dioxide is made by adding _____ acid to _____. It is _____ dense than air. This means it _____ into a gas jar. It puts out a lighted _____ or burning _____. It is used in fire _____. It could not put out a fire of burning _____.

   Magnesium burns in carbon dioxide. The equation is:
   magnesium + carbon dioxide → _____ + _____. Carbon dioxide _____ in water. The solution is a weak _____. It is used in making _____ drinks. Solid carbon dioxide is very _____. It turns to gas at −_____ °C. It is used to transport _____.

2. A test tube contains a gas. It is hydrogen, oxygen, carbon dioxide or nitrogen. How would you find out which? Describe the results you might see.

Water for us

When we need water we turn on a tap. Clean water comes out. It has no harmful substances in it. It has no bacteria which carry disease.

Where does our water supply come from? It first falls as rain or snow. This soaks into the earth. Some of it may collect underground. Much of it runs into streams. These grow into rivers. Rivers flow into the sea.

Sea and rivers evaporate. Water vapour rises into the air. As it cools it turns back into drops of water. We see these drops as clouds. If the drops get big enough they fall as rain. If it is cold enough, ice crystals fall as snow. We are back to where we started. This series of changes is called the Water Cycle.

We need water all the time. We store it in reservoirs. Even these may run dry in hot weather. They are filled by rivers and rain. The water from them is made clean. It passes into pipes called mains. These take it to the taps.

All the used water goes down the drain. It is cleaned up and put back into the rivers or the sea.

Underground water is also used. A hole is drilled down to it. A pipe is passed down the hole. The water can then be pumped up the pipe.

We can add these three changes to the Water Cycle. We shall split the Cycle into sections. Then we can study each section in more detail.

The water cycle.

From rain to reservoir

Water is a solvent. Many solids, liquids and gases dissolve in it. As rain falls it will dissolve gases out of the air. One of these gases is carbon dioxide.

The rain soaks into the earth. It runs over rocks. Two common ones are chalk and limestone. The map on page 100 shows where they occur in Britain. They are both calcium carbonate.

On page 89 we passed carbon dioxide into milky lime water. Three substances met in the beaker. They were chalk, water and carbon dioxide.

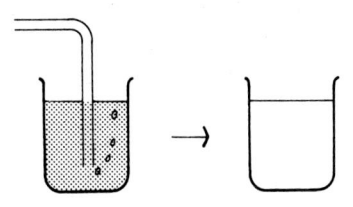

The chalk dissolved. It did this by turning into a new substance. This new substance is soluble. It is calcium hydrogencarbonate.

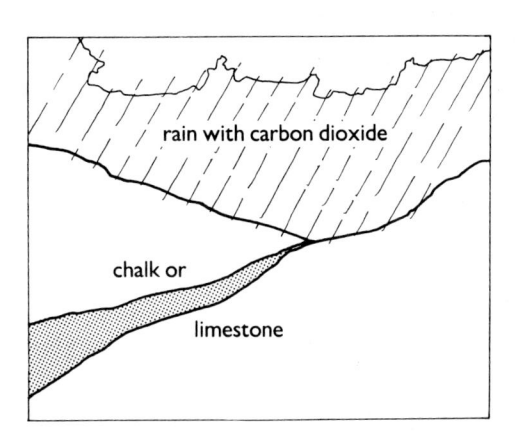

Rain falls on chalk or limestone. The same three substances meet. Some chalk or limestone dissolves. This puts calcium hydrogencarbonate into rivers and streams.

The rain and rivers feed reservoirs. These supply our tap water. In many parts of Britain tap water contains calcium hydrogencarbonate.

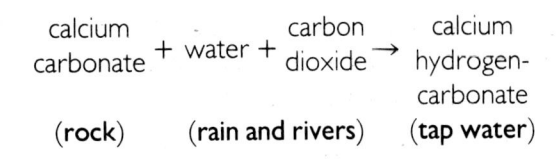

calcium carbonate + water + carbon dioxide → calcium hydrogencarbonate

(rock)   (rain and rivers)   (tap water)

Rain and rivers pass over other rocks. Some of these dissolve. Calcium sulphate is one of them. Tap water will have this in it too.

We drink tap water. We wash in it. We boil it. It evaporates if we leave it in the air.
What effect will the calcium compounds have?
How will calcium compounds affect these changes?

Drinking

Our bodies need calcium compounds. Having them in our drinking water is useful. They are used in forming bones and teeth. They may also give water a more pleasant taste.

MALVERN

AVERAGE ANALYSIS
DISSOLVED SOLIDS PARTS PER MILLION

Calcium Carbonate	100
Magnesium Sulphate	38
Magnesium Chloride	32
Sodium Chloride	26
Silica	10
Sodium Nitrate	6
Potassium Nitrate	2
Organic Carbon	0.1
Fluoride	0.1
Iron	0.05
Trace Heavy Metals	less than 0.01
pH 8.0	

The label from a bottle of Malvern Spring Water. The water contains more calcium carbonate than any other substance.

What about washing?

We wash with soap and water. We use detergents to wash clothes and dishes.

Experiment 6.1 The effect of soap on water

We shall compare distilled water and tap water. We need to measure how much soap we use. The best way to do this is to use soap solution. This is soap dissolved in ethanol and water.

Use a small conical flask or a large test tube. Put in 10 cm^3 of distilled water. With a dropper add one drop of soap solution. Stopper the tube or flask. Shake it.

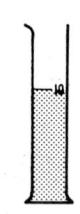

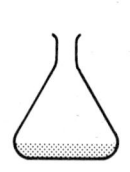

The bubbly froth which forms is called lather. If it lasts for two minutes, add no more soap. If not, add another drop of soap solution. Count the drops needed to get a lasting lather.

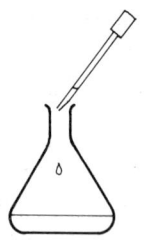

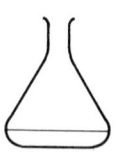

Do this again with 10 cm^3 of your tap water. Do it with 10 cm^3 of tap water from a limestone area. If you cannot get this, make hard water by the method shown.

> Which needs least soap to form a lasting lather?
> Which water stays clear and which becomes cloudy?
> What happens to tap water when soap is added?
> Does water from a limestone area give the same result?

To form a lather:
distilled water needs little soap and the water remains clear.
tap water from a limestone area needs much more soap. It becomes cloudy. A white curd or scum forms on it.

Hard water

With some water it is hard to form a lather using soap. We say that this water is **hard**. Substances dissolved in it react with soap. This forms a white scum. No lather forms until the dissolved substances are used up. Much more soap is needed. Some water needs little soap. A lather forms at once. No scum forms. We say this water is **soft**.

To make hard water:
Shake calcium sulphate in water. Filter it. Pass carbon dioxide into lime water until it is clear. Mix equal volumes of each solution.

*Willie said to his Dad, 'Would you rather
Shave in hard or soft water, Father?'
Dad said, 'Don't be dumb!
Hard water forms scum
And needs far more soap for a lather.'*

The two kinds of hardness

Hard water wastes soap. It uses it to form scum. Scum is a nuisance. It sticks to baths and wash basins.

Distilled water would be best to wash in. It has no dissolved substances to react with soap. No soap is wasted in making scum. Lather forms straight away.

To make distilled water needs heat. This makes it expensive. Can you think of a cheap substitute? Water evaporates. The vapour rises into the air. Cooling turns it back to water. This falls as rain. Catch it before it has a chance to dissolve rock. **Rainwater is soft** (and cheap, too).

Carbon dioxide makes lime water cloudy then clear. In the solution is calcium hydrogencarbonate. Can you remember what happened when we boiled it? Hard tap water contains calcium hydrogencarbonate, too.

Experiment 6.2 The effect of boiling on hardness

Put hard tap water into a beaker. Gently boil it for ten minutes. Let it cool. Put 50 cm^3 of it in a conical flask.

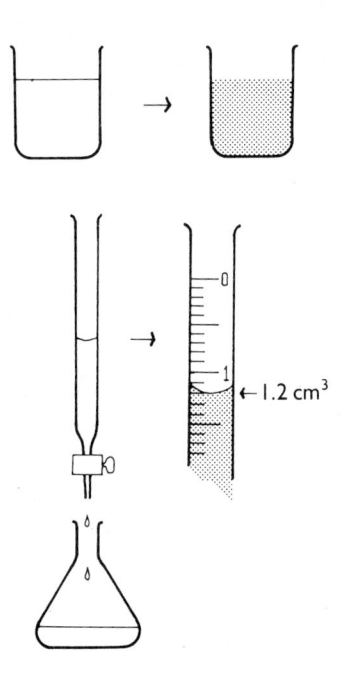

Lather produced by soap in hard and soft water.

Add soap solution from a burette. Stopper the flask. Shake it. Add just enough soap to get a lasting lather. The burette measures how much soap this needs.

Do the same with 50 cm^3 of hard tap water. Test 50 cm^3 of distilled water in the same way.

Water from a limestone area gave these results:

	tap water	boiled tap water	distilled water
Soap used	15.0 cm^3	5.4 cm^3	1.4 cm^3
Water was	very cloudy	fairly cloudy	clear

Read the results. Use them to fill the gaps.

In distilled water soap forms no _____. All the soap is used in forming _____. Tap water needs about _____ times as much soap. Most of this soap is wasted in forming _____. Boiled water needs less soap than _____ water. This means boiling must have removed some _____.

Boiled tap water needs more soap than _____ water. This means that it is still _____. Boiling gets rid of calcium hydrogen _____. It turns this substance into _____. Tap water must have a second substance dissolved in it.

How do soap and detergents work?

Experiment 6.3 To compare soap and detergents in hard water

Put hard water into two test tubes.
To one add three drops of washing-up liquid.
To the other add 1 cm^3 of soap solution.
Stopper both tubes. Shake them.

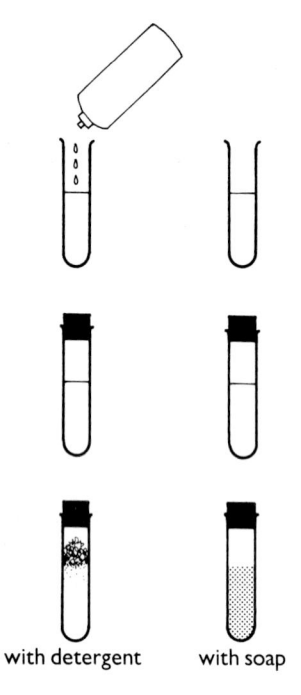

with detergent   with soap

In what ways are the two results different?

Soap is made by heating oils or fats with alkali. The alkali used is sodium hydroxide. Glycerol is formed as well.

oil or fat + sodium hydroxide → soap + glycerol

A simple name for soap is sodium stearate. In soft water it froths, or makes a lather. In hard water it forms scum first.

calcium compounds (hard water) + sodium stearate (soap) → calcium stearate (scum) + sodium compounds

Enough soap turns all the calcium compounds into scum. Adding more soap will now make a lather. A lather shows that soap is there, ready to wash with.

The word detergent comes from a Latin word. It means 'to clean'. Soap and detergents do the same job. They both remove dirt.

Detergents are made from oils too. They are heated with sulphuric acid. Detergents are not sodium compounds. They do not react with calcium compounds. So they do not form scum in hard water. They can remove dirt straight away.

Later on we shall make soap and a detergent.

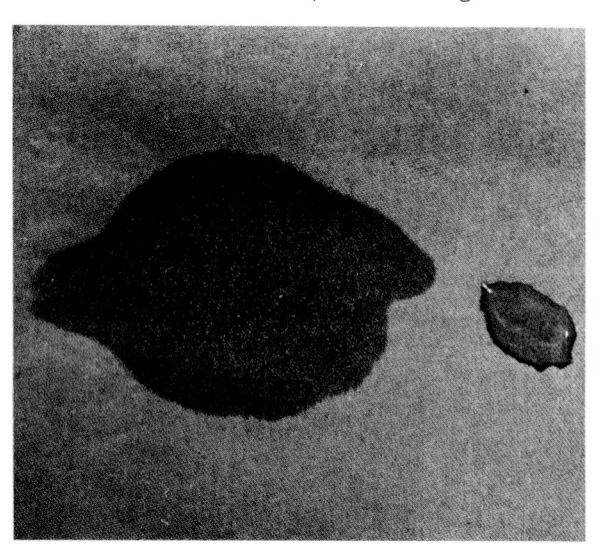

Drops of water on a cloth. The one on the left has detergent on it.

Experiment 6.4 To find out how a soap and detergent work

1. Fill a dropper with distilled water. Put a drop on the back of your hand. Tilt your hand. Carefully put a drop on a piece of cloth.

Half fill small test tubes with distilled water. Put drops of detergent in one. Put soap solution in the other. Put drops of these on the back of your hand. Put drops of each on cloth.

Do the drops of water wet your hand evenly?
Do they spread out and wet the cloth?
Do soap and detergent make a difference?

2. Set up three test tubes as shown. In one put two drops of liquid detergent. In the second put soap solution. Leave the third.

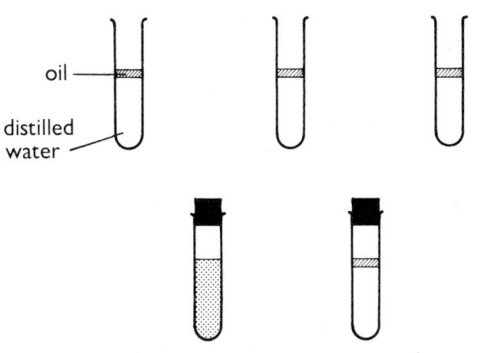

Stopper all three tubes. Shake them well. Leave them to stand. Pour the liquids away.

In which tubes do oil and water mix?
In which do they stay mixed after standing?
When each liquid is poured off is any oil left?

3. In the beakers are strips of cloth. Each is smeared with oily dirt. Rub them hard in the liquids. Pour the liquids out of the beakers.

In which beakers is dirt removed?
In which do oil, dirt and water mix?
Is the oily dirt poured away with the liquid?

Our skins produce an oily substance. Oil and water do not mix. This is why water does not 'wet' our hands. It does not spread evenly over the skin. The oily layer prevents this.

The oily substance on the skin collects dirt. Oily dirt collects on clothes too. Water alone will not remove it. The oily layer and the water do not mix.

Soap and detergents alter this. They help oil and water mix. Experiment 6.4 part 2 shows that they stay mixed. Pouring the liquid away leaves no oil behind. After washing we rinse. This takes oil, dirt and soap (or detergent) away.

Summary

Most dirt is oily. Water does not mix with oil. So washing with water alone is not enough. It leaves most of the dirt on skin or clothes. Some may rub off on the towel we use to dry!

Soap and detergents make oil and water mix. With the oil and dirt they form one liquid. Rinsing this away takes the dirt as well. Skin and clothes are left clean.

The compounds in hard water react with soap. They do not react with detergents. This means that detergents form no scum. They lather at once. They mix oil and water straight away. Lather shows that soap or detergent is there.

Dispersing an oil slick at sea.

Getting rid of hardness

Calcium compounds make water hard. So do magnesium compounds. To make water hard they must be dissolved in it.

There are two kinds of hardness. One is caused by calcium hydrogencarbonate. Boiling the water turns this into chalk. Chalk does not dissolve in water. So the hardness has gone.

Hardness removed by boiling is called **temporary hardness**.

Boiling does not remove the second kind. It is caused by calcium sulphate and magnesium sulphate. These dissolve in water. They did so when the water ran over rocks.

Hardness not removed by boiling is called **permanent hardness**.

We can get rid of both kinds. We use substances called water softeners. Washing soda, ammonia and permutit are softeners.

Experiment 6.5 To test water softeners

Take seven conical flasks. Put 50 cm³ of hard tap water in each. Add drops of washing soda solution to six of them. Give each flask a different number of drops: 1, 2, 4, 6, 8 or 12 drops. Let the flasks stand overnight.

Do this again. Add ammonia solution instead of soda. Use 2, 4, 6, 8, 12 or 16 drops.

Let hard tap water run through permutit. Collect it. Put 50 cm³ into a conical flask.

Run soap solution into each flask. Find out how much is needed to get a lasting lather.

Tap water from a limestone area gave the results below. They are also shown as a graph.

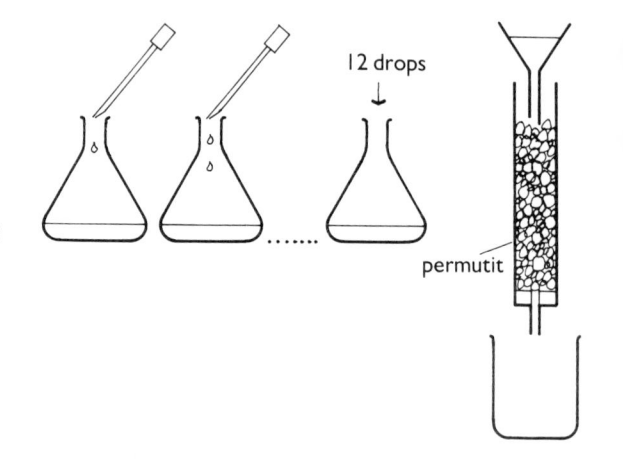

Using soda solution (sodium carbonate):

Drops added	none	1	2	4	6	8	12
Soap needed in cm³	15.0	13.1	10.3	4.1	3.1	2.7	1.7

Distilled water needed 1.3 cm³.
Boiled tap water needed 5.4 cm³.
Water passed through permutit needed 1.7 cm³ of soap solution.

Using ammonia solution:

Drops added	none	2	4	6	8	12	16
Soap needed in cm³	15.0	13.9	9.1	6.7	6.3	5.6	5.5

Boiled water needs less soap. Water with ammonia needs the same amount. Both methods get rid of temporary hardness only.

Questions

1. Using soap, rainwater is better for washing than tap water. Give two reasons for this.

2. Water from three towns is tested with soap. The amounts needed, in cm^3, are shown:

Place	Tap water	Boiled tap water
Bultown	10	4
Cowtown	4	1
Dogtown	6	6

What kinds of hardness are present in each?

3. Copy this into your book. Fill in the blanks.

Calcium and _____ compounds make water hard. To do so they must be _____ in the water. Removing these compounds makes water _____. Boiling water removes _____ hardness. This is caused by calcium _____. Boiling turns this into calcium _____ (chalk). _____ hardness is not removed by boiling. It is caused by calcium _____.

All hardness is removed by _____ and by _____. Ammonia gets rid of _____ hardness only. The best softener is _____.

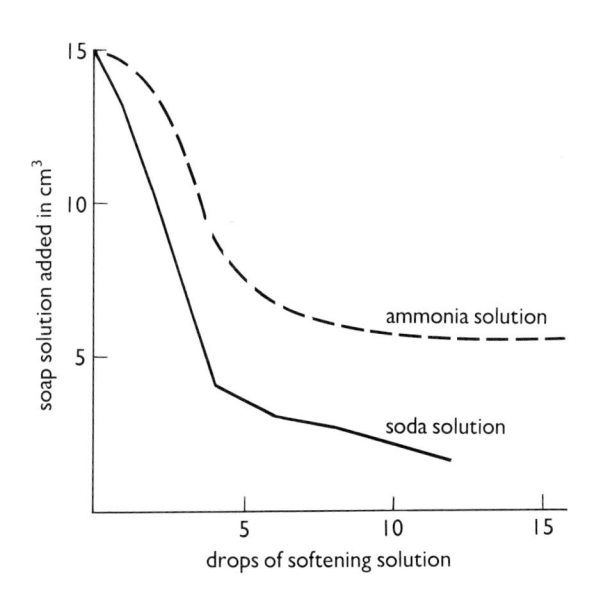

Look at the results and the graph. Answer these questions.

How much soap does distilled water need?
Which other solutions need almost the same amount?
What softeners get rid of all hardness?
How much soap does boiled tap water need?
Which other solution needs almost the same amount?
Which hardness does this softener remove?
Why is permutit the best softener?

Two solutions need the same soap as distilled water. Permutit removes all hardness. So does washing soda if enough is added. Permutit is a mineral. It contains sodium compounds. Hard water is run through it. An exchange happens. Calcium in the water is swopped for sodium from permutit. So the water comes out soft. This is called 'ion exchange'.

Washing soda is sodium carbonate. In hard water it forms chalk.

sodium carbonate (soda) + calcium compounds (hard water) → calcium carbonate (chalk) + sodium compounds

Things to do

1. Collect rainwater. Test its hardness with soap. (Try soap solution at school, flakes at home.)
2. Find out if bath salts soften water.
3. Try washing a greasy plate with cold water. Then use hot water and water + soap.

Evaporating hard water

In limestone areas tap water contains calcium hydrogencarbonate. Boiling the water turns this into chalk or limestone. The same change happens when the water evaporates.

The map shows the areas in England and Wales where water is hard. Do you live in one of them?

Limestone has dissolved for millions of years. This has formed deep valleys and caves. The valleys are called gorges. The passages down to the caves are called potholes.

Water drips from the roofs of the caves. Each drop evaporates a little. It leaves a small deposit of limestone. This slowly grows. After millions of years a pillar of it has formed.

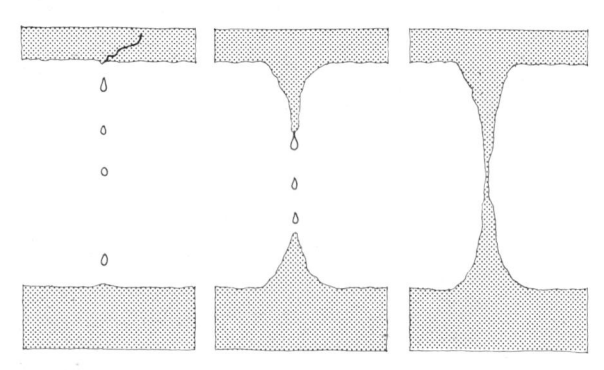

The drops fall to the floor of the cave. As each evaporates, limestone forms. This grows, too. A pillar grows upwards. The two pillars may meet. Water runs down. The whole thing grows thicker.

The pillar on the **c**eiling is called a stala**c**tite. The one on the **g**round is a stala**g**mite. They are often coloured. The colour comes from other substances in the water.

Dripping taps often form limestone in the same way. You may see it on baths and wash basins.

Heating hard water gives the same effect. Limestone collects in kettles. It forms a solid layer of 'fur' or 'scale'. It also forms in hot water pipes. They may be blocked by it.

This is one more disadvantage of hard water. Water is made soft for use in boilers in industry. If not, they need 'de-scaling' regularly. Water softeners are also used in the home.

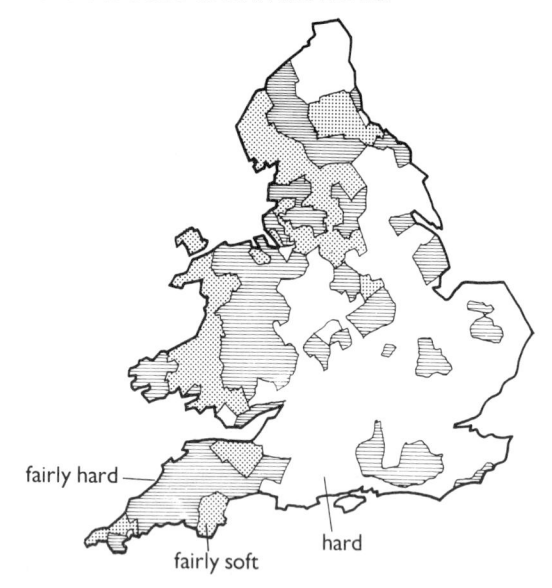

fairly hard

fairly soft

hard

Stalactites and stalagmites in an underground cave.

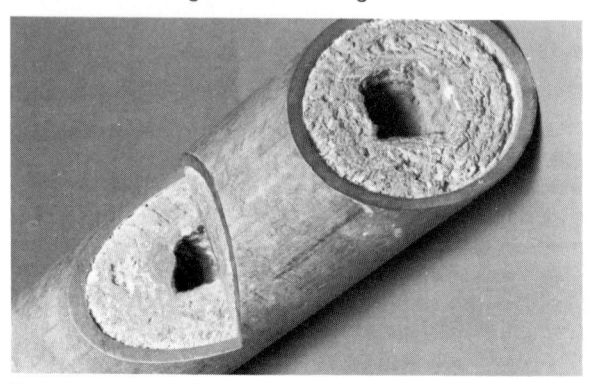

Scale in a water pipe.

Reversible reactions ⇌ elbisreveR snoitcaer

Water, chalk and carbon dioxide react. Calcium hydrogencarbonate is formed in the water.

calcium carbonate + water + carbon dioxide → calcium hydrogencarbonate

We heated this solution. It gives back calcium carbonate, water and carbon dioxide.

calcium hydrogencarbonate → calcium carbonate + water + carbon dioxide

This change can happen either way. Substances react to form new ones. The new ones can react. They give the substances we began with.

This kind of change is a **reversible reaction**.

Permutit is an ion-exchange compound. It contains sodium compounds. Substances like it can be man-made. They are 'ion-exchange resins'. When hard water passes through them, we get:

calcium compounds (hard water) + sodium X (exchange resin) → sodium compounds + calcium X

The sodium compounds go on with the water. All the hardness has been taken out. But the resin slowly becomes a calcium compound. It can no longer soften water.

A strong solution of salt is passed through it.

sodium chloride (salt) + calcium X (used-up resin) → calcium chloride + sodium X (resin)

In modern softeners this happens automatically. The resin is renewed. The change is reversible. Calcium chloride is washed out by the water.

We have used an arrow to show chemical change. To show a reversible change we use half arrows.

For example: mercury heated in air gives mercury oxide. Heating the red oxide gives mercury and oxygen.

mercury + oxygen ⇌ red mercury oxide

Scale in a hot water tank.

An automatic water softener which uses Permutit.

101

Clean and pure

Our water comes from rivers and streams. It is often stored in reservoirs. These can be natural or man-made. A dam built across a valley makes a reservoir.

Water also comes from underground. It may rise naturally as springs. Holes may be bored down to it. Pipes are placed in the holes. The water is then pumped up. This water is cleaner than water from rivers. Concrete reservoirs may be used to store it.

All water needs some treatment. How much depends on where it comes from. Before reaching our taps it goes through a water works.

It may need to be screened. Wire screens take out floating objects. River water contains solids. It may stand in tanks. This allows the solids to settle. All water drains through filter beds. These are large tanks. At the bottom are stones and gravel. Over these is a layer of fine sand. The bed acts as a filter. It takes out mud and similar matter. It needs to be cleaned and re-made regularly.

The water is now clean. It may still contain bacteria. These may cause disease. As the water leaves the works, chlorine is added. This kills bacteria. The amount of chlorine is too small to affect us.

Water must come out when we turn the tap. So it must be stored above the area it serves. In flat country, water towers do this. Pumping is needed in many cases.

Cleaning filter beds.

Chlorinators add chlorine to water to kill germs.

A natural reservoir.

Building a man-made reservoir.

Where does the waste go?

We each use about 250 litres of water a day. We drink it. We wash with it. We use it to flush WCs. The used water is called waste. It goes down the drain. It takes with it soap, detergent, dirt and organic matter.

Factories also use water. Their waste may contain harmful substances.

All this waste is called **sewage**. It was once put straight into the nearest river. In some places it went into the sea. It made the water dirty and smelly. It also spread disease.

Bacteria in the river broke down the sewage. This used up the oxygen in the water. Fish and plants living in the water died as a result.

Now sewage passes through a sewage works. It is screened to take out large objects. Grit and sand are removed. They are useful. They can be used for hole-filling.

The sewage then stands in large tanks. Solids settle to the bottom. This is crude sludge. It is taken out and treated separately.

The liquid sewage goes to aeration tanks. Bacteria grow in these tanks. They feed on the waste matter and destroy it. As in the river, this process needs oxygen. So air is bubbled through. This is called aeration.

The sewage has gone. The water contains only bacteria. These settle out in more tanks. They are put back into the aeration tanks. They are used again. The water is clean enough to be put into the river or the sea.

The crude sludge is also treated with bacteria. No air is allowed in. Breakdown of the sludge takes about 30 days. It gives off gas. This is used as a gas fuel in the works. The liquid is dried and used to improve the soil.

Beddington sewage works from the air.

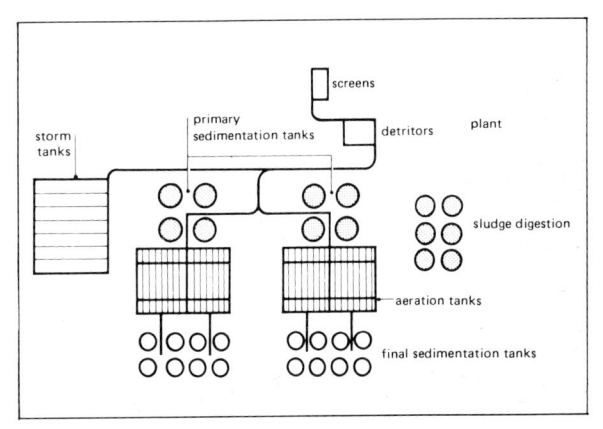

Ideas in chemistry

How well have you spent your time in Chemistry?
What have you learnt so far?

First We have looked at substances. We have done experiments. Experiment and observation have given us facts.

Ice melts at 0 °C. Water boils at 100 °C. Oxygen relights a glowing splint. Salt has cubic crystals. Plants use carbon dioxide and produce oxygen. A light will make a hydrogen–air mixture explode. Water is hydrogen oxide. Mercury oxide breaks down into mercury and oxygen.	Facts

Second Hundreds of facts like these have led to ideas.

Boiling turns water into steam. Steam and water are the same substance. No new substance is formed. Boiling is a **physical change**. It is a **change of state**.	Physical change
Calcium burns in air. A new substance is formed. Calcium and oxygen have combined. Calcium oxide is a **compound**. This is a **chemical change** or **reaction**.	Chemical change
Mercury oxide breaks down on heating. It splits up into simpler substances, mercury and oxygen. No one has ever broken down mercury. It cannot be split up into simpler substances. Mercury is an **element**.	Elements
The world is made up of 92 elements. They fall into two classes. Those in one class are shiny. They conduct an electric current. These elements are **metals**.	Metals
Elements in the other group are **non-metals**. They differ from metals. Most of them have low density. Most are non-conductors. These are **physical properties**.	Non-metals Physical properties
Elements have other properties. Many react with oxygen. Oxides are formed. What the element has done gives a new substance. This is a **chemical property**.	Chemical properties
Elements are placed in two classes. This is an example of **classification**. We can classify inside a group. All metals are similar. However, some react more strongly than others. We can put them in order of activity. Classification helps us to learn and remember.	Classification Activity Series
Some substances speed up chemical changes. They are called **catalysts**. They are still there at the end of the reaction.	Catalysts

Questions

Look at the photographs. Find words to fill the blank spaces below. Write them down in your book.

1. The balloons contain gas. The gas could be _____ or _____. A flame under the balloon makes it explode. The gas must be _____. The explosion is a _____ change. The equation for it is:
   _____ + oxygen → _____.
   The balloon rises because _____ is _____ dense than air. This is a _____ property.

2. This is an _____ platform. It drills for a liquid called _____ _____. The liquid is piped ashore. It goes to an oil _____. It is a _____ of many liquids. They are separated by _____. Two liquids formed are _____ and _____. Both burn. They are liquid _____. They burn to form _____ and _____ dioxide. This change takes _____ out of the air. Green plants put _____ into the air. They take out _____ _____. This is _____synthesis.

3. Metal compounds in the earth are called _____. Malachite is one. It is _____ in colour. On heating it turns _____. It gives off a _____. This turns lime water _____. It is _____ _____. The black powder may be copper _____. Hydrogen is passed over it while it is heated. The solid formed will _____ an electric current. The mass of 1 cm^3 of it is 9 grams. It is likely to be a _____. It has a _____ density.

    copper _____ + hydrogen → _____ + _____

   Removing oxygen from a substance is _____. Hydrogen is a _____ agent. It reduces copper o_____ to form the metal, _____. Charcoal is a form of the element _____. It reduces lead oxide to _____. This is a metal. It has a _____ density. It has metallic _____.

Movement of matter

*Experiment 7.1 Movement in liquids and gases

1. Set up two gas jars as shown. Slide the lids out from between them. Count up to five. Separate the jars. Test each for carbon dioxide.

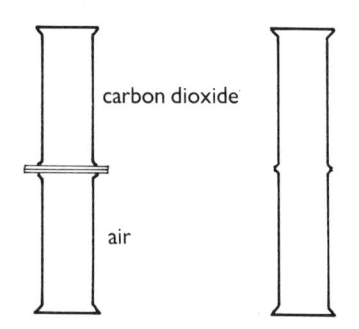

Which test did you use for carbon dioxide?
In which gas jars is it found?
Can you explain this result?

Take fresh jars of each gas. Do the same experiment again. This time, put the jar of air on top.

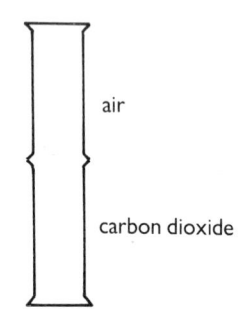

Is there carbon dioxide in the top jar?
If so, how does it get there?

2. Grease round the edge of a gas jar lid. Put three drops of bromine on the middle of it. Cover it at once with a gas jar. Put a white screen behind it. Let it stand. Record results.

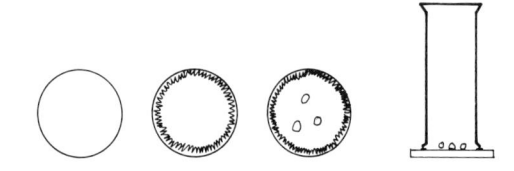

What happens to the drops of bromine?
What other change happens in the jar?
Can you explain why this happens?

In 1. there is carbon dioxide in both jars. We know carbon dioxide is more dense than air. We expect it to fall out of the top jar. However, it also rose from the bottom jar into the top. It did so in five seconds. How do we explain this?

In 2. the liquid bromine evaporates. Its vapour is orange-brown. A vapour is gas coming from a liquid. It slowly moves up the jar. In the end it fills it.

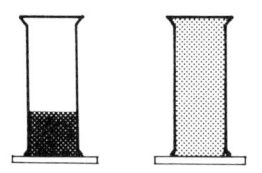

Do gases and vapours stretch like elastic?
Or do they grow upwards like plants?
Or are they made up of tiny moving bits?

Movement like this happens every day. We can smell good food from a long way away. The perfume of flowers comes in through the window. Why and how does it happen?

We can smell good food from a long way away!

Did you guess the answer? All substances consist of small bits, or particles. They are called atoms and molecules. Those in gases move freely. They travel fast in all directions.

*Experiment 7.2 To find out if particles all move at the same speed

Use a glass tube about 1 metre long and 3 cm in diameter. Support it in a stand.

Take a pad of cotton wool. Wet one side with concentrated ammonia solution. Wet a second pad with concentrated hydrochloric acid. Hold the pads about 3 cm apart.

The smoke ring is nearer the acid pad. The ammonia has travelled farther. It must have been moving faster. The gases take a long time to meet. They seem to travel slowly. Remember that the tube is full of air. It has molecules too. They are also moving.

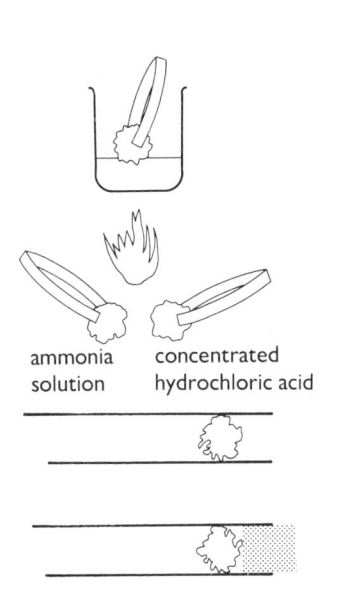

Push one pad, wet side first, into one end of the tube. At the same time push the second pad into the other end. Stopper the ends. Time how long it takes to get a result.

- What happens when the pads are close?
- What do you see inside the glass tube?
- Did you smell any gas coming from the pads?

Each liquid gives off a gas. The gases form white smoke when they meet. A gas comes from each pad of cotton wool. The gases pass along the tube. Where they meet a smoke ring forms.

- Is the smoke ring half-way along the tube?
- If not, is it nearer to ammonia or acid?
- Which of the two gases travels the faster?

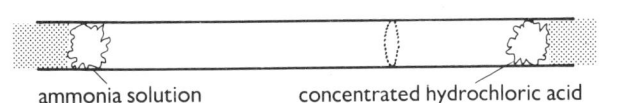

Willie, a rapid runner, reckons
To run this street in 20 seconds.
Brother George is not so swift. He
Runs the street in over 50.
Start one at each end of the street.
Who's run the furthest when they meet?

Atoms and molecules

The idea that atoms exist is an old one. Democritus first suggested it in about 400 BC.

Take a strip of copper. Cut it in half. Now cut one of the halves in two. This gives a quarter. Cut this piece in two. Suppose the cutting goes on.... Can it go on for ever? Or shall we come to a 'smallest bit'?

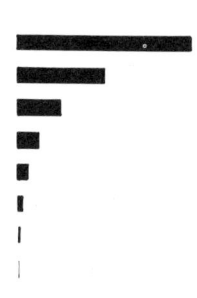

Democritus believed the 'smallest bit' idea. The smallest bit was called an **atom**. The name comes from Greek words meaning 'not cuttable'. Ideas about atoms make up the Atomic Theory.

No one had ever seen an atom. No one could explain what held atoms together. The Atomic Theory fell flat. John Dalton revived it again.

We now know that all matter is made of atoms. **An atom is the smallest piece of an element**. The smallest bit of carbon is a carbon atom. The smallest bit of oxygen is an oxygen atom.

Carbon burns in oxygen. In the flame carbon and oxygen atoms meet. They join together. This gives bigger particles. Each of these is a **molecule** of carbon dioxide.

A molecule consist of two or more atoms bonded together.

Atoms and molecules are always moving.

In a solid they move very little. They stay in fixed positions. This is why a solid keeps its shape. Heating a solid gives it energy. Energy makes molecules move faster. They break out of their fixed positions. The solid is hot enough to melt to a liquid.

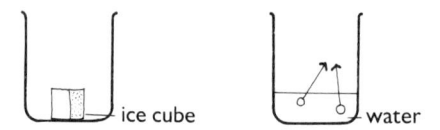

ice cube   water

In the liquid the molecules move freely. They move anywhere inside the liquid. Some strike the surface. Some break through the surface. The liquid is evaporating.

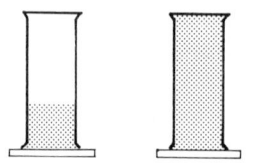

These gas or vapour molecules move freely. They move in all directions. Heating gives a liquid energy. Its molecules move faster. More of them break through the surface. These ideas explain the gas jar experiments. Bromine evaporates. Its molecules pass into the air. They go on moving. They spread to fill the gas jar.

Gas molecules move. They strike the gas jar lid. Take away the lid. The molecules which would have hit it now go straight on. They pass into the top jar. So carbon dioxide passes out of the bottom jar into the top one.

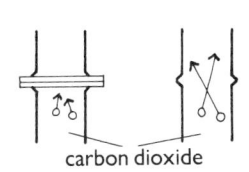

carbon dioxide

Solids contain atoms or molecules. They may be in a regular pattern. If so, the solid consists of crystals. Put the solid in water. Molecules can break out of their fixed positions. They spread through the water. The energy for this comes from the water. The solid has dissolved.

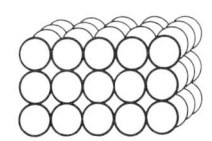

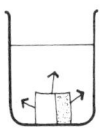

Experiment 7.3 To find out about the mass of a molecule

Fill a beaker with water. Let it stand. Take a crystal of potassium manganate(VII). Use a balance to find its mass. Drop it into the water.

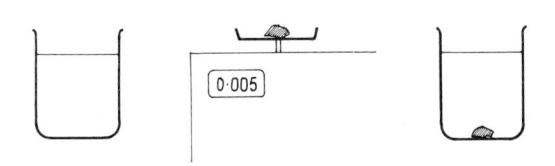

What happens in the first ten minutes?
What has happened after one hour?
What is the result a day later?

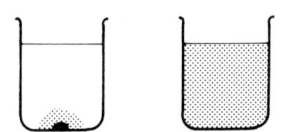

Look at a drop of solution with a microscope. Count the drops needed to make 1 cm^3 of solution. Use a dropper and measuring cylinder.

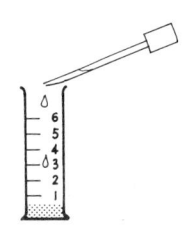

Purple solution slowly forms round the crystal. It very slowly spreads. At the end all the water is pink.

No solid can be seen in the drop. Still, every drop is pink. So each drop has some substance in it.
What mass of the substance is there in one drop?

The mass of the crystal is, say, 0.005 grams.
The volume of water is, say, 250 cm^3.

1 cm^3 of solution contains
0.005 g ÷ 250 = 0.000 02 grams.

Suppose there were 20 drops in 1 cm^3.
Then each drop contains
0.00002 ÷ 20 = 0.000 000 1 grams.

One hundredth of the drop is pink, too. It will contain 0.000 000 001 grams. This must be at least one molecule. The mass of a molecule is less than 0.000 000 001 grams.

Atoms and molecules are very, very, very small.

How thick is a molecule?

The mass of a molecule is very small. So is the mass of an atom. Think of a molecule as a sphere, like a tennis ball. How can we measure its thickness, or diameter?

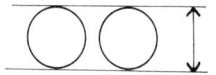

Think of a rope loop on a pond. Take a bucket of tennis balls. Pour them into the loop. Do they fill it? If not, the side of the loop can be pushed in, or dented.

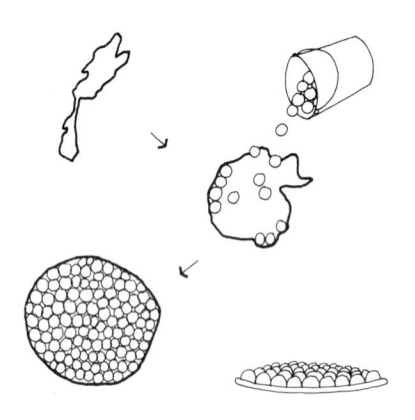

Try to fill the loop. It may need several buckets full. The layer will be one tennis ball thick all over. The loop will not dent.

We can make a layer of oil molecules. The oil is stearic acid. We use a solution of it. We use 0.1 cm^3 of oil in 1000 cm^3 of a solvent.

*Experiment 7.4 The diameter of a molecule

1. Put a drop of the oil on one watch glass. Put a drop of petroleum ether on another. Put a drop of oil in petroleum ether on a third.

   Which of the three liquids evaporates away?

2. Fill a large funnel with water. Cut a 30 cm length of cotton. Tie the ends to form a loop. Grease it very lightly. Drop it on the water.

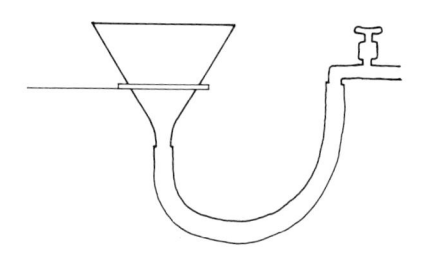

Put a drop of oil solution inside the loop. Go on adding drops until the loop is just full. Test this by tapping it with a pencil. Count the number of drops of oil solution needed. Measure the distance across the full loop.

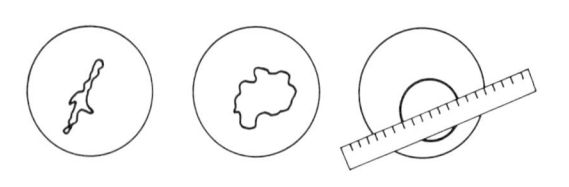

Which part of the solution will evaporate?
Which part of it will be left on the water?
What, roughly, is the area of oil in the loop?

3. Find out how many drops of solution make 1 cm^3.

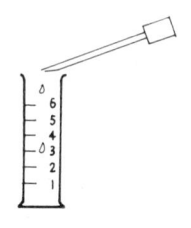

Work out the thickness of the oil layer from the results.

Petroleum ether evaporates at once. The oil does not. The drop of solution evaporates. The petroleum in it turns to vapour. The oil is left on the watch glass.

The same thing happens to the drops on water. The ether evaporates. The oil in the drop is left inside the loop. It spreads over the water. The full loop is a circle.

The ruler measures the radius of the circle. From the radius we can find its area.

area of oil layer = 3 × (radius)^2 (roughly!)

1000 cm^3 of solution has in it 0.1 cm^3 of oil.
1 cm^3 of solution contains 0.0001 cm^3 of oil.
We know how many drops there are in 1 cm^3.
We can work out the **volume of oil in one drop**.

$$\text{volume} = \frac{0.0001 \text{ cm}^3}{\text{number of drops}}$$

We know how many drops we put into the loop. We can work out the **volume of oil in the loop**. The volume of the oil layer is its area × its thickness

$$\text{So the } \textbf{thickness of the layer} = \frac{\text{its volume}}{\text{its area}}$$

The usual result is about one ten-millionth of a centimetre. This is a thousand-millionth of a metre. No one has ever seen a molecule. This is the diameter of a molecule.

Why do we believe that atoms and molecules exist?

First: We cannot see atoms and molecules. However, we can see what they do. Modern methods show them in action. A jet plane flies very high. It may be too small to see. We can see its vapour trail. Its effects tell us it is there.

Second: The Atomic Theory answers **why?** questions very well. It answers **how?** questions too. It explains why crystals have a definite shape, why gases spread, why liquids evaporate, why . . .

Summary

All matter is made up of atoms. An atom is the smallest part of an element which can exist. Atoms join together in small groups. Each group is called a molecule. Atoms and molecules are very small in mass and diameter.

Molecules in solids are almost stationary. This explains why solids keep their shape. It explains the regular shape of crystals.

Heat gives energy to a substance. Its molecules move faster. They break out of the solid. The solid melts. Molecules move freely inside the liquid. Some will break through the surface. This explains evaporation and boiling.

Gas molecules move freely in all directions. This explains why gases mix completely, as in air.

If a plane flies high in the sky we may not be able to see it but we know it is there because we can see its vapour trail.

The Atomic Theory

Ideas about atoms were revived in the 17th century. John Dalton put these ideas together. He also added new ones. These were to explain results from experiments. He began in 1803. The explanation was called Dalton's Atomic Theory.

The Atomic Theory

Every element is made up of atoms. They are very small and indivisible.

Atoms of the same element are alike. They have the same size and mass. (These are not quite true. We shall find out why later.)

Atoms combine together to form molecules. The smallest part of a compound is a molecule. It contains atoms of different elements.

Atoms of one element are different from the atoms of others. They differ in size and mass.

Chemists make pure substances. These are either elements or compounds. Carbon, oxygen and hydrogen are elements. The smallest particle of each is an atom.

Sugar is a compound. The smallest possible piece of it is a molecule. It contains carbon, hydrogen and oxygen atoms. These atoms are joined, or bonded, together in the molecule.

Dalton used a picture to represent each atom. The picture for one atom of oxygen was ◯. For a carbon atom it was ●. Copper was ⓒ. He used the pictures to show molecules, too.

The mass of an atom is very small. Dalton was sure no one would ever measure it. But he used compounds to compare the masses of atoms.

For example, black copper oxide is a compound. It contains copper and oxygen. The simplest molecule would have one atom of each. Dalton's picture of it would be ⓒ◯. He thought that the simplest molecule was the most likely.

John Dalton.

A page from Dalton's notebook.

*Experiment 7.5 To compare the masses of copper and oxygen atoms

Dry some black copper oxide in an oven. Gently warm a reduction tube. Let it cool. Use a balance to measure its mass in grams.

Put into it a layer of dry copper oxide. Find its mass again. Hold it in a clamp and stand.

Pass hydrogen through it. Light the hydrogen at the hole. Gently heat the oxide. Start at the stopper end. When it has all changed, let it cool. Measure its mass again.

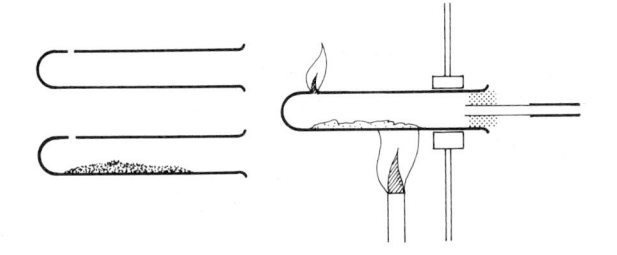

This is a set of results.
Mass of the tube and copper oxide = 18.97 g
Mass of the tube and copper = 18.17 g
Mass of the empty tube = 14.97 g

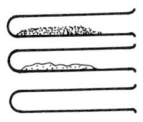

Hydrogen reduces copper oxide. Oxygen is taken away from it. Copper is formed instead.

Use your own results or the set given above.
How much oxygen is taken away by the hydrogen?
How much copper is left in the tube?
How many grams of copper combine with one gram of oxygen?

Taking oxygen away makes the mass less. It falls from 18.97 grams to 18.17 grams. So the mass of oxygen in the oxide is 0.80 grams. The copper formed is 18.17 − 14.97 grams.

Mass of oxygen = 0.80 g
Mass of copper = 3.20 g

The copper oxide has in it 3.20 g of copper and 0.8 g of oxygen.

If 0.80 g of oxygen combine with 3.20 g of copper, then 1 g of oxygen would combine with 3.20 ÷ 0.80 grams.

One gram of oxygen combines with **four** grams of copper.

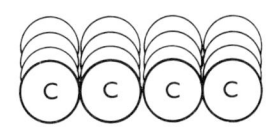

Dalton's guess was one atom of oxygen for each atom of copper. The copper and the oxygen have the same number of atoms. A copper atom has four times the mass of an oxygen atom.

Symbol and formula

Dalton used a different sign for each element. In his time few elements were known. Not many signs had to be learnt. Now we should need to learn over one hundred.

The signs made simple molecules easy to show. Copper oxide is

Large molecules were less easy. We now know that a sugar molecule has 12 carbon atoms
    22 hydrogen atoms
    11 oxygen atoms

A better method took the place of Dalton's signs. The name of the element was used. The first letter of it stood for one atom.

    H stands for one atom of hydrogen.
    O stands for one atom of oxygen.
    C stands for one atom of carbon.

What letters would you use for the atoms of sulphur, nitrogen, phosphorus and iodine? (Check your answers from the list on the right.)

Each letter is the **symbol** of the element. Choose symbols for calcium, cobalt and copper.

All three names start with the letter C. But C is the symbol for a carbon atom. So an extra letter from the name is added. The symbol for an atom of calcium is Ca. The symbol used for an atom of cobalt is Co.

In Dalton's time, many people knew Latin. The symbol for copper comes from its Latin name, cuprum. The symbols for some other elements come from their Latin names, too. Find copper, silver, sodium and lead in the list.

Dalton's guess was right. In black copper oxide one atom of copper is joined to one atom of oxygen. It is written CuO. CuO is called the **formula** of copper oxide.

A molecule of sugar has a formula. It is $C_{12}H_{22}O_{11}$. The symbol shows the element. The number after it shows the number of atoms of it. C_{12} means 12 carbon atoms. H_{22} means 22 hydrogen atoms.

The **symbol** is the letter or letters standing for one atom. A **formula** shows the number of atoms in a molecule.

Element	Symbol	RAM
Aluminium	Al	27
Argon	Ar	40
Bromine	Br	80
Calcium	Ca	40
Carbon	C	12
Chlorine	Cl	35.5
Chromium	Cr	52
Cobalt	Co	59
Copper	Cu	64
Helium	He	4
Hydrogen	H	1
Iodine	I	127
Iron	Fe	56
Lead	Pb	207
Lithium	Li	7
Magnesium	Mg	24
Nitrogen	N	14
Oxygen	O	16
Phosphorus	P	31
Potassium	K	39
Sodium	Na	23
Sulphur	S	32
Tin	Sn	119
Zinc	Zn	65

In Experiment 7.5 we used hydrogen to reduce copper oxide.

copper oxide + hydrogen → copper + water

We found that
  mass of a copper atom = 4 × mass of oxygen atom.

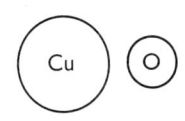

Other atomic masses can be compared. Alter this last experiment a little. Collect the water formed by the reduction. Anhydrous calcium chloride will absorb water. Put the black copper oxide in a narrowed tube.

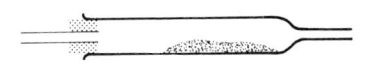

*Experiment 7.6 The masses of hydrogen and oxygen atoms

Put anhydrous calcium chloride in a U-tube. Use a balance to measure its mass. Find the mass of the dry tube with dry copper oxide.

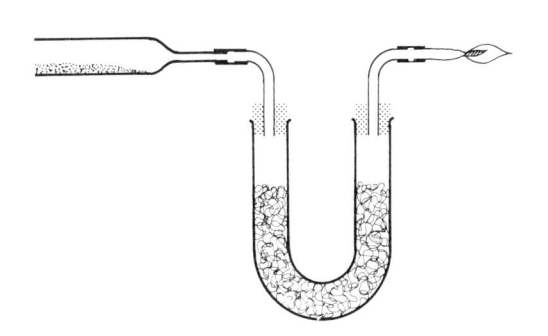

Set up the apparatus. Pass hydrogen through it. Collect it in test tubes at the other end. Test it with a lighted splint. When it burns quietly, light it at the jet.

Heat the oxide until it is all reduced. Let it cool. Keep the hydrogen passing through. Find the masses of tube and U-tube separately.

  What is the mass of the water formed?
  (the gain in mass of the U-tube)

  How much oxygen is there in this water?
  (the loss in mass of the oxide tube)

  What is the mass of hydrogen in the water?
  (the difference between these two)

This is a sample set of results:
Loss in mass of copper oxide = 0.80 g
Gain in mass of U-tube = 0.90 g
Oxgen in this water = 0.80 g
Mass of water formed = 0.90 g

The water formed is (0.80 g of oxygen + 0.10 g of hydrogen).

Dalton guessed that a water molecule is ⊙O, or HO. He was wrong. The formula of water is H_2O. It has two atoms of _____ for each atom of _____.

So: the mass of oxygen is 8 times the mass of hydrogen.
One oxygen atom is 8× the mass of **two** hydrogen atoms.
One oxygen atom is 16× the mass of **one** hydrogen atom.

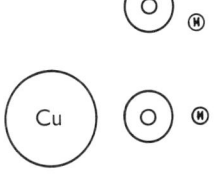

The hydrogen atom is the smallest. All other atoms have a larger mass. How many times larger is the mass of a copper atom?

Relative atomic mass and formula

Look at the photograph. The mass of the marble is 5 g. The mass of the golf ball is 45 g. Its mass is 9 times as big. If M is 1, then Gb is 9. The mass of the cricket ball is 155 g. This is 31 times the mass of the marble. If M = 1 and Gb = 9, then Cb = 31. The numbers 1, 9 and 31 are called the **relative**, or compared, **masses**.

A hydrogen atom has the smallest mass. We know the mass of an oxygen atom is 16 times as big. If H is 1, then O is 16. A copper atom has 4 times the mass of an oxygen atom. If O = 16 then Cu = 64. These numbers are called the **relative atomic masses**. We write them as   Mg = 24.

Relative atomic masses are listed on page 114 under RAM. They are given to the nearest whole number. More accurate values will be given later. We can use them to find the formula of a chemical compound.

Experiment 7.7 The formula of magnesium oxide

Use a clean crucible and lid. Heat it gently. Let it cool. Use a balance to find its mass.

Clean a 30 cm strip of magnesium ribbon. Fold it loosely into the crucible. Find the mass.

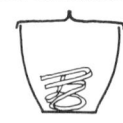

Stand the crucible on a pipe clay triangle. Heat it gently, then strongly. Lift the lid with tongs. Put it back before smoke escapes. Go on doing this. When all the metal has burnt, let it cool. Find its mass once more.

> How many grams of magnesium were used?
> How much oxygen did it combine with?
> How much magnesium would 1 g of oxygen need?
> How much would combine with 16 g of oxygen?

My result is: 24 g of magnesium combine with 16 g of oxygen.

16 g of oxygen is a huge number of atoms. Call this number L. 16 grams of oxygen contains L atoms.

But O = 16 and Mg = 24. An Mg atom has a mass $1\frac{1}{2}$ times as big as an oxygen atom. L atoms of magnesium contains 24 grams. Magnesium oxide is MgO.

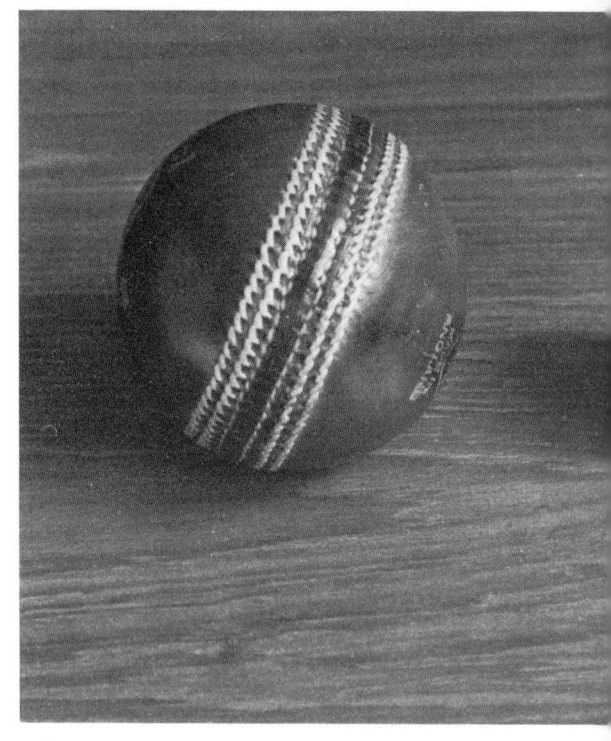

My results

mass = 15.52 g

mass = 16.72 g

mass = 17.52 g
1.20 g
0.80 g
1.50 g
24.0 g

This last idea is very important. Try it again.

Pretend we can pick up atoms with tongs. Put an oxygen atom on one balance. Put a magnesium atom on the other. The magnesium atom has a bigger mass. It is $1\frac{1}{2}$ times as big as the oxygen atom. The second balance shows this.

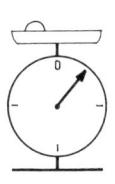

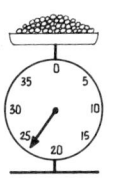

Pile on oxygen atoms until the mass is 16 grams. We shall need 602 300 000 000 000 000 000 000. Call this number L.
L is known as **Avogadro's Constant Number**.

Put L atoms of magnesium on the other balance. Their mass will be $1\frac{1}{2}$ times 16 grams, or 24 g. But our result said:

    24 g of magnesium combine with 16 g of oxygen

So: L atoms of magnesium combine with L atoms of oxygen

    One magnesium atom combines with **one** oxygen atom

The formula of magnesium oxide is MgO.

Summary

The smallest piece of an element is an atom. An atom is shown on paper by a symbol. This is the first letter of the name of the element. The Latin name is sometimes used. A second letter is added if it is needed. The symbol for sulphur is S and for silicon Si.

The hydrogen atom is the smallest. Any other atom has a bigger mass. The number of times bigger is called its relative atomic mass. If H = 1, then C = 12, Fe = 56, Pb = 207 and so on. Fe comes from the Latin name for iron, ferrum

1 g of hydrogen, 12 g of carbon and 56 g of iron contain the same number of atoms. This number is called Avogadro's Constant Number, L. We can use it to find the formula of a substance.

Questions

1. Fill in the blanks as you copy this out.
   An atom is the smallest piece of an _____.
   An atom is shown on paper by a _____.
   The symbol for an atom of nitrogen is _____.
   The symbol for nickel must have an extra _____.
   S is the symbol for one atom of _____.
   S = 32 shows its relative _____ _____.
   The mass of L atoms of sulphur is _____ grams.

2. Use the list on page 113. Which atom in the list has
   a) the highest relative atomic mass?
   b) twice the mass of an oxygen atom?
   c) four times the mass of an oxygen atom?
   d) twice the mass of a calcium atom?
   What is the relative mass of
   e) a lead atom + an oxygen atom?
   f) two oxygen atoms + a carbon atom?

3. Yellow lead oxide can be reduced to lead. 2.23 g of oxide contain 2.07 g of lead. Work out the formula of the oxide. Pb = 207, O = 16.

4. The formula of sulphuric acid is H_2SO_4. Write down what this tells us about the acid. Use the words symbol, atom, formula and molecule. Say what each of these words means.

The mole

We have dealt with many chemical changes. In them new substances are formed. For example, magnesium burns in oxygen.

The reaction is summed up by a word equation. For example:

magnesium + oxygen → magnesium oxide

But a piece of magnesium is a huge number of atoms. It is the atoms which react. Each of them joins to an oxygen atom. We can write an equation to show this: Mg + O → MgO

An equation must be based on fact. Experiment tells us that
    24 g of magnesium combines with 16 g of oxygen
So L atoms of magnesium react with L atoms of oxygen.
One atom of Mg reacts with one atom of O. It is Mg + O.

We need a name for L atoms of an element. 100 of anything is a century. 12 of anything is a dozen. L atoms or molecules is called a **mole**.

24 g of magnesium contains a mole of magnesium atoms.
16 g of oxygen contains a mole of oxygen atoms. How many MgO particles will they give? Each atom of magnesium gives one MgO. So there will be one mole of MgO formed.

What will its mass be? Mg = 24 and O = 16. MgO = 40. The mass of one mole of magnesium oxide is 40 grams.

The smallest bit of oxygen we can get is an atom, O. In oxygen gas the atoms are not single ones. In the gas the smallest piece of oxygen is a molecule. It contains two atoms joined together. It is written O_2. If H = 1, O = 16. If O = 16 then O_2 = 2 × 16. This is 32. Molecules have a **relative molecular mass**, or **formula mass**.

Most gas elements exist as molecules. A molecule with two atoms in it is **di**atomic. Hydrogen is like this. It is written H_2.

This alters the equation for burning magnesium.
    Mg + O → MgO
Oxygen atoms are in pairs. The formula is O_2.
    Mg + O_2 → ?
So for each O_2 we need two magnesium atoms.
    2Mg + O_2 →
They are separate atoms so we write them 2Mg, just as we write 2 eggs or 2 . . . .
Each Mg and O give one MgO. This makes 2MgO.
    2Mg + O_2 → 2MgO

Two moles of magnesium atoms and one mole of oxygen molecules react. They form two moles of magnesium oxide.

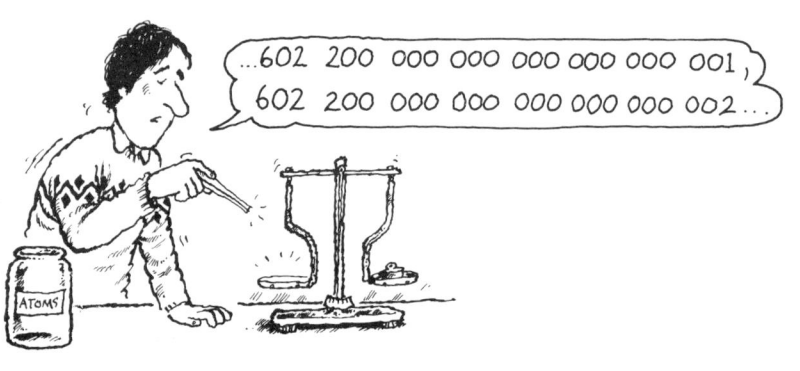

12 is a dozen, 20 is a score,
Avogadro's Number, L, is many millions more.
Are you counting particles? When you call the roll.
Just remember L of them is always called a mole.

...602 200 000 000 000 000 000 001, 602 200 000 000 000 000 000 002...

Building an equation

First check what you know.

The formula of sulphuric acid is H_2SO_4. The symbols show the elements in it. What are they?

Numbers come after the symbols. They show how many atoms. How many hydrogen atoms? How many of sulphur? Oxygen?

H_2SO_4 is a molecule. Its mass is small. What is its relative molecular mass? $H = 1$, $S = 32$, $O = 16$.

H_2 means two hydrogen atoms. $H_2 = 2$.
S means that there is only one sulphur atom.
$S = 32$.
O_4 means four oxygen atoms.
At 16 per atom this comes to 64.
$H_2SO_4 = 2 + 32 + 64 = 98$.
So 98 grams of sulphuric acid is one mole because it contains L molecules.

To set up a word equation

Experiment 7.8 Word equations for reactions

1. Put a little chalk into a test tube. Add dilute nitric acid with a dropper. Find out what gas is formed. Boil the liquid away.
2. Add copper to dilute sulphuric acid.
3. Add black copper oxide to dilute sulphuric acid in a test tube. Gently warm it. Add oxide until no more will dissolve. Filter. Evaporate.

4. Put a little lead nitrate solution into a test tube. Add drops of potassium iodide solution. Filter the mixture.

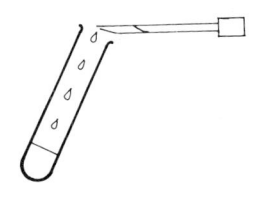

What substances are formed in each case?
Write a word equation for each change.
In which case is no equation possible?

Chalk and acid give carbon dioxide. A solid is formed when the liquid is boiled away. The equation will be:

$$\text{calcium carbonate} + \text{nitric acid} \rightarrow \text{carbon dioxide} + \text{calcium?}$$

In 4. a yellow solid is formed. A filter takes it out. It does not dissolve in water. We know that metals replace metals.

$$\text{lead nitrate} + \text{potassium iodide} \rightarrow \text{lead iodide} + \text{potassium nitrate}$$

The insoluble substance in the solution is a **precipitate**.

Building a formula equation

The reaction of nitric acid with chalk

The formula of nitric acid is HNO_3.
Copy this out. Fill in the blanks.
In the formula HNO_3:
The number of hydrogen atoms is _____.
The number of nitrogen atoms is _____.
There are _____ oxygen atoms.
H = 1, N = 14, O = 16 are relative _____ _____

The formula mass of the acid is _____.
One mole of nitric acid has a mass of _____ grams.
The formula of chalk, calcium carbonate,
is $CaCO_3$. Ca = 40   C = 12
Work out its formula mass.
$CaCO_3$ is Ca + C + O + O + O.
One mole of calcium carbonate is 100 grams of it.
200 g is _____ moles. 1 g of it is _____ mole.

HNO_3 means H + N + O + O + O. The relative atomic masses add up to 63. One mole of nitric acid is 63 grams.

In the reaction we used dilute acid. This is acid with water added. Measuring its mass will not tell us how much acid.

Experiment 7.9 To find the formula equation

Measure 63 g of acid. Put it into distilled water. Add more water. Make the volume up to 1000 cm³.

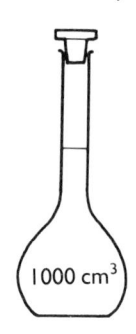

We have one mole of acid in 1000 cm³ of solution. This is called a **molar** solution, or M solution.

We can measure how many moles of acid we use. We simply measure its volume. 1000 cm³ of M solution contains 1 mole. Suppose we use 100 cm³. Then we have used 0.1 mole. 10 cm³ will contain 0.01 mole, and so on . . . .

Chalk is a solid. We can measure its mass. 100 g is one mole, 200 g is 2 moles, 1 g is 0.01 mole.

The word equation is

calcium carbonate + nitric acid → carbon dioxide + calcium nitrate + ?

$CaCO_3$ + HNO_3 → CO_2 ?   ?

A molar solution?

On a balance measure exactly 1 g of pure chalk. Put it in a conical flask. Fill a burette with M nitric acid solution. Take the reading.

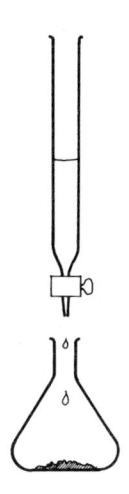

an oven at 200 °C. Find the mass of the dish and dry solid.

It is difficult to measure the mass of a gas.
*Set up the apparatus. Put 30 cm³ of M acid in the flask. Put 1 g of chalk in the small tube. The cotton keeps it out of the acid. Measure the mass of the whole apparatus.

Tilt the flask to mix acid and chalk. Anhydrous calcium chloride takes in water. So only dry carbon dioxide escapes. At the end measure the mass. Loss in mass = carbon dioxide formed.

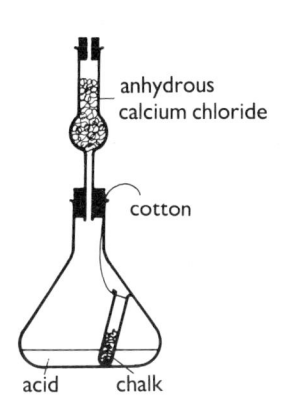

Run acid slowly into the flask. Swirl the mixture. Add just enough acid to dissolve the chalk. Towards the end add the acid in drops. Give the last bits of chalk time to dissolve.

Take the reading of the burette. Find out how much acid is used. Work out how much is needed for one mole of chalk, 100 grams.

Find the mass of an evaporating dish. Pour the solution into it. Gently boil off most of the water. Put the dish in

---

<u>My results were:</u>

I used 1g of chalk. This ⎰ reacts with 20.1 cm³ of M nitric acid
⎱ gives 1.60g of solid by evaporation
⎱ loses 0.45g of carbon dioxide

Now 1 mole of chalk is 100g.

So multiply all the quantities by 100 ⎰ 100 × 20.1 = 2010 cm³ of nitric acid
⎱ 160 g of calcium nitrate
⎱ 45 g of carbon dioxide

M acid has 1 mole in 1000 cm³. So there are 2 moles in 2010 cm³
   Therefore: 1 mole of calcium carbonate reacts with 2 moles of acid

The equation begins $CaCO_3 + 2HNO_3 \rightarrow$
Roughly 1 mole of carbon dioxide is formed so $CaCO_3 + 2HNO_3 \rightarrow CO_2$

CO_2 from CO_3 leaves an O atom. With 2H from the acid this gives H_2O.
2H from the acid leaves 2 × NO_3. The solid must be $Ca + NO_3 + NO_3$.

The full equation must be: $CaCO_3 + 2HNO_3 \rightarrow Ca(NO_3)_2 + CO_2 + H_2O$

Non-metals

All metals, except mercury, are solids. Their atoms have fixed positions. They are close together. They move very little.

At normal temperatures many non-metals are gases. They exist as molecules. Many of these are diatomic. Each of them contains two atoms. The atoms are bonded together. Hydrogen is like this. Its formula is H_2.

Some non-metals are solids. We shall study two of them, carbon and sulphur. We know a great deal about carbon already.

Carbon

In Experiment 1.14 we heated wood out of air. The solid formed is charcoal. It is one form of carbon.

Experiment 8.1 The properties of charcoal

1. Nearly fill a test tube with water. Add a few drops of litmus solution. Take half of this solution. Add powdered charcoal. Boil the solution gently. Filter it. Compare it with the unused solution. Now use activated charcoal.

2. Dissolve brown sugar in water. Shake half of the solution with activated charcoal. Filter it. Compare it with the unused half.

*3. Fill a test tube with the gas ammonia. Invert it in a trough of mercury. Use a fume cupboard. Push pieces of charcoal into the gas. Push them through the mercury.

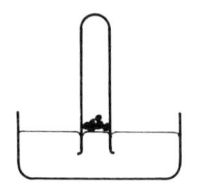

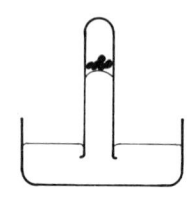

Put two drops of bromine in a gas jar. Cover it. Let it fill with vapour. Crush charcoal into small pieces. Put some into the gas jar.

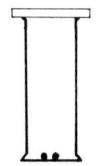

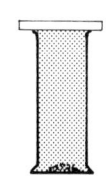

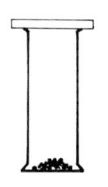

Charcoal is used in gas masks.

4. Find out if charcoal conducts a current. Try to find the mass of 1 cm³ of it (Expt. 4.1).

5. Heat a mixture of black copper oxide and charcoal. Pass any gas into lime water.

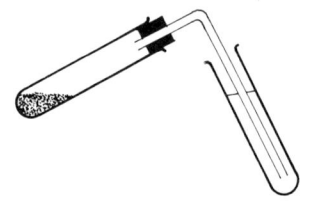

These properties decide what charcoal is used for. Some of them you have met before. Can you write down some of its uses?

The uses of charcoal

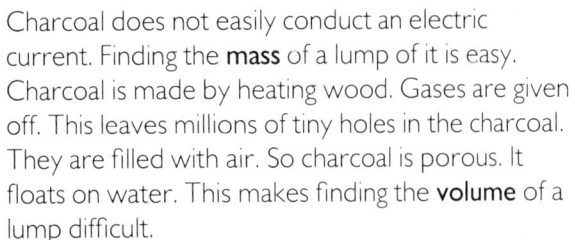

Charcoal does not easily conduct an electric current. Finding the **mass** of a lump of it is easy. Charcoal is made by heating wood. Gases are given off. This leaves millions of tiny holes in the charcoal. They are filled with air. So charcoal is porous. It floats on water. This makes finding the **volume** of a lump difficult.

Mercury rises into the test tube. Some ammonia must have gone. Bromine vapour disappears too. Charcoal takes in, or absorbs, gases and vapours. It does so because it is porous.

Charcoal is used in gas masks. Activated charcoal is best. The person wearing the mask breathes in. The air passes through charcoal. Poison gases and smoke are absorbed. The rest of the air goes through. It has been made pure.

Charcoal absorbs dyes. It takes litmus out of solution. It takes the brown colour out of sugar solution. It is used in making white sugar.

Charcoal can reduce metal oxides to the metal. The arrows show what happens to each reactant. Which arrow shows reduction?

$$2CuO + C \rightarrow 2Cu + CO_2$$

Charcoal was used in early times to make iron. It reduced iron oxide. It was also one of the substances in gunpowder.

Charcoal was made in the forests. Wood was piled up. The pile was covered with turf. Burning wood was dropped through a hole in the top. The hole was covered with turf. Some wood in the pile burnt. It turned the rest into charcoal.

Charcoal is a smokeless fuel. It is still used – in barbecues! Like other forms of carbon, charcoal makes marks on paper.

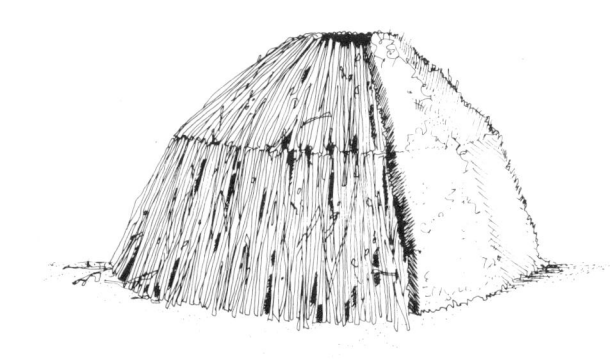

Two other forms of carbon

Diamond and graphite are well known forms of carbon. Both are found in nature. Both are made by man.

Graphite

Experiment 8.2 The properties of graphite

1. Rub some graphite on paper. What do you see?

2. Twist the glass stopper in a bottle neck. Rub graphite on the stopper. Twist it in the neck of the bottle again.

3. Find out if graphite can conduct an electric current.

Graphite consists of grey-black crystals. It is soft and greasy to the touch. The crystals look shiny. It is a form of carbon. So it is a non-metal. But its shine is almost like metallic lustre. It is a conductor. It has some of the properties of metals.

Graphite is used as a conductor in electrodes. Carbon is one electrode in dry cells (batteries).

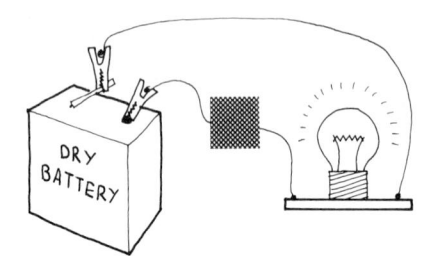

Graphite makes a mark on paper. It is the 'lead' in a pencil. In making leads, graphite is mixed with clay. The mixture is made into a wet paste. It is then forced through holes. The long pieces are baked dry in an oven. They are cased in wood to keep them from breaking.

Making pencil lead.

Graphite is soft. It leaves a trail of crystals on the paper. This is a pencil mark. A pure graphite pencil would be used up quickly. Clay makes it harder. It lasts longer.

H pencils have more clay in the mixture. B pencils have more graphite. They give a blacker mark.

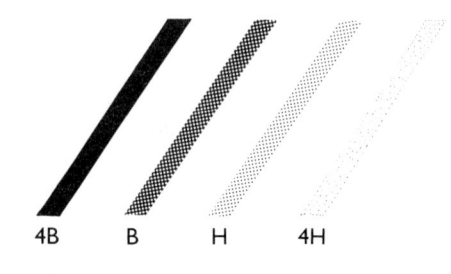

4B   B   H   4H

A stopper twisted in a bottle squeaks. Coated with graphite it moves more smoothly.

Rough surfaces grate over each other. If your bicycle squeaks, two metal parts are touching. Oil is put between them. The film of oil keeps them apart. Oil lubricates the moving parts. Layers of graphite keep surfaces apart. Alone, or mixed with oil, graphite is a lubricant.

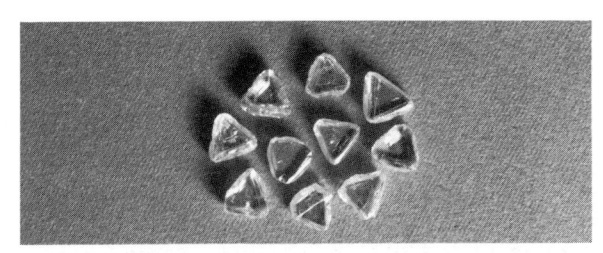

Diamond

Diamond is a form of carbon. Small pieces of it are called diamonds. They are found in many countries. Most of them come from South Africa. They are found in some kinds of rock. The rock may be part of a long dead volcano.

Some diamonds are clear with no colour. Some are dull and coloured. They all have uses. Uses depend on properties.

Diamond is the hardest known natural substance. It makes scratches on glass. It does this to other hard minerals such as sapphire. Both are used as the stylus (needle) in record players.

Diamond is used in glass cutters. Drills can be studded with diamonds. They are then hard enough to cut through rock. Saws for cutting other hard materials carry diamonds.

Diamond has a definite crystal shape. Its surface reflects light. Light also passes into the transparent crystal. It is reflected inside as well. This is why a diamond sparkles. It is used in jewellery.

Diamond and graphite have many uses. We need far more of both than we find in nature. Graphite is made from sand and coke. They are mixed and heated to 2500 °C. This needs an electric furnace. After some hours, the coke has changed to graphite.

Natural diamonds may have formed in volcanoes. High temperature and pressure might make them. Last century, many people tried to make them. Some cheated. They took natural diamonds and pretended they had made them.

Now graphite is put into a small vessel. It is subjected to huge pressure and temperature. The diamonds formed are small. They are used in drills, glass cutters and so on.

Look at the table. It shows properties of diamond and graphite. They are forms of the same element. Both are carbon.
How can they be so different?

Diamond crystals.

A diamond saw blade cutting hard limestone.

A diamond saw blade cutting fossil footsteps out of rock.

Property	Diamond	Graphite
appearance	transparent	grey-black
mass of 1 cm^3	3.5 g	2.2 g
conductor?	no	yes
hardness	very hard	very soft

The coal industry

Coal was used at least 2000 years ago. It was mined in this country in Roman times.

Where did it come from?

Coal was formed about 240 million years ago. The climate was hot. Areas where rivers ran into the sea were marshy. Giant trees, ferns and rushes grew well there. They died and others grew. This gave layers of rotting vegetation.

Bacteria slowly turned the layers into peat. The rivers covered it with mud and silt. This put pressure on the peat. Water and oxygen compounds were squeezed out. Most of the peat was now carbon. It finally formed coal.

The layers of coal are called seams. They are found at various depths in the earth. Some seams are near the surface. They may even show through it. Then they are called 'outcrops'. They were the first coal to be discovered.

Coal mining began early in Britain, around Newcastle. Records show that it was sent to London by sea. Using it as fuel began air pollution.

By 1700 AD three million tonnes a year were mined. By 1810 it was 10 million tonnes a year. Miners hacked it out of underground seams. They worked as much as fifteen hours a day. So did women and young children.

Mining was dark and dangerous work. Naked flames were the only lighting. Gas came out of the coal seams. The lights made it explode. The gas carbon monoxide was formed. It killed the miners. So did falls of rock and flooding.

Conditions of work were dreadful quite late in this century. By 1913 Britain was mining 287 million tonnes a year. Amounts used are shown:

Year	1925	1950	1960	1970	1975	1979
Million tonnes	176	204	198	150	116	105

A primeval forest.

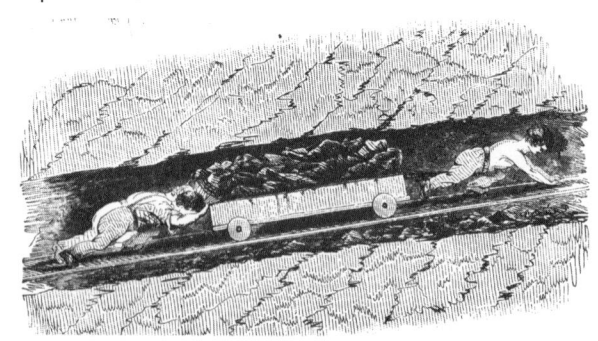

Children working in a coal mine.

Cutting coal by hand.

Miners in a cage waiting to go underground.

A coal cutting 'shearer' machine at work.

Lea Hall colliery and Rugeley power station.

A gas works producing gas from coal.

A coke oven discharging coke.

The uses of coal

Coal was first burnt as fuel. This wasted useful substances. It put smoke and dust into the air.

In Experiment 1.15 we heated coal out of the air. It gives a gas which burns. It leaves coke. This is a smokeless fuel. Coal tar forms in the tube. So does a watery liquid with ammonia in it. This can be used to make fertilizers.

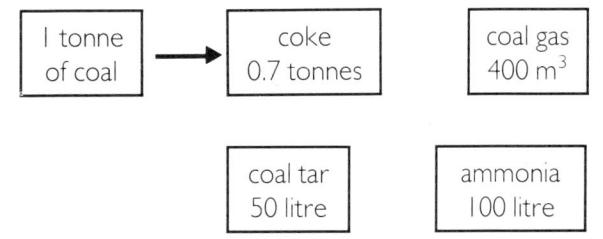

| 1 tonne of coal | → | coke 0.7 tonnes | coal gas 400 m³ |

| coal tar 50 litre | ammonia 100 litre |

For many years coal gas was the only gas fuel. About 50% of it was hydrogen, 35% methane and 10% carbon monoxide. This made it poisonous.

The coal tar is collected. Distilling it gives many substances. From them other substances such as dyes and explosives are made. Distillation leaves pitch. This is used in road making.

Coke is carbon. It is used in extracting metals. Other fuel gases are made from coke. Air blown through hot coke makes it burn. This gives carbon monoxide and heat. Then steam is blown through the hot coke.

$$C + H_2O \rightarrow CO + H_2$$

Carbon monoxide and hydrogen are both gas fuels. The mixture is called 'water gas'.

Coal and its products are very important. The rise of the oil industry made it less so. Gas and liquid fuels are easier to transport. They can be piped from place to place. However, the supply of crude oil may run out. Coal as a form of energy is becoming more important.

Allotropy

It is easy to show that graphite contains carbon. We can burn it. If it has carbon in it, carbon dioxide will form. Burning it does give carbon dioxide. So graphite contains carbon.

Sir Humphrey Davy was the first to burn diamond. (He had a rich wife!) Diamond gave carbon dioxide too. It must contain carbon.

How can we show that they contain *only* carbon?

The equation for burning is $C + O_2 \rightarrow CO_2$. Work out the atomic and molecular masses.

$C = 12$ $O = 16$
$O_2 = 32$ $CO_2 = 44$

They show that 12 g of carbon use up 32 g of oxygen.
The mass of carbon dioxide formed is 44 grams.

Now can you see the answer to the question? Burn 12 grams of graphite. Collect the carbon dioxide. Measure its mass. Is it 44 grams? If it is, graphite must be all pure carbon.

Suppose graphite is not all carbon. Then it contains other elements. Only part of the 12 g will be carbon. Burning will give less than 44 grams of carbon dioxide.

Diamond can be burnt in the same way. 12 g of it gives 44 g of carbon dioxide. Like graphite, it contains only carbon atoms. They differ because their atoms are not joined in the same way.

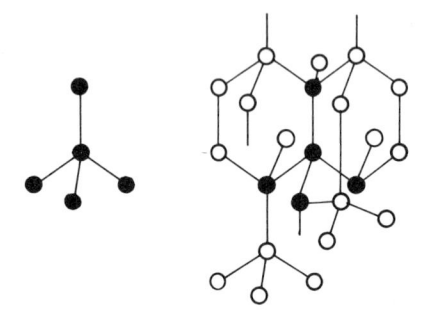

In diamond, each carbon atom is joined to four others. Each of these is joined to four more. This goes on in every direction. Each piece of diamond is one huge molecule.

In graphite each atom is joined to three others. Each of these is joined to three more. The atoms form layers. The layers lie on each other like cards in a pack. Cards in a pack slide over each other. So do the graphite layers.

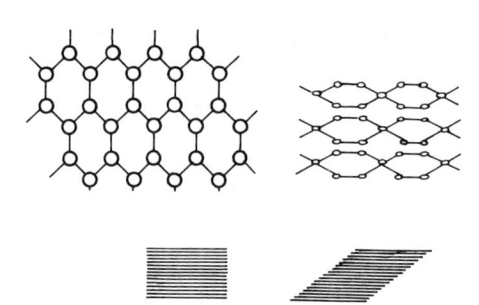

This explains why graphite is soft. If it is rubbed on paper, the layers peel off. This leaves a trail of crystals, as a black line.

The atom pattern in diamond makes it hard. The atoms are closer together. There are more in 1 cm³. The mass of 1 cm³ is larger.

Sulphur can appear in many different forms. These are monoclini

Allotropy and sulphur

Pure diamond and graphite contain only carbon atoms. But these are arranged in different patterns. This effect is **allotropy**.

Allotropy is the existence of an element in different forms. These crystalline forms are called **allotropes**. They differ in appearance and in physical properties.
Other forms of carbon have no regular atom pattern.

Sulphur

Many elements have allotropes. Sulphur has. So has tin. Sulphur is a non-metal. It is found in the earth. We buy it as a powder. This is called flowers of sulphur. It can be bought as lumps. This is roll sulphur.

ystals.

Experiment 9.1 The action of heat on sulphur

1. Fill a test tube two-thirds full of powdered sulphur. Heat it gently for fifteen seconds. Stop heating. Shake the tube. Gently heat and shake until all the sulphur melts. Try to avoid any great change in colour.

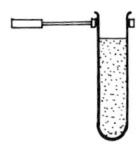

Fold a filter paper into a cone. Hold it by the rim. Pour in the liquid sulphur. Wait until the top becomes solid. Slowly open the cone. Do not let any liquid run out.

2. Take a second test tube. Melt sulphur in it gently in the same way. Use a test tube holder. Go on heating the sulphur. When it is red-brown in colour, turn the test tube upside down.

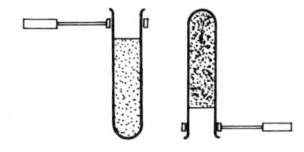

Turn the test tube right way up. Heat it until the sulphur boils. Pour the liquid into cold water in a beaker. Pour away the water. Pick up the solid. Hold its ends and pull. Try this again later.

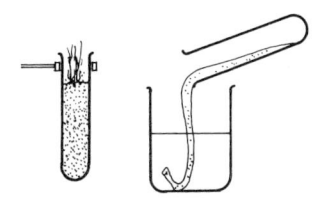

Is the melting point of sulphur low or high?
What did you see on the filter paper?
What happens when liquid sulphur is heated?
What happens when the tube is upside down?
Describe the solid left in the cold water. Are the crystals and the brown solid both sulphur?

More about sulphur

Sulphur needs little heat to melt it. It turns into an orange-yellow liquid. Its melting point seems likely to be low. It is a non-metal. Most non-metals have low melting points.

In the filter paper liquid sulphur cools. It turns back to a solid. The solid consists of yellow crystals like needles.

If liquid sulphur is heated its colour darkens. It becomes orange, red and red-brown. Now the tube is turned upside down. No liquid runs out. It is like very thick treacle.

More heating makes the sulphur runny again. It is black when it boils. The water cools the boiling sulphur suddenly. A soft, dark brown solid forms. It stretches like elastic. It goes back slowly to its first length. In time it gets hard and yellow.

*Experiment 9.2 To check the melting point of sulphur

Take a 12 cm length of glass tubing. Heat the middle of it. Rotate it in the flame. When it is soft take it out of the flame. Pull it out into a narrow tube.

Cut off a 3 cm length of this. Seal one end in a bunsen flame. Let it cool. Powder some roll sulphur. Jab the open end of the tube in it. Tap the sulphur down the tube. Tie it to a 200 °C thermometer close to the bulb. Half fill a large test tube with medicinal paraffin. Hold the thermometer upright in it.

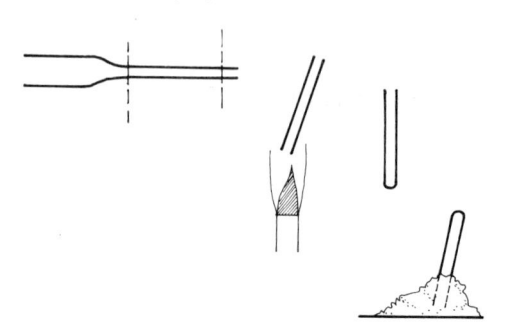

Gently warm the paraffin. Stir it all the time. Keep the temperature rising very slowly. Note what it is when the sulphur melts. Take out the thermometer. The sulphur turns to a solid. Find its melting point in the same way again.

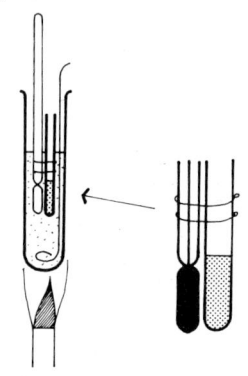

What is the first melting point of sulphur?
Will sulphur melt if put into boiling water?
What is the second melting point?
Is it different from the first?

Sulphur melts at 113 °C. Boiling water is at 100 °C. It cannot melt sulphur. The second melting point is higher, about 119 °C.

Rubber tyres after vulcanization.

Where does sulphur come from?

Sulphur is found native. This means that the element itself is found in nature. Many metal ores are sulphur compounds.

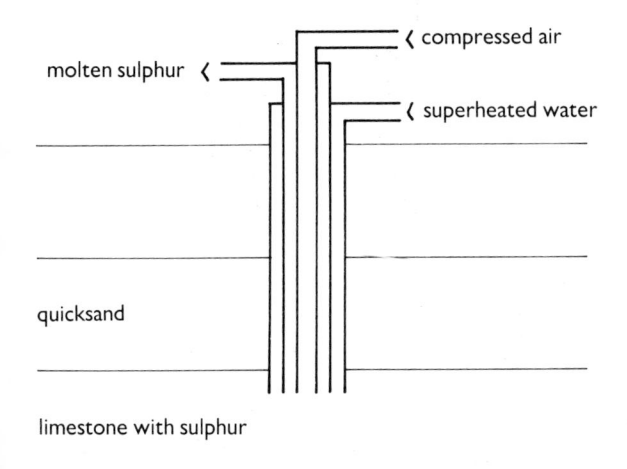

Sulphur is found in the southern states of the USA. Most of the world's sulphur comes from there. It was found by accident. People drilling for oil discovered it. It is in a layer of limestone. This begins about 150 metres down.

It was nearly thirty years before the sulphur was mined. The problem is quicksand. There is a layer of it between the sulphur and the surface. This prevents normal mining.

In 1890 a man named Frasch found the answer. The boiling point of a liquid can be altered. If air pressure is higher than normal, boiling point is higher too. Water boils at 100 °C.

Frasch heated water at fifteen times normal pressure. It is still liquid at 170 °C. It is called superheated water. It can melt sulphur.

A hole is bored down to the limestone. Three steel pipes are fitted into it. They are one inside the other. Superheated water is forced down the outer one. It spreads through the limestone. The sulphur melts.

Compressed air is blown down the inside pipe. This forces the liquid sulphur up the middle one. The water going down keeps it hot. It is run into huge tanks. It turns back to a solid.

What is sulphur used for?

Very large amounts are used to make sulphuric acid. We shall deal with this later.

It is used in vulcanizing rubber. Rubber comes from the sap of the rubber tree. Man-made rubber comes from petroleum gases. Both of them are soft. Sulphur makes them harder and more elastic. The method is called vulcanization.

Sulphur is used in making matches and fireworks.

Are there other allotropes of sulphur?

We have made spiky crystals from liquid sulphur. We have also made a soft brown solid. Both may be allotropes of sulphur.

How did we make crystals of salt? We evaporated a solution of it in water. We might make sulphur crystals from solution.

But does sulphur dissolve in water? We know it does not. We poured boiling sulphur into water. It did not dissolve. We need to find other solvents.

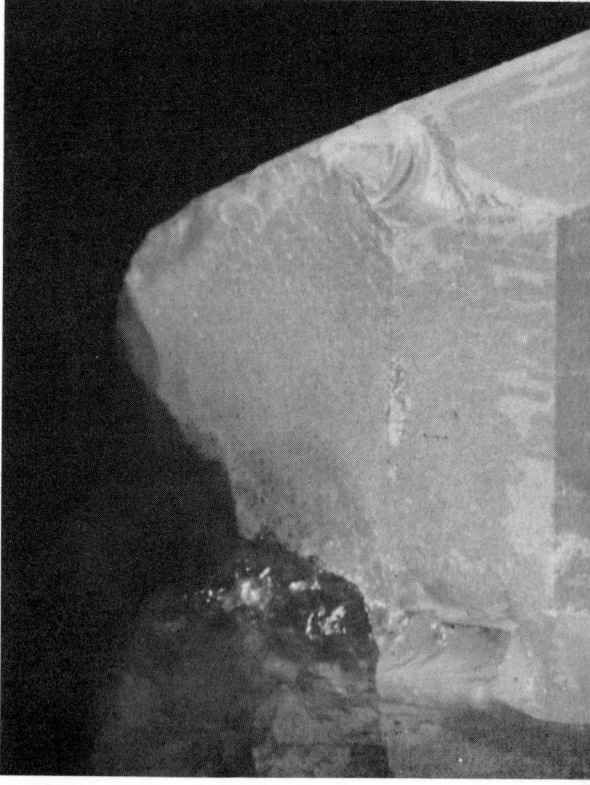

Experiment 9.3 To make sulphur crystals

1. Do the experiment in a fume cupboard. Put some flowers of sulphur in a test tube. Add carbon disulphide. Stopper the tube. Shake it well.

Filter the mixture. Put drops of filtrate on a glass slide. Look at them through a microscope. Pour the rest into a petri dish. Cover it with a sheet of paper. Leave it to evaporate.

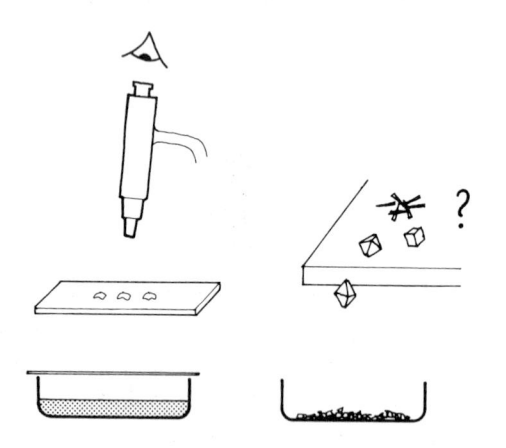

A rhombic sulphur crystal.

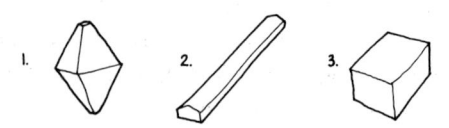

Carbon disulphide evaporates. It needs no heating. Crystals form in the dish. They are not thin and spiky. They are like drawing 1. Not all the sulphur dissolves. The filter paper holds a pale yellow powder. We may not have used enough solvent to dissolve it. Or it may be an allotrope.

*2. Crush some roll sulphur. Measure about 20 g. Put it in a 250 cm^3, round-bottomed flask. Pour 60 cm^3 of methylbenzene into it. Stand it on a sand tray. The flask has a long neck.

Dimethyl benzene gives the same results. It does not need a fume cupboard.

Does all the sulphur dissolve in the solvent?
What is left on the filter paper?
Crystals of sulphur are formed. Draw one of them in your book. Is it like 1, 2 or 3?

What happens to the boiling point of the liquid?
What happens to the sulphur in the flask?
What is the shape of the crystals formed?
Where have you seen this shape before?
Why was the tube packed in cotton wool?

The liquid first boils at about 112 °C. Sulphur dissolves in it. This raises the boiling point. As it rises above 113 °C the sulphur melts. The solution becomes yellow.

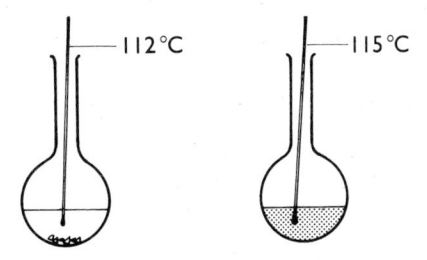

The solution cools. The cotton wool cuts down loss of heat from it. It cools slowly. This gives time for large crystals to form. They are thin and spiky, like needles. The same crystals are formed when we cool molten sulphur.

Heat the tray on a tripod. When the liquid boils, take its temperature. Boil it gently for five minutes. Take its temperature again. The long neck condenses vapour. None escapes.

Put 20 cm³ of methylbenzene into a large test tube. Bring it to the boil. Put the tube into a large beaker lined with cotton wool.

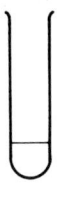

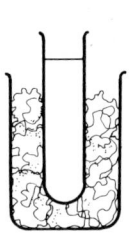

The crystals are **monoclinic sulphur**. They are always formed above 96 °C. The crystals from the cold solution are different. They are shaped like two pyramids. They are **rhombic sulphur**. These two crystal forms are allotropes.

There are two other forms. The brown elastic solid is **plastic sulphur**. We had a pale yellow powder in Experiment 9.3. These forms are not usually called allotropes.

How can we show that all four contain sulphur?
How can we show that they are sulphur *only*?

Put out the bunsen flame. Pour the boiling liquid from the flask into the test tube. Keep undissolved sulphur out of the test tube. After three minutes take it out of the beaker.

Can you remember burning elements in oxygen? Two of them were carbon and sulphur. What is formed by the burning? What does the equation
$$S + O_2 \rightarrow SO_2$$
mean?

The patterns of sulphur atoms

Sulphur allotropes do not look alike. Their physical properties are not the same. For example, their melting points differ.

In Experiment 9.2 we melted sulphur. We used rhombic sulphur. It melted at 113 °C. We let it cool. It turned to solid again.

The solid is monoclinic sulphur. This always forms above 96 °C. We found the melting point again. It was 119 °C. This is the melting point of monoclinic sulphur. The melting points differ.

We can show that all forms contain sulphur. When sulphur burns, its atoms combine with oxygen. Molecules of sulphur dioxide are formed. This is what the equation means. We have added one thing. We have put in the states of the substances. (s) means solid; (g) means gas.

$$S + O_2 \rightarrow SO_2$$
$$S(s) + O_2(g) \rightarrow SO_2(g)$$

The gas dissolves in water. An acid is formed. (l) means liquid and (aq) is solution in water.

$$SO_2(g) + H_2O(l) \rightarrow H_2SO_3(aq)$$

Experiment 9.4 Burning sulphur

Put roll sulphur in a combustion spoon. Hold it in a bunsen flame. Put the burning sulphur into a gas jar of oxygen. Let it burn.

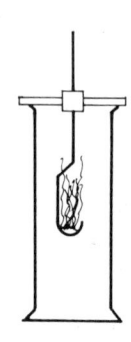

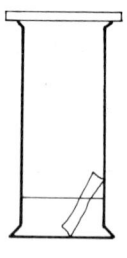

Burn some of the spiky crystals in oxygen. Do the same with brown plastic sulphur. Try burning the pale yellow powder in oxygen.

> Do they all burn more brightly in oxygen?
> Would you recognize the smell of the gas?
> Is the flame the same colour for all four?
> What is the name of the acid formed in water?

The allotropes all burn with the same mauve flame. The oxide formed is a gas. It has a choking smell. It is sulphur dioxide.

Remove the spoon. Add water to the jar. Put a lid on it. Shake the jar. Add litmus paper. Pour in drops of Universal Indicator.

Sulphur dioxide dissolves in water. The solution contains an acid. It comes from sulphur. It is called sulphurous acid. Its formula is H_2SO_3. Have you heard of a similar acid?

Burning shows that the allotropes contain sulphur.

$S + O_2 \rightarrow SO_2$ Relative atomic masses: $S = 32$; $O = 16$.

What is the formula mass of O_2? Of SO_2? $O = 16$. $O_2 = ?$
A mole of sulphur atoms is 32 grams. $SO_2 = (S + O + O) = ?$
What mass of sulphur dioxide will it give if we burn it?

Burn 32 grams of sulphur. Collect the sulphur dioxide formed. Find its mass. Is it 64 grams?

If it is, what we burnt was sulphur only. If not, it has other elements in it. The allotropes prove to be sulphur only. (We need not burn 32 g. We can burn far less. We can work out how much sulphur dioxide it should give.)

Why are the allotropes different?

The sulphur atoms are joined up in rings. Each ring has eight atoms. Rhombic sulphur is made up of these rings. They are packed in a regular pattern. This gives the crystals their shape.

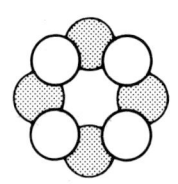

Above 96 °C the pattern changes. Rhombic crystals change to monoclinic crystals. These are long and spiky. The crystal shape is different.

Heat the sulphur. Heat gives energy. The rings move faster. They break out of the pattern. The sulphur melts. The rings move freely in the liquid. More heat makes the rings move faster.

The rings break up into chains. These join to form longer ones. The long chains get tangled, like strings of beads. This makes the liquid stiff. It is non-runny. More heating breaks the long chains. The liquid becomes runny again.

Water cools liquid sulphur suddenly. The chains stop moving. They are left in a tangled mess. This is solid plastic sulphur. Pulling it will stretch the tangled chains. They go slowly back again. The solid behaves like weak elastic.

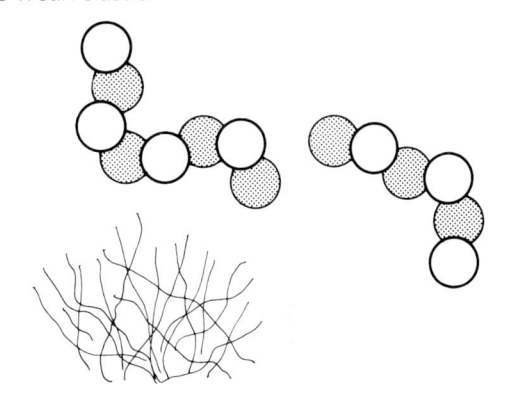

Cooling sulphur vapour gives no time for chains to form. The result is a fine powder. It does not dissolve in carbon disulphide. This is what was in the filter paper.

More of sulphur and sulphur dioxide

Sulphur and metals

Experiment 9.5 Iron and sulphur

Powder some roll sulphur. Add an equal volume of fine iron filings. Mix them thoroughly. Put the mixture in a test tube. Heat it gently. Let the mixture cool. Scrape it out of the tube.

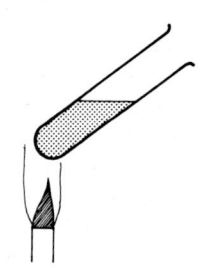

Add dilute sulphuric acid to the manganate (VII) solution. Dip filter paper into it. Put this in the mouth of the tube.

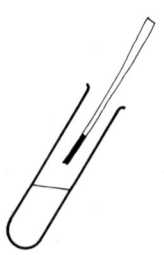

What happens in the test tube?
Do you think a new substance has been formed?

A red hot glow spreads through the mixture. This shows that heat is produced. Nearly all chemical changes produce heat. Those which do are called **exothermic reactions**.
A new substance is formed. It contains iron and sulphur. It has in it two elements. Its name will end in -ide. It is iron(II) sulphide, FeS.

Fe + S → FeS

Sulphur reacts with metals. Iron and sulphur become red hot. Magnesium is more active than iron. How would it react with sulphur? Look at the Thermit reaction (page 67). How did we start it?

What gas is formed in the test tube?
What does the litmus paper show?
What happens to the strips of filter paper?

The gas has a choking smell. The wet litmus paper shows an acid. These two tests suggest sulphur dioxide.

Manganate(VII) is purple. In sulphur dioxide the colour goes. The paper is white again. The manganate(VII) has been reduced to colourless compounds. With manganate(VII) alone the change is slow. With sulphuric acid present it happens at once.

Sulphur dioxide makes a manganate(VII)-acid solution colourless.

It does this by taking away oxygen. It can take the colour from dyes too. It bleaches them by reduction:

$$SO_2(g) + H_2O(l) + \text{oxygen from a dye} \rightarrow H_2SO_4(aq)$$

Experiment 9.6 Another property of sulphur dioxide

Put a few sodium sulphite crystals into a test tube. Add drops of concentrated hydrochloric acid. Have ready (a) a moist litmus paper, (b) a strip of filter paper dipped in potassium manganate (VII) solution. Hold each in the mouth of the tube. Smell the gas with very great care.

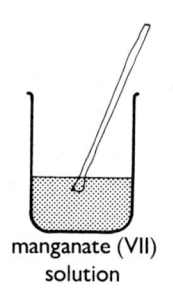

Sulphur dioxide can be oxidized to sulphuric acid.

This points out two uses of sulphur dioxide.
1. It is used to bleach. Wood pulp, straw and wool are bleached white. Wood pulp is used to make paper. The effect does not last. In light, air slowly puts back oxygen. Paper and straw slowly turn yellow again.
2. It is used to manufacture sulphuric acid.

Summary

Some elements exist in more than one form. Each form is the pure element. Each is an allotrope. Allotropes have the same chemical properties. All the forms of carbon burn. They all give carbon dioxide. All the allotropes of sulphur react with metals. They form sulphides.

Allotropes differ in physical properties. Their densities are not the same. Graphite is a conductor; diamond is not. Some are crystals and some are not. There are two crystalline allotropes of sulphur. They differ in shape.

Allotropes of an element contain the same atoms. But they are 'packed' in different patterns. The whole effect is called allotropy. We talk of the 'allotropy of carbon'.

All forms of sulphur burn. They all give sulphur dioxide. It has a choking smell. It dissolves in water. The solution contains sulphurous acid, formula H_2SO_3. It takes oxygen from substances. It reduces them. It may turn them colourless. This is bleaching.

$$SO_2(g) + H_2O(l) + oxygen \rightarrow H_2SO_4(aq)$$

(g) = gas, (l) = liquid, (aq) = in water.
Sulphur dioxide makes manganate(VII) colourless.

Questions

1. What is meant by 'the allotropy of carbon'?

2. Write down three ways in which diamond and graphite differ. What uses do they suggest?

3. How would you make monoclinic crystals from sulphur? What is plastic sulphur?

4. Where is mineral sulphur found? Why is ordinary mining impossible? What method is used?

5. Fill in the blanks.
   $S(s) + O_2(g) \rightarrow SO_2(g)$ tells us that _____ burns in oxygen forming _____. (s) stands for _____. (g) stands for _____. Sulphur dioxide has a _____ smell. It turns moist litmus _____. This shows an _____ called _____ acid.
   $SO_2(g) + H_2O(l) \rightarrow H_2SO_3(aq)$
   (l) stands for _____. (aq) means _____ _____. Moist sulphur dioxide takes away _____. It _____ other substances. By taking away colour it _____ the dye. It can _____ wood pulp.
   $SO_2(g) + H_2O(l) + O \rightarrow H_2SO_4(aq)$
   H_2SO_4 is the formula of _____ acid.

6. Explain why (a) we do not prod electrical equipment with a pencil, (b) we burn sulphur in a greenhouse, (c) paper goes yellow in air.

Diamond is hard and glitters,
Graphite's soft as soap.
Odd that each of them should be
A carbon allotrope.

Pollution

What is it?

We put harmful substances into the air we breathe. Some find their way into the rivers and the sea. All this is pollution.

There is air pollution. Burning fuels are the main cause of this. Water is polluted by sewage and other waste. Substances used in farming can pollute. They are washed into rivers by rain.

Air pollution

Burning fuels may give smoke. They may put dust and grit into the air. We can see these. We cannot see harmful gases mixed with them. However, we breathe them.

Is it a new problem?

No. It is as old as the burning of fuel. A law was passed in 1273 AD. It banned the burning of coal in London. In 1307 people still broke the law. They were punished with 'great fines'. In 1661 there was still smoke. It made London like a 'suburb of Hell'. It was blamed for causing diseases such as 'coughs and cathars'.

How big is the problem?

Solid fuels are not always completely burnt. The products of burning pass into the air. In them may be bits of unburnt fuel. Part of the fuel may not be able to burn. This adds grit and dust to the smoke.

Burning fuels form carbon dioxide, CO_2. With not enough oxygen, carbon monoxide forms (CO). Even less oxygen gives carbon. This appears as black smoke. Sulphur in the fuel may give sulphur dioxide. This, and carbon monoxide, are the gases which cannot be seen. Transport uses mainly liquid fuels. They give the same products, particularly carbon monoxide. Leaded petrol puts poisonous lead compounds into the air.

Before the Clean Air Act (1910).

After the Clean Air Act (1970).

Pollution damages buildings.

The effects of pollution

The grit, dust and carbon fall. About 200 tonnes fall on a square km of a city every year. Buildings, clothes and people get dirty. More soap and detergent are used. These solids in air absorb light. Smoky areas are darker. They get less sunlight. They use more electricity.

Buildings suffer in other ways. Gases such as sulphur dioxide dissolve in rain. The acids formed dissolve limestone and marble. Stonework crumbles. Metals corrode faster. Repair and decoration are needed more often.

We breathe air. Our lungs take in solids and harmful gases. More people suffer from lung diseases. So people are more often away from work. Smog and fog are also bad for the lungs. The death rate rises. Fog is a mixture. It is tiny drops of liquid with solid particles. Smog is a mixture of fog and smoke. It holds on to the solids and harmful gases. They increase until the smog goes.

In 1952 there were four days of dense smog in London. Traffic was halted. Accidents increased. There were 4000 more deaths than usual.

The cost of pollution

Pollution damages people and buildings. More cleaning and repairs are needed. It causes fog and smog. More people are ill and more working time is lost. It may cost us as much as £500 million a year. Plant life suffers too. Plants prefer clean air.

The Clean Air Act of 1956 banned black smoke. Solids had to be taken out of it. Fuel had to be used more efficiently. The figures show the smoke put into air in a year. They are in millions of tonnes. They show the change the Act made. In 1938, 2.7; in 1966, 1.3; in 1972, 0.5.

Water pollution comes mainly from using the land. Fertilizers and other substances are used. Rain dissolves them. They are carried by the rain into rivers. They may harm river life.

Foggy day in London—Tower Bridge.

Acids and salts

Check what you know about acids.

Some acids are made by adding water to a non-metal oxide. If this dissolves, an acid is formed. How do we settle its formula?

$$SO_2 + H_2O \rightarrow H_2SO_3$$
$$\uparrow \qquad \uparrow \qquad \uparrow$$
non-metal + water → acid
oxide

Water contains hydrogen. Then so will the acid. It is hydrogen which makes it an acid. So we put hydrogen first in the formula.

The oxide contains a non-metal. Then so will the acid. The non-metal is put next in the formula. Any other elements come last.

Look at the formula H_2SO_4. It tells us that:

it is an acid   it contains sulphur   it has oxygen, too

It is the formula of **sulphuric acid**. This reacts with metals.

Experiment 10.1 The action of acid on metal

Put magnesium in a test tube. Add dilute sulphuric acid. Test any gas with a lighted splint.

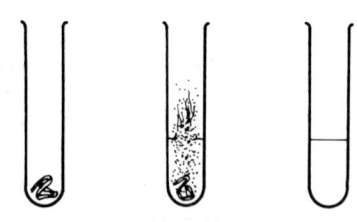

The mixture effervesces. What gas is it?
What happens to the magnesium?
Is it reacting with the water or the acid?
Did you notice any other change?
Try to write an equation for the reaction.

The gas is hydrogen. It gives the well-known 'squeaky pop'. The magnesium disappears. It must be in the solution. Magnesium reacts very slowly with water. This reaction is fast. Magnesium is reacting with the acid. The test tube gets very hot. It is an **exothermic** reaction.

Has all the acid been used up in the reaction? How shall we know? Add litmus. It will turn red if any acid is left. We could add more magnesium. It will react with any acid. If some magnesium is left over, then all the acid has gone.

Experiment 10.2 To get a solute out of the solution

Add more magnesium to the test tube. Wait until no more will dissolve. Filter off the unused metal. Evaporate the filtrate. When most of the water has gone, let it stand. Put some hot solution on a slide. Use a microscope to watch it.

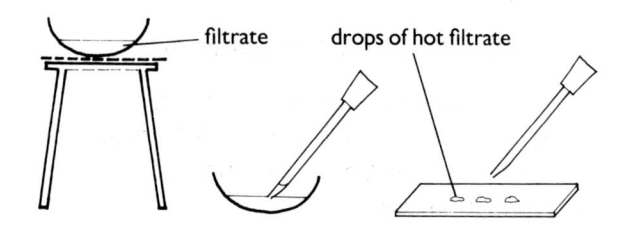

filtrate   drops of hot filtrate

What is a salt?

Did you write an equation for the reaction?
First: work out the word equation
   magnesium + sulphuric acid → ? + hydrogen
Next: put in each symbol and formula
   Mg + H_2SO_4 → ? + H_2

Hydrogen is diatomic. Each molecule contains two atoms. The formula of hydrogen gas is H_2. Mg pushes out H_2. This seems right. Metals can replace hydrogen. We used this to set up the Activity Series. And magnesium is an active metal.

The likely equation is

Mg + H_2SO_4 → $MgSO_4$ + H_2

We can show, by experiment, that this is correct. $MgSO_4$ is in the solution. The SO_4 part of sulphuric acid is called **sulphate**. $MgSO_4$ is the formula of **magnesium sulphate**.

Salts

Magnesium sulphate is a salt. It belongs to the same family as common salt. All compounds like them are salts. How was it made? A metal pushed hydrogen out of an acid.

A salt is the substance formed by replacing the hydrogen of an acid with a metal.

Salts are common compounds. We have used many of them. Each of them needs a name. Old names said little about the salt. Magnesium sulphate was found in springs at Epsom. It was called Epsom salt. Some names came from people and plants. An example is Glauber's salt. Glauber was the first man to make it.

An acid has two parts. One is hydrogen. The rest of the acid is called the **anion**. A salt is named from its metal and anion. Common salt is sodium chloride.

Making salts by other methods

Will copper and dilute sulphuric acid give copper sulphate? No! Copper is low in the Activity Series. It is less active than hydrogen. It cannot push hydrogen out of the acid.

We can use black copper oxide. It contains oxygen. Then the metal may be able to replace hydrogen.

Acid	Anion
acetic	acetate
carbonic	carbonate
hydrochloric	chloride
hydrobromic	bromide
nitric	nitrate
phosphoric	phosphate
sulphuric	sulphate
sulphurous	sulphite

What is a policeman on night duty paid? Copper nitrate?

Acid + base

Experiment 10.3 To make copper sulphate

Take a 100 cm³ beaker. Fill it a quarter full with dilute sulphuric acid. Add black copper oxide. Gently heat it. Stir with a glass rod.

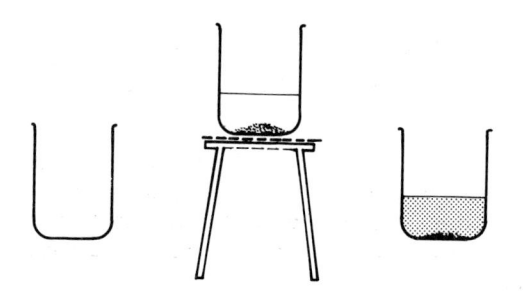

If all the oxide dissolves, add more. Do this until some oxide is left in the liquid. Let it cool. Filter it into an evaporating dish.

Gently heat the dish. When about half the water has gone, stop heating. Pour the solution into a flat dish. Cover the dish and leave it.

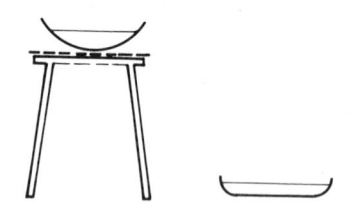

Copper oxide + sulphuric acid → copper sulphate + ?
$$CuO + H_2SO_4 \rightarrow CuSO_4 + ?$$
H_2 from the acid and O from the oxide give water, H_2O.

Black copper oxide is a basic oxide, or base. A base reacts with an acid. A salt and water are formed.

The copper sulphate crystals are small. It is not easy to see their shape. We shall try to make a large crystal.

Experiment 10.4 To make larger crystals

Take a glass tube drawn out at one end. Use a good crystal from Experiment 10.3. Drop it into the tube so that it sticks out at the end. Drop in more crystals. Hold the tube upright.

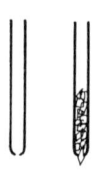

Warm some distilled water. Dissolve as much copper sulphate in it as you can. Put the solution into a beaker. Let it cool.

Lower the crystal into the solution at night. Raise it in the morning. Dry the crystal gently. Lower the tube again at night.

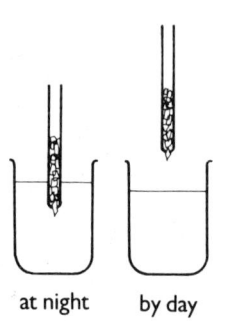

at night   by day

Do the oxide and acid give a gas?

Pick out well-shaped crystals from the dish. Draw one of them in your book. Write a word equation. Put under it a formula equation.

Why do we use too much oxide in the beaker?

No gas is formed. Blue solution passes through the filter paper. Crystals appear. They have a definite shape. They are copper sulphate.
Some oxide was left in the beaker. This means that all the acid has been used up.

Acid and alkali

An alkali is a base. It is a base which dissolves in water. It reacts with an acid. The products are a salt and water.

Experiment 10.5 To make sodium sulphate

1. Fill a burette with dilute sulphuric acid. Hold it over a sink. Run out some acid. This brings the acid level on to the scale. It also fills the part below the tap. Support the burette in a stand. Note the level of the acid.

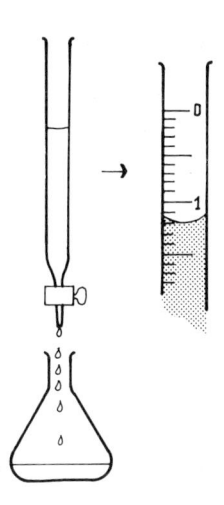

Take a pipette bulb. Practice with it using water. Then pick up 25 cm^3 of sodium hydroxide solution. Put this into a conical flask. Add three drops of methyl orange indicator.

Run acid into the flask. Swirl the mixture. Add more acid. Stop when the colour shows signs of change. Now add acid in drops. Swirl the flask after each drop. Stop when the colour just turns pink. Take the reading on the burette.

The acid and alkali react. The solution contains a salt. It is neutral. At most it has one drop of acid too much.

> How can we get the salt from the solution?
> What colour will the crystals be?

We can evaporate the solution. However, the indicator is still there. So the crystals will be pink. The indicator has done its job. It has told us how much acid is needed.

2. Take a clean flask. Put in 25 cm^3 of alkali solution. Do not add an indicator. Take the burette reading. Run in the same volume of acid as before. Evaporate this solution.

A copper atom can replace two hydrogen atoms. A sodium atom can replace only one. H_2SO_4 has two hydrogen atoms. It needs two sodium atoms to replace them. Sodium hydroxide is NaOH. The equation will be

| Na | OH | + | H | SO$_4$ |
| Na | OH | | H | |

$$2NaOH + H_2SO_4 \rightarrow Na_2SO_4 + 2H_2O$$

Willie's sister's teacher taught her,
Acid + base gives salt and water.

This is what copper sulphate crystals look like when they are taken from the earth before they are made pure.

143

A fourth method

This method also uses an acid. Again we replace the hydrogen in it by a metal. To do this we use a metal carbonate.

To make calcium chloride we need: hydrochloric acid, HCl
                                    calcium carbonate
One form of calcium carbonate, $CaCO_3$, is chalk.

Experiment 10.6 To make calcium chloride

Use a 100 cm³ beaker. One-quarter fill it with dilute hydrochloric acid. Add powdered chalk. Wait until reaction stops. If no chalk remains, add more. There must be some left at the end.

Filter off the excess chalk. Heat the filtrate in a dish. Try to get crystals in the normal way. Then heat the dish again. Gently drive off all the water. Leave the dish to stand in air. Look at it some days later.

> What does the word 'effervescence' mean?
> Why do chalk and acid effervesce?
> Why do we use an excess of chalk?
> Do crystals of calcium chloride form?
> What happens to the dry salt left in air?

If chalk remains all the acid has gone. It has reacted to form a salt. Crystals of it are not easy to get. Driving off all the water gives a white solid. This turns to solution in air.

The solid is **anhydrous** calcium chloride. Anhydrous means 'without water'. The solid takes water vapour from the air. It dissolves in it. It goes into solution. Substances which do this are **deliquescent**. They are used to dry gases and liquids.

Effervescence is gas bubbles. The gas is carbon dioxide. So the word equation is

calcium carbonate + hydrochloric acid → calcium chloride + carbon dioxide + ?

$CaCO_3$ + HCl → ? + CO_2 + ?

A calcium atom can replace two hydrogen atoms. To get two H atoms we need HCl + HCl, or 2HCl. CO_3 gives CO_2 + O. Two H atoms + O give H_2O.

The equation is $CaCO_3 + 2HCl \rightarrow CaCl_2 + CO_2 + H_2O$.

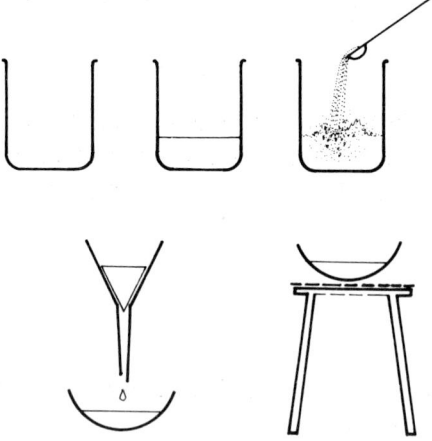

> Willie, finding life a bore,
> Drank some H_2SO_4.
> Willie's teacher saw that he
> Was filled with $MgCO_3$.
> Now he's neutralized, its true,
> But he's full of CO_2.

What is wrong with the verse?

144

Insoluble salts

We now have four methods of making a salt. Each uses an acid. The acid is neutralized. Its hydrogen is replaced by a metal. To do this we use four kinds of substance.

acid
{
+ metal → salt + hydrogen
+ metal oxide → salt + water
+ metal hydroxide → salt + water
+ metal carbonate → salt + carbon dioxide + water
}

Which method do we choose? The one which works best. Each method gives a solution. The salt is dissolved in water. Heating it gives the salt. Most salts appear as crystals.

Experiment 10.7 To make salts which do not dissolve

1. Put sodium chloride solution into a test tube. Add drops of silver nitrate solution.

> What do you see?
> Is silver nitrate a salt?
> Does it contain a metal and an anion?
> What new substances might be formed?

We have mixed solutions of two salts. Remember that metals can replace metals. Suppose the two metals change places?

sodium chloride + silver nitrate → sodium nitrate + silver chloride ↓

The two salts may react. If so, they form two new salts. This will happen only if one new salt is insoluble. Then it will appear in the water. We shall see it. An insoluble substance formed in solution is called a **precipitate**.

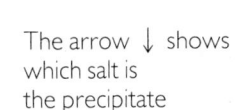

The arrow ↓ shows which salt is the precipitate

2. Add drops of silver nitrate solution to other salt solutions. Use potassium chloride, potassium iodide, calcium chloride, magnesium chloride, sodium carbonate, potassium carbonate. Warm each tube. Add dilute nitric acid.

> Are precipitates formed in each case?
> Are they all white or are some coloured?
> Which of them dissolves in nitric acid?

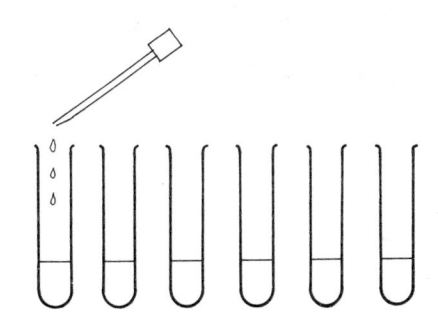

Which salt is it?

All the salts we used react with silver nitrate. All of them give precipitates. These are all white except one. Precipitate is a long word. We shall shorten it to ppt.

Say the letters p p t.

Write your results in the form of a table.

First salt	Second salt	Names of new salts formed	Name of ppt	Colour of ppt
sodium chloride	silver nitrate	sodium nitrate silver chloride	?	white

It will help to know that all nitrates dissolve in water
all sodium salts are soluble
all potassium salts dissolve

The precipitate is either sodium nitrate or silver chloride.
It is not sodium nitrate. All nitrates dissolve in water.
The ppt is silver chloride. Complete your table of results.

Check these results. All the chlorides give a white ppt. So do the carbonates. The silver carbonate ppt dissolves in nitric acid. The silver chloride ppt does not.

Now take *any* chloride solution. Add silver nitrate solution.

X chloride + silver nitrate ⟶ X nitrate + silver chloride ↓
So any chloride + silver nitrate ⟶ a white ppt.
This ppt does not dissolve in nitric acid.
This test shows that the salt is a chloride.

Can we find out which metal the salt contains? Look at page 77. Some metal compounds give flame colours.

On page 12 we made crystals from rock salt. How do we know that the crystals are salt, sodium chloride? They are white. They are cubic crystals. They taste salty. We also know that tasting can be dangerous (page 19).

Now we can recognise the substance by tests.
It colours the flame orange-yellow. All sodium compounds do.
It gives a white ppt with silver nitrate. The ppt does not dissolve in nitric acid. The salt is a chloride, sodium chloride.

Analysis

A salt contains a metal and an anion. Tests tell us which metal. Flame colour is one of the methods. We can find out which anion. Getting a ppt is one way.

This kind of finding out tells us which salt we have. It is called **analysis**. We can analyse a substance by tests.

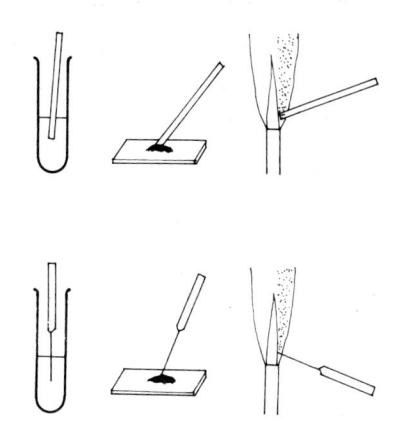

Experiment 10.8 Tests for sulphites and sulphates

Put sodium sulphate solution in a test tube. Put sodium sulphite solution in a second tube. Add barium chloride solution to both. Then add dilute hydrochloric acid.

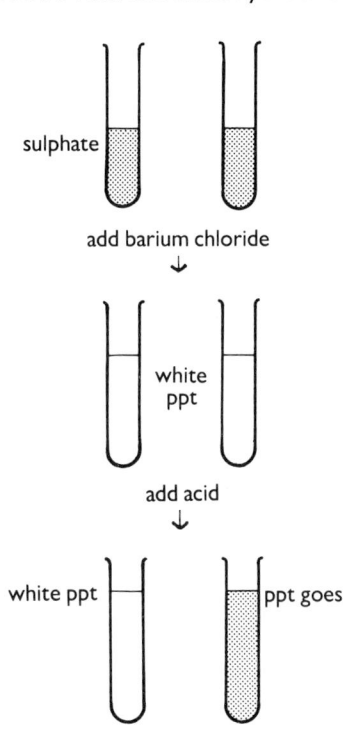

Are barium chloride and sodium sulphate salts? Write the names of two new salts they could produce. What are the names of the ppts in the test tubes? Can you tell the difference between them? Which one of them dissolves in the acid?

sodium sulphate + barium chloride → sodium chloride + barium sulphate

Which is the ppt?

Sodium chloride is common salt. It is also a sodium salt. So we know that it dissolves in water. The white ppt must therefore be barium sulphate. The ppt in the other tube is white. It is barium sulphite. The ppts look alike.

This is why we add acid. It decides which ppt is which. The sulphite ppt dissolves in the acid. The sulphate ppt does not. (Barium chloride gives a white ppt with a carbonate. This dissolves in acid too. Carbon dioxide is formed as well.)

Remember that this is a fifth way of making salts. Solutions of two salts are mixed. They form two new ones. One of these is soluble. It will be in the solution. The other new salt is insoluble. It appears as a precipitate.

Filter the mixture. The solution passes through. Evaporate it. The ppt is on the filter paper. Wash it with water. Dry it.

This method is not much used for making salts. It is used in analysis.

147

Equations

We can work out equations for these reactions.
We know the names of the substances we start with.
We can find out what substances are formed.
This gives the word equation.

Metals replace hydrogen. They also replace other metals. One atom of sodium can replace one atom of hydrogen. A copper atom can replace two H atoms. An aluminium atom can replace three. Numbers for other atoms are given in the table.

Number of H atoms one atom can replace:

One	Two	Three
lithium Li	barium Ba	aluminium Al
potassium K	calcium Ca	chromium Cr
silver Ag	copper Cu	iron Fe
sodium Na	iron Fe	
	lead Pb	
	magnesium Mg	
	zinc Zn	

We can use this to work out a formula. Nitric acid is HNO_3. A silver atom, Ag, can replace one hydrogen atom, H. The formula of silver nitrate is $AgNO_3$. A lead atom, Pb, can replace two hydrogen atoms. It will join to two NO_3 radicals. Lead nitrate is $Pb(NO_3)_2$.

We shall work out equations for two reactions.

Word equation: sodium chloride + silver nitrate → sodium nitrate + silver chloride

Formula: $NaCl + AgNO_3 \rightarrow$? + ?

The table: one Na atom can replace one H atom
one Ag atom can replace one H atom
So one Na atom can replace one Ag atom

Final equation: $NaCl + AgNO_3 \rightarrow NaNO_3 + AgCl \downarrow$

Barium chloride solution is added to sodium sulphate solution. A white ppt forms. Sodium chloride dissolves. The white ppt must be barium sulphate.

Sulphuric acid is H_2SO_4. One Na atom can replace one H atom. The formula of sodium sulphate is Na_2SO_4.
One Ba atom can replace two H atoms. Barium chloride is $BaCl_2$.

sodium sulphate + barium chloride → sodium chloride + barium sulphate

$Na_2SO_4 + BaCl_2 \rightarrow 2NaCl + BaSO_4 \downarrow$

An equation like this sums up a reaction. It tells us what happens. It does not say *how* or *why* it happens. We shall find that out later.

Summary

Every acid contains hydrogen. This is what gives it acid properties. So hydrogen comes first in its formula. The rest of the acid is called the anion.

The formula of nitric acid is HNO_3. N shows that it contains nitrogen. The anion is NO_3. It is called nitrate.

A salt is formed by putting a metal in place of the hydrogen of an acid. So a salt has two parts, metal and anion. A sodium atom can replace one hydrogen atom. The formula of the salt sodium nitrate is $NaNO_3$. A lead atom can replace two H atoms. Lead nitrate is $Pb(NO_3)_2$. Notice the bracket.

A salt is made from an acid in four ways.

Add a metal. This usually gives a salt and hydrogen. Some metals cannot replace hydrogen. Very active metals may react too vigorously.

Add a metal oxide. This gives a salt and water.

A metal hydroxide also gives a salt and water. A metal oxide and hydroxide are both bases. So
   acid + base → salt + water
An alkali is a base which dissolves in water.

Metal carbonates react with acids. The result is a salt, water and carbon dioxide.

A fifth method uses two salts. Their solutions are mixed. Two new salts may be formed. They will be if one of them does not dissolve. It will appear as a precipitate (ppt). It can be taken out by filtering. The second new salt is in the filtrate. The method is used to make insoluble salts.

This method is also used in **analysis**. Analysis means finding out what a substance contains. For a salt we find out which metal it has in it. We also find out which anion it contains.

In all these reactions: metals replace hydrogen or metals replace other metals. We need to know how many H atoms an atom of a metal can replace. We can then work out equations.

Questions

1. Sodium hydroxide is an alkali. What does this mean? It can react with (a) nitric acid, (b) sulphuric acid. Name the salts formed. Describe how you would make one of these salts.

2. What is a salt? They are made from acids. What four types of substance are added to an acid? Which would you use to make (a) copper sulphate, (b) magnesium sulphate? How would you know if all the acid had been used up?

3. A salt gave a lilac colour to the flame. Its solution and silver nitrate gave a white ppt. This did not dissolve in nitric acid. Which salt is it? Write down its formula.

4. Complete this as you write it in your book. All acids contain _____. The formula of an acid stands for one _____ of it. An acid has the formula HPO_3. One molecule of it contains _____ hydrogen atom, one atom of _____ and _____ oxygen atoms. The formula of its sodium salt is _____. Its magnesium salt is $Mg(PO_3)$ _____.

Why does a magnesium atom replace *two* hydrogen atoms?
Is there anything smaller than an atom?
Why is this called the Plastic Age?
What is an explosive?
Where does a Coke tin come from?
Find out in Book Two!

Questions

In each question five answers are given. They are labelled A, B, C, D and E. Only one answer is correct. Choose this one. Write its letter on your answer sheet.

1. Water is
   A an element.
   B a compound of carbon and oxygen.
   C a mixture of hydrogen and oxygen.
   D a compound of hydrogen and oxygen.
   E a compound of hydrogen and carbon.

2. Both diamond and graphite
   A conduct an electric current.
   B form carbon dioxide when they burn.
   C are black and crystalline.
   D have the same density.
   E are used to drill through rock.

3. Oxygen is made in industry by
   A heating black copper oxide.
   B photosynthesis.
   C heating red mercury oxide.
   D using hydrogen peroxide solution.
   E boiling liquid air.

4. Which of these changes is a chemical one?
   A dissolving salt in water.
   B changing rhombic to monoclinic sulphur.
   C melting ice to water.
   D burning petrol in a car engine.
   E evaporating salt solution.

5. In pure water, Universal Indicator is A red, B orange, C green, D blue, E violet.

6. In alkali, Universal Indicator is coloured A red, B orange, C yellow, D green, E blue.

Questions 7 to 12 are about five methods used in Chemistry. They are: A filtration, B distillation, C chromatography, D crystallization, E using a magnet. Which of the five is used to:

7. get pure water from a salt solution

8. make salt crystals from salt solution

9. separate the coloured substances in flower petals

10. get iron from a mixture of iron and tin

11. get clear water from muddy water

12. take unused copper oxide from copper sulphate solution

Questions 13 to 18 are about five kinds of chemical change. They are: A reduction, B combination, C decomposition, D neutralization, E forming a precipitate. Which one describes each change shown below?

13. tin oxide + carbon → carbon dioxide + tin

14. magnesium burning in oxygen

15. acid + alkali → salt + water

16. mercury oxide heated → mercury + oxygen

17. silver nitrate + sodium chloride (both in solution in water)

18. hydrogen peroxide → oxygen + water

19. A certain metal: (i) does not react with dilute sulphuric acid to give hydrogen, (ii) becomes coated with copper when put into copper sulphate solution. In the Activity Series this metal would be placed
    A above sodium
    B below sodium and above magnesium
    C below iron but above hydrogen
    D below hydrogen but above copper
    E below copper

20. Another metal: (i) does not react with cold water but does react with steam. Hydrogen is formed. (ii) can be used to reduce iron oxide to iron. In the Activity Series this metal would be placed
    A above sodium
    B below sodium but above iron
    C below iron but above hydrogen
    D below hydrogen but above copper
    E below copper

In Questions 21 to 25 use C = 12, O = 16, Ca = 40.

21. C = 12 shows
    A the atomic number of carbon
    B the formula mass of carbon
    C the relative atomic mass of calcium
    D the formula mass of calcium
    E the relative atomic mass of carbon

22. The mass of a calcium atom is
    A three times the mass of oxygen atom
    B 2.5 times the mass of an oxygen atom
    C twice the mass of an oxygen atom
    D equal to the mass of an oxygen atom
    E less than the mass of an oxygen atom

23. The formula mass of carbon dioxide, CO_2, is:
    A 12, B 28, C 44, D 56, E 60.

24. One mole of chalk, $CaCO_3$, is:
    A 68, B 124, C 100, D 100 grams, E 116.

25. Heat decomposes chalk: $CaCO_3 \rightarrow CaO + CO_2$
    One mole of chalk gives
    A one mole of carbon dioxide
    B 28 grams of carbon dioxide
    C 2 moles of carbon dioxide
    D 3 moles of carbon dioxide
    E one mole of calcium dioxide

Questions 26 to 31: each question has four statements. One or more of them is correct. Decide which are the correct ones. Then write down:

    A if only 1, 2 and 3 are correct
    B if only 1 and 3 are correct
    C if only 2 and 4 are correct
    D if only 4 is correct
    E if some other statement or group of statements is correct

26. The gas hydrogen
    1 is less dense than air
    2 can reduce some metal oxides
    3 forms an explosive mixture with air
    4 has a choking smell

27. Acids can be neutralized by
    1 sodium hydroxide
    2 sodium chloride
    3 sodium carbonate
    4 sodium sulphate

28. The atmosphere contains
    1 about 21% nitrogen
    2 more carbon dioxide than oxygen
    3 more nitrogen than oxygen
    4 about 1% hydrogen

29. The reaction of an acid with an alkali produces
    1 an element
    2 a salt
    3 hydrogen
    4 water

30. Substances which lose mass on heating include
    1 copper carbonate
    2 black copper oxide
    3 copper sulphate crystals
    4 copper metal

31. Calcium oxide is also called
    1 limestone
    2 slaked lime
    3 chalk
    4 quicklime

Questions 32 to 35: the apparatus is shown in the drawing. We used it to find the volume of oxygen in the atmosphere. Choose the best answer.

32. The two pieces of apparatus labelled X are
    A test tubes
    B measuring cylinders
    C glass tubing
    D syringes
    E condensers

33. The metal in the tube is: A magnesium, B copper, C mercury, D iron, E tin.

34. This metal takes out of the air: A nitrogen, B carbon dioxide, C water vapour, D oxygen, E some other gas.

35. At the start the apparatus contains 50 cm^3 of air. The metal removes all possible gas. The volume left at the end is: A 40 cm^3, B 30 cm^3, C 20 cm^3, D 10 cm^3, E some other volume.

151

More questions

1. Here is a list of elements. They are in order of chemical activity. The most active element comes first.

   calcium, aluminium, iron, lead, hydrogen, copper, gold

   Use the list to answer these questions:
   a) Which element in the list is not a metal?
   b) Which element combines best with oxygen?
   c) What is likely to happen when aluminium is heated with lead oxide? Write a word equation for any change.
   d) Which elements will not liberate hydrogen from dilute acid?
   e) Which metal in the list is most likely to be found 'native'?
   f) Will iron displace copper from copper sulphate solution?
   g) Which metals have oxides which can be reduced by hydrogen?

2. Three towns, A, B and C, have different water supplies. 50 cm^3 samples of each are taken. Soap solution is added until a lasting lather forms. 50 cm^3 samples of each are boiled. Soap solution is added. Each is passed through a water softener. Soap solution is added to 50 cm^3 of this water. In each case enough is added to give a lasting lather. The results are given in the table below in cm^3 of soap solution needed:

	Town A	Town B	Town C
Tap water needs	20	15	10
Boiled tap water needs	16	15	1
Softened water needs	1	1	1

   Which town has the hardest water? Which types of hardness does each town supply contain? What substance causes hardness in water from town B? What substance causes the hardness of town C? How much of this soap solution would distilled water need? Rain in town A falls into a beaker. How much soap would 50 cm^3 of it need to give a lasting lather?

3. Salts can be made by several methods. Here is a list of salts: zinc sulphate, copper sulphate, silver chloride, sodium chloride, magnesium carbonate. From it, choose:
   a) one which can be made by the action of acid on metal
   b) one made by the action of an acid on an oxide
   c) one made by precipitation
   d) one made by mixing acid and alkali.
   Describe in detail how you would make crystals of one of them.

4. Substance A is a white solid. It is heated strongly in a bunsen flame for a long time. It colours the flame brick red. A white solid B is formed. Its mass is less than the mass of A. With water, B crumbles to a powder C. Steam is formed. C is shaken with water. The mixture is filtered. Carbon dioxide is passed into the clear filtrate. It becomes cloudy.
   a) Name the substance A.
   b) Explain why it loses mass on heating.
   c) What does the flame colour mean?
   d) Name the substance B.
   e) What tells you that B reacts with water?
   f) Name the substance C.
   g) The filtrate is a solution of C. Why does it become cloudy?
   h) What effect would the filtrate have on litmus?
   j) Give one everyday use of B and one of C.

5. Hydrogen is burnt in air. The products are cooled. A clear, colourless liquid is formed.

   What is its chemical name?
   What is its everyday name?

   The liquid turns to a solid at 0 °C. What will be its boiling point? Salt is dissolved in the liquid. How will its boiling point alter? How would you get salt crystals from the solution? What will be the shape of the crystals? Describe briefly how you would make pure water from tap water.

6. These are relative atomic masses: $Cu = 64$, $O = 16$, $H = 1$, $S = 32$.
   Which atom has 64 times the mass of a hydrogen atom? 64 g of copper form 80 g of black copper oxide. Work out the formula of the oxide. What is one mole of it? The formula of sulphuric acid is H_2SO_4. What is its relative molecular mass? What is the mass of one mole of it? Write an equation for the reaction between the copper oxide and sulphuric acid. How much acid is needed to react with 8 g of the oxide? How much copper sulphate will be formed?

7. Write one sentence, in each case, to explain what is meant by:
   an allotrope; reduction; an element; a chemical change; an atom; a molecule; a mole.

List of elements

Element	Symbol	Atomic number	Relative atomic mass
Aluminium	Al	13	27
Argon	Ar	18	40
Barium	Ba	56	137
Bromine	Br	35	80
Calcium	Ca	20	40
Carbon	C	6	12
Chlorine	Cl	17	35.5
Chromium	Cr	24	52
Cobalt	Co	27	59
Copper	Cu	29	64
Fluorine	F	9	19
Gold	Au	79	197
Helium	He	2	4
Hydrogen	H	1	1
Iodine	I	53	127
Iron	Fe	26	56
Lead	Pb	82	207
Lithium	Li	3	7
Magnesium	Mg	12	24
Manganese	Mn	25	55
Mercury	Hg	80	201
Neon	Ne	10	20
Nickel	Ni	28	59
Nitrogen	N	7	14
Oxygen	O	8	16
Phosphorus	P	15	31
Platinum	Pt	78	195
Potassium	K	19	39
Silicon	Si	14	28
Silver	Ag	47	108
Sodium	Na	11	23
Strontium	Sr	38	88
Sulphur	S	16	32
Tin	Sn	50	119
Uranium	U	92	238
Zinc	Zn	30	65

Word games

Word changing

Example: Change sand to salt in three moves.
Change one letter at each move to make a new word.
Alchemy! change lead into gold in three moves.

LEAD
. . . .
. . . .
. . . .
GOLD

SAND
SAN<u>E</u>
SA<u>L</u>E
SAL<u>T</u>

Change salt into lime in four moves.
SALT
. . . .
. . . .
. . . .
LIME

Make up your own word changes. COPPER into CARBON?
BOIL into MELT?

Symbol chain

Write down any symbol such as Pb. Use its second letter to start a new symbol: Pb .. Ba. Now use this second letter for the next: Pb .. Ba .. Al .. Li .. How long can you make the chain?

Anagrams

Arrange the letters of each phrase to make one word. The meaning of the word you are to make is given. For example:

P.C. ROPE	A metal used as a conductor in wire form	COPPER
TRIFLE	To separate a solid from a liquid	_____
PARE A VOTE	To get rid of a liquid by heating it	_____
SEND ONCE	To turn steam back into water	_____
LAST CRY	Lump of solid with a regular shape	_____
BIG RUIN	The scientific name for it is combustion	_____
CURE ED	To take oxygen from a substance	_____
BE RAKE	Vessel for holding liquids	_____
MEET THE MORE	It measures temperature	_____
GO DRY HEN	Gives squeaky pop with lighted splint	_____
LANE RUT	Neither acid nor alkaline	_____

Chemist's alphabet

The smallest bit of an element is an	A _____
Effervescence means	B _____
Dyes in ink are separated by	C _____
One allotrope of carbon is	D _____
A substance which cannot be split up into others is an	E _____
The liquid which runs through a filter paper is the	F _____
A yellow, noble metal is	G _____
The chemical name of water is	H _____
The element which gives violet vapour on heating is	I _____
If you think this alphabet is easy you must be	J _____
The symbol for the element potassium is	_____
To find out if a liquid is an acid use	L _____
L atoms or molecules of a substance is called a	M _____
78% of the air we breathe is	N _____
21% of the air we breathe is	O _____
Green leaves of plants make starch by	P _____
There are two limes. Calcium oxide is	Q _____
Taking oxygen from a substance is called	R _____
A yellow non-metal is	S _____
The simplest piece of apparatus is a	T _____
To find out how strong an acid is use	U _____
In strong alkali Universal Indicator is	V _____
Hydrogen oxide is	W _____
One of the noble gases is called	X _____
The colour of gold and sulphur is	Y _____
A more active metal than copper is	Z _____

Now invent an alphabet of your own.

Words

Put one letter in front of each four-letter word to make a five-letter word. The letters you use must make the name, in the right order, of a well-known metal.

___rack   Add a letter to each three-letter word to make a four-letter word.
___bout   The added letters make the name of a metal.
___earn   ___top
___lean   ___van
___deal   ___air
___sing   ___ale
___over   ___den
            ___oar

Crosswords

Across

1. A non-metal, often black. (6)
5. A mineral found in the earth. (3)
6. Fine powder. (4)
8. The symbol for lead. (2)
9. The symbol for nickel. (2)
11. To take oxygen from a substance. (6)

Down

1. Pink metal used as a conductor. (6)
2. Symbol of the noble gas argon. (2)
3. Colour of litmus in acid. (3)
4. Metals found in the earth are this. (6)
7. The symbol for the metal tin. (2)
10. The symbol for the metal copper. (2)

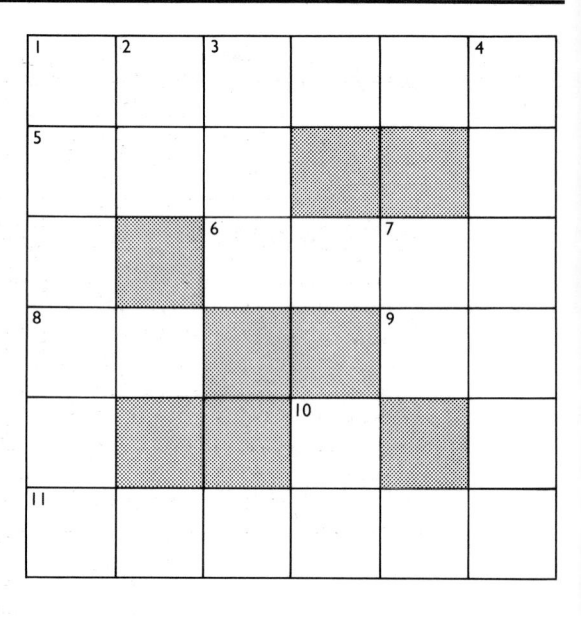

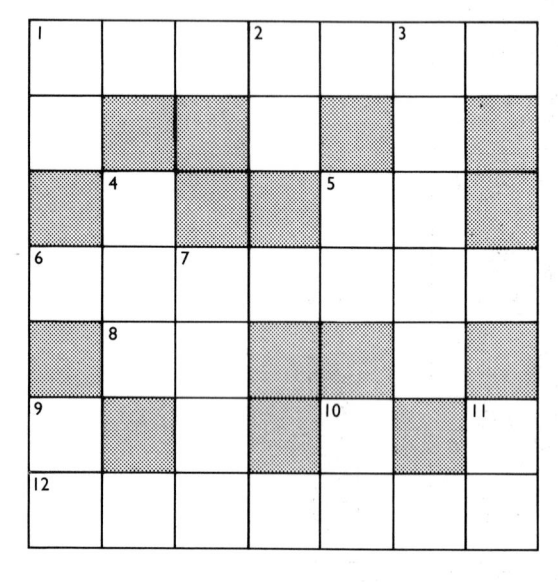

Across

1. A piece of solid with a regular shape. (7)
5. The symbol for the metal silver. (2)
6. The element with the symbol Si. (7)
8. The symbol for the metal nickel. (2)
12. A single simple substance. (7)

Down

1. The symbol for the metal calcium. (2)
2. The symbol for the metal tin. (2)
3. A noble gas which is 1% of air. (5)
4. A silvery metal. (3)
5. Guess the symbol of actinium! (2)
7. Calcium oxide or calcium hydroxide. (4)
9. Symbol for the metal iron. (2)
10. Symbol for the noble gas neon. (2)
11. Symbol for the metal platinum. (2)

Periodic table

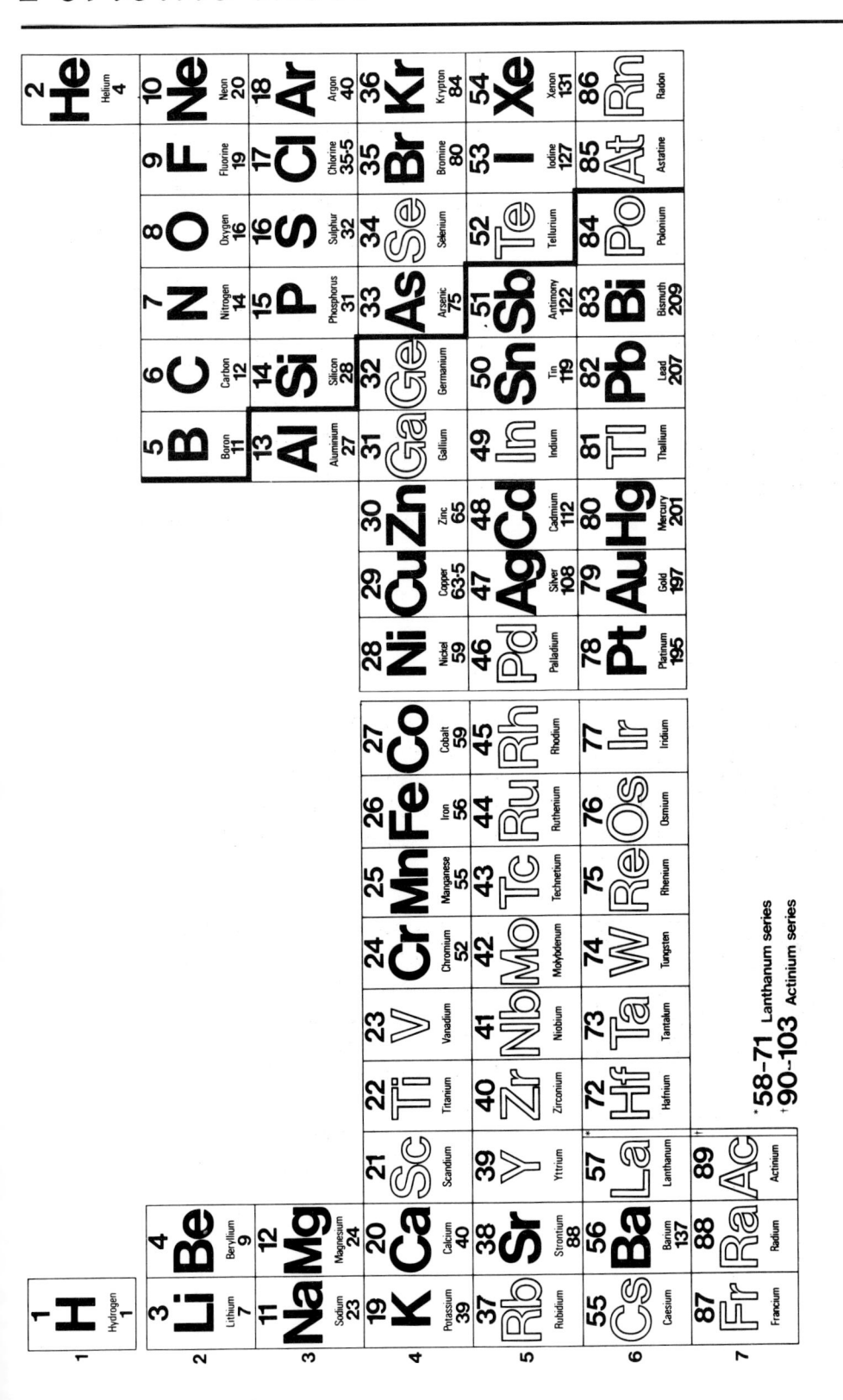

1 H Hydrogen 1																	2 He Helium 4
3 Li Lithium 7	4 Be Beryllium 9											5 B Boron 11	6 C Carbon 12	7 N Nitrogen 14	8 O Oxygen 16	9 F Fluorine 19	10 Ne Neon 20
11 Na Sodium 23	12 Mg Magnesium 24											13 Al Aluminium 27	14 Si Silicon 28	15 P Phosphorus 31	16 S Sulphur 32	17 Cl Chlorine 35·5	18 Ar Argon 40
19 K Potassium 39	20 Ca Calcium 40	21 Sc Scandium	22 Ti Titanium	23 V Vanadium	24 Cr Chromium 52	25 Mn Manganese 55	26 Fe Iron 56	27 Co Cobalt 59	28 Ni Nickel 59	29 Cu Copper 63·5	30 Zn Zinc 65	31 Ga Gallium	32 Ge Germanium	33 As Arsenic 75	34 Se Selenium	35 Br Bromine 80	36 Kr Krypton 84
37 Rb Rubidium	38 Sr Strontium 88	39 Y Yttrium	40 Zr Zirconium	41 Nb Niobium	42 Mo Molybdenum	43 Tc Technetium	44 Ru Ruthenium	45 Rh Rhodium	46 Pd Palladium	47 Ag Silver 108	48 Cd Cadmium 112	49 In Indium	50 Sn Tin 119	51 Sb Antimony 122	52 Te Tellurium	53 I Iodine 127	54 Xe Xenon 131
55 Cs Caesium	56 Ba Barium 137	57 La* Lanthanum	72 Hf Hafnium	73 Ta Tantalum	74 W Tungsten	75 Re Rhenium	76 Os Osmium	77 Ir Iridium	78 Pt Platinum 195	79 Au Gold 197	80 Hg Mercury 201	81 Tl Thallium	82 Pb Lead 207	83 Bi Bismuth 209	84 Po Polonium	85 At Astatine	86 Rn Radon
87 Fr Francium	88 Ra Radium	89 Ac† Actinium															

* 58–71 Lanthanum series
† 90–103 Actinium series

Glossary

The glossary is a list of important words or terms. The first number refers to the first page on which it is mentioned. Other page numbers refer to important uses.

Acid:	A substance which turns litmus red and has a sour taste. It is often formed by dissolving a non-metal oxide in water/42, 44, 64
Alkali:	A substance which turns litmus blue/42, 44, 65
Allotropes:	Different forms of the same element/128
Allotropy:	The existence of allotropes of an element/127, 128
Analysis:	Tests to find out what a substance is made up of/147, 149
Anhydrous:	Without water/48, 144
Appearance:	What a substance looks like/19
Atom:	The smallest particle (bit) of an element/108
Atomic theory:	The idea that all matter is made up of atoms. Using the idea to explain the facts of science/111, 112
Avogadro's Constant Number:	The number of atoms in 1 gram of hydrogen/117
Behaviour:	What a substance can do/19
Boiling point:	The temperature which a liquid boils at/18, 64
Carbon cycle:	The changes which keep the amount of oxygen in the air the same all the time/52, 53
Catalyst:	A substance which alters the speed of a reaction and is still there at the end of the reaction/41, 104
Change of state:	Change from solid to liquid to gas or the reverse/104
Chemical change:	A change in which at least one new substance is formed/31, 64, 104
Chemical properties:	The properties of a substance which can make a new substance/104
Chemical reaction:	Another name for a chemical change/31, 64, 104
Chromatography:	Separating substances by washing them through a solid/22, 64
Classification:	Grouping things of the same kind together/72, 104
Combine:	Join substances together to form a new substance/36, 80
Compound:	Two or more elements joined up in one substance/36, 72, 104
Condense:	Turn a gas or vapour back into a liquid/20
Condenser:	The apparatus used to condense/20
Conductor:	A substance which allows an electric current to pass through it/67
Corrosion:	The loss of metallic lustre (surface shine) by a metal forming a compound/78
Crystals:	Pieces of a substance which have the same regular shape/13, 64
Decompose:	Break down a substance into different substances/36, 64, 80
Deliquescent:	Taking water vapour from air and forming a solution/144
Displacement reaction:	Another name for replacement reaction/75
Dissolve:	What a substance does when it disappears into a liquid/13, 64
Distillation:	Boiling a liquid so that the vapour formed can be condensed/20, 64
Distilled water:	Pure water made by distillation/20, 94
Effervescence:	The escape of bubbles of gas from a liquid/88
Element:	A single substance which cannot be split up into simpler substances/36, 72, 104

Endothermic reaction:	A reaction where heat is taken in when the substances react. The opposite of an exothermic reaction/136, 140
Energy cycle:	Another name for the carbon cycle/52, 53
Evaporation:	Turning a liquid into gas or vapour/13, 64
Exothermic reaction:	A reaction which gives out heat when the substances react/136, 140
Experiment:	A test to find out by doing something/10, 64, 104
Filter:	Something used to separate a solid from a liquid (or gas)/13
Filtrate:	A liquid which passes through a filter/13
Filtration:	Using a filter/13
Flame colouration:	The colour which a metal compound gives to a flame/77
Formula:	The symbol way of showing the atoms which are in a molecule/114, 148
Formula mass:	Relative molecular mass as shown by the formula/118
Fuel:	A substance burnt to give heat and energy/46, 64
Hard water:	Water with dissolved compounds in it which affect soap/94
Heat of reaction:	The amount of heat when moles of reacting substances react/136, 140
-ide:	The name ending for a compound with only two elements in it/36
Indicator:	A substance which has one colour when it is in acid and a different colour when it is in alkali/40, 42, 64
Insoluble:	Unable to dissolve/15, 64
Insulator:	A substance which does not allow an electric current to pass through it/67
Mass:	The amount of matter in a substance or object/33, 123
Matter:	The 'stuff' that the world is made of/8, 64
Melting point:	The temperature which a solid melts at/18, 64
Metallic lustre:	The surface shine which all metals have/30
Metal oxide:	A compound which contains a metal and oxygen only/64
Mineral:	A substance found in the earth/16
M solution:	Another name for a molar solution/120
Molar solution:	One mole of solute in 1000 cm^3 (1 dm^3) of solution/120
Mole:	Avogadro's Number L of atoms or molecules/118
Molecule:	A particle of an element or compound which contains two or more atoms/108
Neutral:	A substance which is not acid or alkali/43, 44, 64
Non-metal oxide:	A compound which contains a non-metal and oxygen only/64
Observation:	Using eyes and ears to find out facts/10, 64, 104
Oxidation:	Oxidizing a substance/51
Oxidize:	Add oxygen to a substance/51
Permanent hardness:	Hardness not removed by boiling the water/98
Photosynthesis:	The chemical change in which the leaves of green plants produce sugar and starch/53
Physical change:	A change in which no new substance is formed/31, 64, 104
Physical properties:	The properties of a substance which do not make a new substance/104
Precipitate (ppt):	An insoluble solid formed in a liquid/119, 145
Products of combustion:	The substances formed by burning/47
Properties:	The appearance and behaviour of a substance/19, 64, 104
Reduction:	Taking away oxygen from a substance/63, 73

Relative atomic mass:	The number which shows the mass of an atom if a hydrogen atom is given a mass of 1/116
Relative molecular mass:	The number showing the mass of a molecule if H = 1/118
Replacement reaction:	A change in which one metal replaces another/75
Reversible reaction:	A reaction where the products react to give the reacting substances/101
Salt:	The substance formed when a metal replaces (displaces) the hydrogen of an acid/141, 149
Saturated solution:	A solution which no more of a substance can dissolve in/14
Sewage:	Used water carrying waste matter/103
Soft water:	Water which lathers at once when soap is added/94
Soluble:	Able to dissolve/15, 64
Solute:	The substance which dissolves/14, 64
Solution:	A liquid with a substance dissolved in it/13, 64
Solvent:	The liquid which a substance dissolves in/14, 64
States of matter:	Matter can be solid or liquid or gas. These are the three states of matter/8
Substance:	One particular kind of matter/8, 64
Symbol:	The letter or letters which stand for one atom of an element/114
Temporary hardness:	Hardness which can be removed by boiling the water/98
Thermit reaction:	The reduction of a metal oxide by aluminium/73
Transition temperature:	The temperature at which one allotrope changes to another allotrope/134
Weight:	The pull of the earth on an object/33
Word equation:	A summary of a chemical change. It names the reaction substances and the products which are formed.